D1596451

Praise for
Rules for ANTI-Radicals

"Sometimes, the first step in getting involved in grassroots advocacy can be the most daunting one, but the fact remains: There is no one in your life more important to protecting your rights than you.

"Paul Valone has written a very important primer that helps all of us recognize where we can best fit our talents and goals to beat the control freaks and prohibitionists at their own game, and that makes the first step a lot easier: Read this book. You'll know what to do next. And for those of us already along the path, this book is an invaluable resource to help guide our efforts for maximum effect."

- David Codrea
"Unauthorized Journalist"
Blogger, WarOnGuns.com
Columnist, *Firearms News*, and Ammoland.com

"Politics is simple but not easy, and simple as it is, it's very complicated because it involves humans, and humans complicate everything.

"In Rules for ANTI-Radicals, Paul Valone exposes the simplicity of politics in all of its human complexity, along with the strategy, tactics, and hard work needed to successfully advance an objective through the political process.

"Paul uses the foil of Saul Alinsky, perhaps the most astute political observer since Machiavelli, to lay out the mechanics of our political process, and explain what it takes to influence that process. This is a must-read book for anyone serious about winning in the political arena."

- Jeff Knox
Director, The Firearms Coalition®
Columnist, *Firearms News*, and Ammoland.com

"Paul Valone and I have many things in common. Both of us have spent years defending the Second Amendment. Both of us see how important to upholding

our Constitution is maintaining the Second Amendment without infringe-ment. Paul's work is a powerful tool for this fight."

- Larry Pratt
Executive Director Emeritus, Gun Owners of America

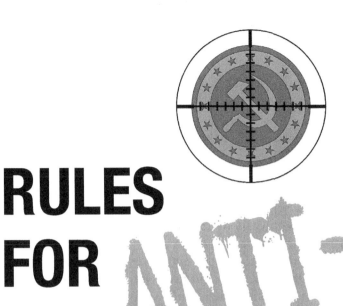

RULES FOR ANTI-RADICALS

RADICALS

A Practical Handbook for Defeating Leftism

F. Paul Valone

Rules for ANTI-Radicals:

A Practical Handbook for Defeating Leftism

By F. Paul Valone

Print ISBN: 978-1-7348824-4-5

E-book ISBN: ISBN: 978-1-7348824-5-2

Library of Congress Control Number: 2022903546

Bacchus USA Publications, LLC

Post Office Box 599

Bryson City, NC 28713

BacchusUSAPublications.com

Rules for ANTI-Radicals
Dedication

Rules for ANTI-Radicals: A Practical Handbook for Defeating Leftism *is dedicated to my loving wife Lori, without whom this book (and a great many other things) would not have been possible. For the first time in my life, I have met someone who embraces my inherent need to address injustice not as competition, but as something we can share.*

I thank you.

Want more information on activist tactics?
Find online seminars or schedule an in-person
seminar for your organization by going to

www.RulesForANTIRadicals.com

# Rules for ANTI-Radicals
Acknowledgments

Thanks go to Larry Pratt, Executive Director Emeritus of Gun Owners of America. When, as a neophyte, I flailed around for how to "do something," he personally took my call and set me on my present course.

My next acknowledgement is to Mike Rothfeld, whose Foundation for Applied Conservative Leadership continues to empower conservatives by teaching the principles I first learned twenty-five years ago. We haven't always seen eye to eye, and he may excoriate me for writing this book, but I would be remiss if I failed to mention his example.

Next, a salute goes to my longtime friend Dennis Fusaro, who as one-time Director of State and Local Affairs for Gun Owners of America, directed us to Rothfeld and the tactics we would use to beat leftists for decades to come.

Gun rights activists everywhere owe thanks to the late Neal Knox who, among many roles in the gun rights movement, served as executive director of the National Rifle Association's Institute for Legislative Action and chairman of the Firearms Coalition, and who routinely greeted adoring crowds with "Hello, gun lobby!" It could be argued that together with Harlon Carter, Neal turned the NRA into the legislative juggernaut it eventually became. He also became my friend and mentor as he educated me on the evils of political organizations gone wrong and helped me defend against efforts by such organizations to destroy me.

And finally, I owe much to the late Walt Dannel, who helped me organize the rally which built Grass Roots North Carolina and was one of its co-founders, and whose somewhat wizened cynicism suffered as the primary sounding board for my youthful naiveté back in the early days.

Beyond these few individuals, however, I would be a fool not to recognize the role of the many dedicated leaders, volunteers and supporters *who have made possible the tremendous impact we have had on the political process over nearly three decades. As I have often said, I am but a lightning rod to channel their energy to the politicians and other players who, quite frankly, need the shock.*

Foreword

"Politics, the crooked timber of our communal lives, dominates everything because, in the end, everything – high and low and, most especially, high – lives or dies by politics. You can have the most efflorescent of cultures. Get your politics wrong, however, and everything stands to be swept away. This is not ancient history. This is Germany 1933 ... Politics is the moat, the walls, beyond which lie the barbarians. Fail to keep them at bay, and everything burns."

– Charles Krauthammer, *Things That Matter: Three Decades of Passions, Pastimes and Politics*

Germany, 1933 ... but also Ukraine, 2022...

This past year has validated Krauthammer's words in dramatic fashion. I doubt there has ever been a time when our nation has experienced a reversal of fortunes as comprehensively as the people of the United States have witnessed the past two years. Some feel that we are witnessing "everything being swept away" by an inept and misguided president and Democrat Party.

Simultaneously, the good order of the entire world is being disrupted by a tyrant in Russia who is taking advantage of our foolish policies while, at home, those who would repeal the Second Amendment are relentless. The barbarians are at the gate, they are desperate, and they mean business. It is up to us to sweep *them* away. This book is your tool box.

As I write this, the assault on Ukraine is raging and the government has issued firearms to its citizens to fight desperately for their families, their cities, and their nation. I can think of no better illustration of the importance of an armed populace – a guaranty made by *our* Second Amendment.

Rules for Anti-RADICALS

I was somewhat surprised that Paul asked me to write the foreword to this book as I am an elected member of the NC General Assembly and, as such, experience activism from various organizations firsthand.

Some of my colleagues, friends of mine, have been displaced from office by Paul's organization. They were warned, they learned. Although some that remain may raise an eyebrow at my endorsement of this book, the Second Amendment is more important than opinion.

If the Second Amendment is important to you, you most certainly *should* read this book. If you want to know how legislation is formed, manipulated, managed and either passed or defeated, you *need* to read this book. If you have aspirations to hold political office, you had *better* read this book.

Paul has compiled not a theoretical, academic narrative, but a truly experiential report of his personal efforts that span the past 28+ years of political combat in defense of our rights. This book is hard core, no holds barred, political reality.

As a legislator I must use a different set of strategies and methods to achieve my goals, but you, as an activist, can amplify your voice and more effectively defend the principles on which our state and nation are built. This book will make your quest more successful and save you a lot of trial and error.

The Second Amendment "brought me to the dance" with regard to politics. I have known Paul for over twenty-five years and I was nearby as the clarion call to political action struck him (and me) in the early 1990s when the Brady Act and the "assault weapon" ban were under consideration. Among other things, flagrant misrepresentations by the mainstream media at the time demanded action.

To some, Paul's modeling his book after Saul Alinsky's *Rules for Radicals* may be somewhat disconcerting, but the fact is Alinsky's methods have been used by the left overtly and covertly for decades. I find it satisfying that Paul has refined Alinsky's methods and turned them mercilessly against the left.

Representative Jay Adams
North Carolina House, District 96

 # About the Author

My passion is delivering pain to politicians.

It all started in 1994, when I watched then-Speaker Tom Foley hold open the vote on the so-called "assault weapon" ban long enough to buy enough votes to pass it. Suitably outraged, I called around for any organization holding rallies for the Second Amendment. (At that time, I still believed rallies to be effective weapons for political change.) Eventually, I found an outfit calling itself The Committee of 1776, whose leaders were organizing coordinated rallies in state capitols around the U.S. on the Fourth of July weekend.

Realizing that was just over a month hence, I asked, "Who is organizing the rally in North Carolina?"

They replied, "You are."

In little more than thirty days and before common use of the Internet, Hugh Adams, Walt Dannel and I put nearly 1,000 people on the steps of the state capitol, had the forethought to collect names and addresses, and used that list to build a gun rights organization which has been kicking tail for twenty-six years.

Circa 1997, I was trained in hard-knuckled political tactics by former right-to-work activists who described what they taught as "political thuggery." Since then, I have modified those tactics to address what I perceive as weaknesses and flaws.

Along the way, I have founded and directed three political non-profits, four political action committees, and a super PAC. When my county decided to build a sewage plant in the cove of the lake on which I lived, I found myself elected president of a citizen's organization that had thus far failed to stop the plant. Sparing you the details, suffice it to say that was twenty years ago, but the land purchased for the sewage plant remains vacant to this day.

My gun rights organization has engineered passage of more pro-gun legislation than space permits me to describe, including concealed carry, Castle Doctrine/Stand Your Ground, concealed handgun reciprocity, statewide firearms preemption, and numerous expansions of our concealed handgun permit law. Meanwhile, we have killed literally dozens of gun control proposals.

Not counting amicus briefs, we have sued cities, sheriffs, an agricultural commissioner, and a sitting governor. We have elected and defeated more politicians than I can recall, up to and including making the margins of victory in several congressional races.

For most of that twenty-six years, I have trained others in legislative tactics based on our grassroots mobilization model, generally rejecting access-based lobbying. Among many, our projects have included not only passing and killing legislation, but also lawsuits, demonstrations (some at the businesses of opposing politicians), boycotts, voter education, building national coalitions, and express advocacy.

Throughout it all, I have taken no money for political organizing, preferring instead to scare the hell out of politicians previously accustomed to comfortably controlling access-based lobbyists via their dependence on money.

When we killed the sewage treatment plant, the leader of another group who had failed in a similar effort said, "You play full body contact politics, don't you?"

"Damned right I do," was my reply.

What is unique about this book?

In researching *Rules for ANTI-Radicals*, I found several books purporting to be the conservative answer to Saul Alinsky's *Rules for Radicals*. I found books written by conservative theorists, satirists, businessmen, and even Tea Party activists; books that lamented the end of our republic and the false flag of utopian socialism.

What I did *not* find, however, were books written by people who spent decades passing and killing legislation, electing and defeating polit-

About the Author

ical candidates, suing politicians, building coalitions, and boycotting corporations. Telling people to pull the levers of power is one thing; showing them *which* levers to pull and in what order to pull them is quite another.

Reprehensible or not, what differentiated Alinsky from the theoreticians was his willingness to jump into the muddy, bloody trenches to slaughter his opponents (metaphorically speaking, of course). That is what I've spent twenty-eight years doing, and after you read this book, you can, too.

You don't have to be a legislative leader to benefit from *Rules for ANTI-Radicals*. Whether you realize it or not, each and every day of your life, leftists bludgeon you into submitting to their agenda – be it at work, in school, in church, in restaurants, or on the street. If you apply the lessons contained in this book, you will no longer be forced to submit.

What *Rules for ANTI-Radicals* offers are the "how to" mechanics of beating leftists and advancing *your* agenda, be the topic guns, abortion, immigration, voter integrity, education, speech, religion, or whatever topic you find crucial to the future of society.

F. Paul Valone
President, Grass Roots North Carolina
Executive Director, Rights Watch International
Radio host, "Guns, Politics, and Freedom"

"Just because you do not take an interest in politics doesn't mean politics won't take an interest in you."

— Pericles (430 B.C.)

"Political tags - such as royalist, communist, democrat, populist, fascist, liberal, conservative, and so forth - are never basic criteria. The human race divides politically into those who want people to be controlled and those who have no such desire."

— Robert A. Heinlein

"A Marxist begins with his prime truth that all evils are caused by the exploitation of the proletariat by the capitalists. From this he logically proceeds to the revolution to end capitalism, then into the third stage of reorganization into a new social order of the dictatorship of the proletariat, and finally the last stage – the political paradise of communism."

— Saul Alinsky

Nearly fifty years ago, Saul Alinsky began **Rules for Radicals** *by saying, "Lest we forget at least an over the shoulder acknowledgment to the very first radical: from all our legends, mythology and history (and who is to know where mythology leaves off and history begins - or which is which), the very first radical known to man who rebelled against the establishment and did it so effectively that he at least won his own kingdom - Lucifer."*

We would do well to consider his choice of role model.

— F. Paul Valone

 # Prologue

In the fifty years since Saul Alinsky wrote *Rules for Radicals*, it has served as a guidebook for aspiring revolutionaries bent on taking over our media, our cultural institutions, and our schools. Judging from our present situation, they have largely succeeded.

Ironically, leftists routinely deny Alinsky, claiming conservatives are overly fixated on him. What radical youngsters fail to understand, however, is that "social justice" tactics taught by the Midwest Academy and others almost invariably derive from Alinsky's.

As one who advocated working within the system, Alinsky himself might be shocked at radical anarchists like those of Antifa. What we are witnessing is nothing less than nascent revolution aimed at ending the values and morals that produced the United States and replacing them with socialist autocracy.

In *Rules for Radicals*, one can see the origins of what is happening today. Yet by current standards, Alinsky's ideas seem almost quaint. Those bent on burning down America's cities are uniformed in "black bloc," riot helmets and gas masks. Far from representing spontaneous protest, their destruction is centrally planned and funded. Trying to stay out of the line of fire, corporations like Walmart, Target, and Home Depot now donate to their revolution.[1]

If Alinsky's claims are to be believed, he might not think much of today's radicals. He correctly said, "Dogma is the enemy of human freedom." Yet dogma is exactly what drives "cancel culture." The system Alinsky claimed to work within is the same system a Black Lives Matter leader threatened to "burn down."[2] It is plausible that Alinsky might not have anticipated the Frankenstein's monster he created.

In my twenty-eight years of political organizing, I've taught that political action divides into four categories: economic, political, legal, and a broad category I call "non-legislative." To that last category, today's radicals have re-introduced violence. I won't be advocating that. Instead, my goal is to give you the tools and tactics to make violence unnecessary. Let's hope that is still possible.

What follows are not just tactics for conservative political activists running organizations, but also practical advice for dealing with leftists you will inevitably endure in your daily routines: the neighbor who calls your American flag "offensive," the school board more interested in ideology than educating children, the corporate employer who demands you accept the LGBTQIA (or whatever they call themselves today) agenda. Winning the battle for our culture and our nation will require you to develop a new mindset – a mindset determined to stop leftists from cowing you into submission.

The thing to remember about Saul Alinsky is that as reprehensible as you may find someone who revered Lucifer as the world's first political activist, he was not wrong about what wins political debate. The difficulty lies in adapting his tactics to preserve our culture without succumbing to their inherently corrupting nature. To steal from Hamlet's soliloquy, "There's the rub."

References:

1. Mercey Livingston, "These are the major brands donating to the Black Lives Matter movement," June 16, 2020, https://www.cnet.com/how-to/companies-donating-black-lives-matter/
2. Mark Moore, "BLM leader: If change doesn't happen, then 'we will burn down this system'," *NY Post*, June 25, 2020, https://nypost.com/2020/06/25/blm-leader-if-change-doesnt-happen-we-will-burn-down-this-system/

 # Introduction

*"It's nice to be nice, and it's good to be right.
But alas, public policy is generally driven by neither."* – FPV

Unfortunately, you are probably ill-suited for political action. "But," you object, "I can name all my legislators and I call them constantly! I keep up on issues and weigh in regularly."

Thank you for your civic responsibility. Sadly, your elected representatives are probably ignoring you for the reasons I am about to describe.

If you are like most conservatives, you are ill-suited for political action because you are honest. Accordingly, you assume the motives of those in the political process are relatively honest or, if not honest, at least responsive to rational incentives. Unfortunately, you are wrong.

Maybe you've said, "If the legislators/media/political opponents just **understood** what is at stake, they wouldn't be doing what they are." You then set about "educating" them. After all, logic and facts are on your side, right?

Trust me when I say they probably **do** understand, and they probably don't care. Neither righteousness nor logic alone will save the day. Worse, if you try to educate members of your political opposition, you are likely ceding tactical advantage.

Because you are ill-suited to political action, the will of others – particularly leftists – is routinely projected upon your life. Your speech is controlled; your heroes' statues are desecrated; your shop is looted or burned; your wealth is given to others; your children are taught to hate your country and culture.

Maybe you have become fatalistic. "The world is screwed," you say, "but what can I do?"

The answer is "plenty." I can teach you the tactics and techniques necessary to *project your will*; to achieve *your* desired outcome by applying leverage to governmental bodies, corporations, and others. On issues ranging from abortion to firearms to vaccine mandates (and beyond), you will learn how to preserve your rights, your wealth, and perhaps your sanity by *decimating your opposition*.

How to use Rules for ANTI-Radicals

Rules for ANTI-Radicals is a practical guide to the tools and tactics for defeating leftism, both organizationally and in your daily life. Whether you are a concerned citizen, a neophyte who wants to get involved, or a grizzled activist, *Rules for ANTI-Radicals* offers information from perspectives you have likely never seen. It is organized into three sections, each comprising several chapters.

❏ **Part I: "Boot Camp for Conservative Activists."** Rather than boring you with the entire history of Marxism, this section details exactly how it has metastasized in America, who your enemies are, and how to defeat them on a personal level. Although Part I is a primer for dealing with leftism, even experienced activists will likely find tactics they had not previously considered.

❏ **Part II: "Activist Tools and Tactics."** Here we detail specific economic, political and legal tactics for defeating leftism, as well as non-legislative operations such as events and demonstrations. It also describes some of the left's favorite dirty tricks and how to counter them.

❏ **Part III: "Grassroots Organization."** This section is for those who are in it for the long haul, and outlines the care and feeding of political organizations, including leadership and fundraising.

Although you will benefit from reading the entire book, it is organized as a quick reference guide, allowing you to readily locate skills for particular projects or activities. The appendices give samples you can readily adapt to your own projects.

A few sad realities

It's nice to be nice, and it's good to be right. But alas, public policy is generally driven by neither.

People are rarely prepared for political battle because they assume the virtue of their position will win the fight. Gun rights activists, for example, expect to prevail because the Constitution is on their side. If you "educate" people about their rights, goes the argument, they will have little choice but to support us. So here are a few truths about issue advocacy. You will see them cited in examples throughout the book.

Four principals of grassroots activism

❏ **Winning is not about being "nice" or civil or even right:** Aggrieved people usually fail to account for their opposition's use of gamesmanship. Through spin, propaganda, deception and redefinition, your opposition—or you—can dominate the game even when dead wrong. In other words, your *motivation* is but marginally related to your *tactics*.

❏ **Politics is *not* "the art of compromise":** The cliché that "politics is the art of compromise" is wrong. In political battles, "compromise" generally defines a process under which you lose slightly less than you would have lost under the opposition's original proposal, *but you still lose*. Those who insist you "compromise" usually want you to cede ground while getting little or nothing in return.

Summing up political "compromise," the late Senator H.L. Richardson, author of *Confrontational Politics*, said:

> *"Consider the bandit who sticks a gun in your ribs and demands your wallet then, with a kindly smile, says, 'Shucks, I don't really need these.' As he hands you your credit cards, he adds, 'Aw, heck, I don't need these either.' With that, he returns the children's snapshots and the wallet itself—minus the cash, of course. Later, you couldn't help telling the police he wasn't such a bad guy after all."*[1]

Politics is a battle of competing ideas in which the landscape of the battlefield might *force* you to cede ground, but you should never do so willingly, never do so without extracting a price, and *never* compromise your underlying principles.

❏ **Politics *is* the adjudication of power:** Whether you like it or not, he who successfully imposes his will on the opposition wins. Period. The only relevant questions are:

- Who wields power? You? Your opposition? A third party?
- What type of power is it? Economic? Political? Legal?
- Who is the target of your effort? A politician? A political body? A corporation?
- What pathway to power is being utilized? The direct path by holding office, or indirect by making office-holders and others do your bidding?

❏ **Politicians respond best to four motivations**: To steal from F. Scott Fitzgerald, politicians are different than you and me. Those drawn to elected office are prone to narcissism, particularly after years of hearing themselves called "The Honorable." As we will later discuss at length, with limited exceptions, educating politicians generally fails. Like rats in a Skinner Box, they respond best to positive reinforcement and punishment – namely, the application or withholding of the four things they value most:

- Votes
- Money
- Power
- Public accolades

Four types of political action

In the past, I described political action as comprising three categories: economic, political, and legal. Given recent events, however, I have added a fourth: a broad category I call "non-legislative," which includes civil disobedience and its recidivist cousin, violence. Below is a summary of the four principal types of political action in order of preference. In following chapters, we'll look at tactics for each.

❏ **Economic action**: Targeting corporations by shaming or boycott tends to be the cheapest and most effective form of action because companies are generally run by bean counters whose chief goal is profit. If you show them you hold the beans, they tend to capitulate. For example, Chick-fil-A had been the target of boycotts since 2012, when CEO Dan Cathy drew fire from LGBT advocates for committing the heresy of saying he believed marriage should be between a man and a woman. Despite the religious orientation of the company, by 2019 LGBT activists forced Chick-fil-A to stop donating to the Salvation Army and Fellowship of Christian Athletes, which they smeared as anti-gay. So adroit at this tactic is the leftist jackal pack that major corporations such as Coca Cola and even Major League Baseball capitulate at even a hint of "woke" pressure.

❏ **Political action:** As the next most desirable option, political action divides into legislative and election operations. Both classify under political action because, as much as politicians want you to believe otherwise, they are two parts of the same process. In the election season, you reward or punish politicians for what they did in the legislative season. While legislative operations can be relatively straightforward, election operations require greater skill and organization. Most activists fail to understand that success in legislative operations is directly proportional to your ability to give or withhold what the politician wants and needs: votes, money, power and public accolades. If a politician knows he can ignore you with impunity, he will.

❏ **Legal action:** This is the most expensive, time-consuming, and risky of the three primary activist tactics. Beyond using lawyers to rattle somebody's cage (i.e. bluffing), you will need activists who have either legal expertise or the time and ability to develop it. They, in turn, will ride herd on the law firm you retain. You might find a lawyer to volunteer services for the short term, but the hours of effort required makes it likely you will eventually have to pay for legal representation. Rest assured your organization will not finance a protracted lawsuit with bake sales and raffles. Worse, even if you raise the necessary tens of thousands of dollars, an activist judge can flush it all down the toilet by imposing *his* ideology on you, regardless of the law.

❏ **Non-legislative operations:** This category is a catch-all that includes everything from mild public rallies to violent street warfare. (I do not advocate the latter.) Among "hard core" tactics, civil disobedience is most popular, but I rank it behind the three other options in desirability because it will cost you. Be it money, your livelihood, or your freedom, the moment you start down the path of civil disobedience, you can count on losing things. As an excuse for apathetic laziness, I routinely hear, "They can ban whatever they want. They ain't gettin' *my* guns." This is civil disobedience not by choice but by default, and will probably end in heartache. My answer is invariably, "But wouldn't you rather *not* be a felon? Do you think that if they ban your AR-15, you will be able to go out and shoot it?"

As a deliberate strategy, civil disobedience is better suited to leftists because, as society's miscreants, they generally have less to lose. To you, an arrest record represents shame and the potential end of your career; to a "black block"-clad Antifite, arrest is a badge of honor.

Civil disobedience can range from private non-compliance to public passive resistance to outright riot. Back in the 1980s "unilateral nuclear disarmament" peaceniks decided to demonstrate in New York City by getting police to arrest them and then refusing to identify themselves, thereby supposedly clogging the legal system. Because this was before leftists in government prevented law enforcement from doing its job, however, the NYPD simply locked up protestors in Rikers Island with rapists and killers until they 'fessed up. It didn't take long.

As I write this, professional truck drivers protesting vaccine mandates in Canada are engaged in civil disobedience via a "Freedom Convoy" which is shutting down Ottawa and various U.S.-Canadian border crossings. Although it is so far successful, I guarantee it will ultimately extract a price from protestors.

What you won't see here

Leftist radicals in the U.S. have recently re-introduced intimidation and violence as mechanisms of political action. Alas, if firebombing an abortion clinic is your idea of a hot Saturday night, you can stop reading; this is not *The Anarchist Cookbook*. Short of outright revolution, such tactics will probably not only fail, but also land you in prison, the hospital, or the morgue. It is no coincidence that recent rioting, looting, and arson thrives in urban centers controlled by leftist mayors, city councils, and district attorneys unwilling to prosecute leftist offenders. As a conservative, I assure you that you will enjoy no such leniency.

That said, as a conservative political activist, you might well be the *target* of radical violence. In, Chapter 13 ("Non-Legislative Operations"), we will discuss how to anticipate and counter potential threats, including communications, designating event marshals, coordinating with law enforcement, and more.

Reviled in all the right places

To deploy the tactics in this book, you must develop a thick skin. My running joke is that I aspire to be reviled in all the right places. I am proud to be more or less equally hated by leadership of both dominant political parties. The organizations I direct have been denounced by politicians in committees, commissions, and on the floor of entire legislative bodies; opposing organizations have painted us as "extremist," generally to our benefit. I am even persona non grata at the headquarters of the National Rifle Association.

Opponents who denounced us have wheedled, whined, and foamed. They have called us incapable of civil discourse, have falsely accused us of threatening them, and have themselves threatened (and filed) lawsuits.

Oh, yes, they have also generally lost.

References:

1.   H.L. Richardson, *Confrontational Politics*, Gun Owners Foundation, 1998.

Rules for Anti-Radicals
Table of Contents

PART ONE:

Boot Camp for Conservative Activists

Chapter 1
Meet Comrade Alinsky

*"...it is not too much to argue that American democracy
is being altered by Alinsky's ideas."* – *Time Magazine*

Born in 1909, Saul Alinsky was not a communist theoretician. In fact, he rejected dogma
and professed intent to work within the system, which would make him an outlier among
the radicals of today. That said, however, as a
mentor to Hillary Clinton and a role model for
Barack Obama, among many others, Alinsky is
undoubtedly the inspiration for radical leftists
of the 21st Century.

Saul learns "ethics" from the Mafia

Alinsky was (and still is) the left's greatest tactician – a tactician who
learned his organizing skills from none other than Frank Nitti and the
Al Capone gang, with whom he effectively apprenticed in the 1930s
after graduating from the University of Chicago. Said Alinsky in a 1972
interview with *Playboy* magazine, "I learned a hell of a lot about the
uses and abuses of power from the mob, lessons that stood me in good
stead later on, when I was organizing."[1]

Alinsky's greatest impact on leftist political action was the deliberate
separation of morals from politics. As suggested in his interview with
Playboy, he learned not only his organizing skills, but also his amorality
from the mob. When asked, "Didn't you have any compunction about
consorting with — if not actually assisting — murderers?" Alinsky replied, "None at all, since there was nothing I could do to stop them
from murdering, practically all of which was done inside the family."[2]

Alinsky's flexible ethics would manifest themselves repeatedly
throughout his career as a community organizer. In *Rules for Radicals*
(hereafter called *Rules*), he makes it clear that he regards the classic

moral question of whether the ends justify the means as "meaningless." He goes on to posit "rules for ethics and means" which are, essentially, free of ethics. Alinsky said, "...the real and only question regarding the ethics of means and ends is, and always has been, 'Does this *particular* end justify this *particular* means.'"[3]

Of particular interest is his third rule of means and ends: "In war, the end justifies almost any means." That sounds reasonable enough until you consider that he also said: "All life is warfare."[4] Applying the transitive law of logic, what he effectively said was, "*In life, the end justifies almost any means.*"

Alinsky's rules of "moral relativism"

Over the past thirty years, it has become popular among leftists to claim that "truth" is not objective, but instead depends on perspective, and that nothing is objectively moral or immoral. To get a feel for where they got those notions, see if any of Alinsky's "rules pertaining to the ethics of means and ends" sound familiar:

1. "...one's concern with the ethics of means and ends varies inversely with one's personal interest in the issue."

2. "...the judgment of the ethics of means is dependent upon the political position of those sitting in judgement."

3. "...in war, the end justifies almost any means."

4. "...judgment must be made in the context of the times in which the action occurred and not from any other chronological vantage point."

5. "...concern with ethics increases with the number of means available and vice versa."

6. "...the less important the end to be desired, the more one can afford to engage in ethical evaluations of means."

7. "...generally, success or failure is a mighty determinant of ethics."

4

8. "…the morality of a mean depends upon whether the mean is being employed at a time of imminent defeat or imminent victory."

9. "…any effective mean is automatically judged by the opposition as being unethical."

10. "…you do what you can with what you have and clothe it with moral garments."

11. "…goals must be phrased in general terms like 'liberty, Equality, Fraternity,' 'Of the Common Welfare,' 'Pursuit of Happiness,' or 'Bread and Peace.'"[5]

Alinksy the "community organizer"

When Barack Obama called himself a "community organizer," he was channeling Alinksy, whose early tactics were honed from labor organizing with the C.I.O. (Congress for Industrial Organizations) under the direction of labor legend John L. Lewis. Alinsky adapted the methods learned there to organize the "Back of the Yards Council" in the slums behind Chicago's Union Stockyards, rallying a mix of mutually hostile Catholic ethnicities, as well as African-Americans, to secure concessions from local meatpackers, landlords, and city hall.

From there, Alinsky decided to go national. In 1940, together with Roman Catholic Bishop Bernard James Sheil and Chicago Sun-Times publisher Marshall Field, he founded the national community organizing network he called the "Industrial Areas Foundation" in order to build coalitions with religious congregations and civic organizations.

He later organized what he called "have-nots" in Buffalo, Detroit, Kansas City, New York, and in Mexican barrios in California and the Southwest. In the 50s, it was the blacks of the Woodlawn of Chicago. In 1945, he wrote *Reveille for Radicals* which, ironically, was panned by the left as too conventional in its stated goal to "revolutionize" from within the existing system.

Fast forward to the 1960s when "Alinsky was again in the national spotlight, constantly on the lecture circuit, but this agitator proved curiously out of tune with the spirit of the 1960's. [Lyndon Johnson's] War on Poverty he declared a 'prize piece of political pornography' that merely spawned a larger 'welfare industry.'"[6]

But it was his battle in Rochester, NY to organize in favor of blacks against Eastman Kodak using corporate proxy battles that gave him the inspiration which dogs America to this day: to organize the middle class against "the system." Said Alinsky in *Rules*:

> *"With rare exceptions, our activists and radicals are products of and rebels against our middle-class society. Our rebels have contemptuously rejected the values and way of life of the middle class ... we must begin from where we are if we are to build power for change, and the power and the people are in the big middle-class majority."*[7]

See if any of that sounds familiar when you next see references to the fact that most Antifa recruiting occurs on college campuses.

Communist or not?

Some have called Alinsky an avowed communist. Andrew Breitbart called him a "pragmatic Marxist." Whether true or not, Alinsky (who admittedly often lied through his teeth) would disagree. In *Rules*, he said, "Today revolution has become synonymous with communism while capitalism has become synonymous with the status quo ... These pages are committed to splitting this political atom, separating this exclusive identification of communism with revolution." If that was truly his goal, he failed.

To give you a flavor for Alinsky's feelings about communism, he said:

> *"Back in the Thirties, the Communists did a hell of a lot of good work; they were in the vanguard of the labor movement and they played an important role in aiding blacks and Okies and Southern sharecroppers. Anybody who tells you he was active in progressive causes in those days and never worked with the Reds is a goddamn liar."*[8]

Yet Alinsky never officially joined the communist party, first because he

6

wasn't a "joiner," and second because he hated dogma. Whether Marxist or not, however, he repeatedly justified socialism, saying of man, "...he will either share part of his material wealth or lose all of it..."[9] Although Alinsky called the tag of communism "irrelevant" due to his claims of pragmatism, to say he wasn't communist because he never officially joined the party would be a distinction without a difference.

In some ways, however, Alinsky would be a poor fit for today's radicals. For example, although he disavowed dogma, preferring instead realistic goals, today's radicals live for nothing *but* dogma as evidenced by cancel culture and the movement to defund police. And when Alinsky divided the world into "Haves," Have-Nots," and Have-a-Little, Want-Mores," we see, if not the first effort to apply class warfare to divide society, certainly one of the most successful.

Misanthropy masked in morality

For the flavor of Alinsky's faith in human nature, consider his statement that "The myth of altruism as a motivating factor in our behavior could arise and survive only in a society bundled in the sterile gauze of New England puritanism and Protestant morality and tied together with the ribbons of Madison Avenue public relations. It is one of the classic American fairy tales."[10] Having bestowed this gem upon us, he goes on to pontificate that all human behavior emanates from self-interest.

But don't expect to hear that from Alinsky or his disciples, who will revert to his tenth rule of means and ends: "...do what you can with what you have and clothe it with moral garments."[11]

He also says, "...drastic shifts of self-interest can be rationalized only under a huge, limitless, umbrella of general 'moral' principles such as liberty, justice, freedom, a law higher than man-made law, and so on."[12] This is precisely the tack his disciples take when they lecture about "saving the planet."

Beyond Alinsky

Saul Alinsky died of a heart attack in 1972, only three months after his famous *Playboy* interview. But his influence lives on in the left, most famously through Barack Obama (who trained at Alinsky's Industrial

Areas Foundation), Hillary Clinton (who interviewed Alinsky for her Wellesley College senior thesis), and equally, if unconsciously, through Antifa, Black Lives Matter, and the rest of today's Marxist radicals.

But much has changed since Alinsky wrote *Rules*. The Internet has revolutionized activism, polarization of American politics has impaired the ability to build bipartisan support for legislative change, and corporations have acclimatized to constant political demands from competing interests.

Moreover, Alinsky spoke in generalizations that fell short on advice for *applying* specific tactics. In the chapters which follow, we will discuss not only how to recognize and counter his tactics, but, more importantly, the nuts-and-bolts of making governmental bodies and corporations do your bidding. We will go beyond Alinsky's tactics, and into what I have proven works in the 21st Century.

But first, here are the rudiments you will see applied, expanded upon, and occasionally disregarded throughout the book.

Alinsky's "Rules for Radicals"

RULE 1: "Power is not only what you have, but what the enemy thinks you have."

RULE 2: "Never go outside the expertise of your people." When an action or tactic is outside the experience of the people, the result is confusion, fear, and retreat."

RULE 3: "Wherever possible go outside of the experience of the enemy. Here you want to cause confusion, fear, and retreat."

RULE 4: "Make the enemy live up to their own book of rules. You can kill them with this, for they can no more obey their own rules than the Christian church can live up to Christianity."

RULE 5: "Ridicule is man's most potent weapon. It is almost impossible to counterattack ridicule. Also it infuriates the opposition, who then react to your advantage."

RULE 6: "A good tactic is one that your people enjoy. If your people are not having a ball doing it, there is something very wrong with the tactic."

RULE 7: "A tactic that drags on too long becomes a drag. Man can sustain militant interest in any issue for only a limited time, after which it becomes a ritualistic commitment, like going to church on Sunday mornings..."

RULE 8: "Keep the pressure on, with different tactics and actions, and utilize all events of the period for your purpose."

RULE 9: "The threat is usually more terrifying than the thing itself."

RULE 10: "The major premise for tactics is the development of operations that will maintain a constant pressure upon the opposition. It is this unceasing pressure that results in the reactions from the opposition that are essential for the success of the campaign. It should be remembered not only that the action is in the reaction but that action is itself the consequence of reaction and of reaction to the reaction, ad infinitum. The pressure produces the reaction, and constant pressure sustains action."

RULE 11: "If you push a negative hard and deep enough it will break through into its counterside; this is based on the principle that every positive has its negative..."

RULE 12: "The price of a successful attack is a constructive alternative. You cannot risk being trapped by the enemy in his sudden agreement with your demand and saying 'You're right—we don't know what to do about this issue. Now you tell us.'"

RULE 13: "Pick the target, freeze it, personalize it, and polarize it."[13]

References:

1. Eric Norden, "Saul Alinsky: Playboy Interview (1972)," https://scrapsfromtheloft. com/2018/05/01/saul-alinsky-playboy-interview-1972/
2. Ibid.

3. Saul Alinksy, *Rules for Radicals: A Pragmatic Primer for Realistic Radicals*, 1971, Vintage Books Edition, 1989, page 24.

4. Op. cit. note 1.

5. Op. cit. note 3, pages 24-45.

6. Nelson Lichtenstein, "It Never Hurts To Have A Few Enemies," *The New York Times*, November 12, 1989, https://www.nytimes.com/1989/11/12/books/it-never-hurts-to-have-a-few-enemies.html

7. Op. cit. note 3, page 185.

8. Op. cit. note 1.

9. Op. cit. note 3, page 23.

10. Op. cit. note 3, page 53.

11. Op. cit. note 3, page 36.

12. Op. cit. note 3, page 55.

13. Op. cit. note 3, page 126.

Chapter 2
Know Your Enemy

"They have the guns and therefore we are for peace and for reformation through the ballot. When we have the guns then it will be through the bullet."
– Saul Alinsky, *Rules for Radicals*

The left is your enemy. Whether you know it or not, you are at war not only for your culture and society, but also for your system of government and with it your very freedom. When people tell me they don't "do" politics, I reply, "That's your choice, of course. But rest assured that if you don't, then politics will 'do' you."

Your enemies will not "compromise" in any meaningful way. Despite grandiose claims, their priority is not truth or enlightenment or the welfare of children; it is power. As such, you will not persuade them of the righteousness of your position. Your only option is to defeat them. If you deceive yourself otherwise, you will lose. *We* will lose.

Maybe you have been calling them "liberals" or "progressives," using the terminology they have inserted into our culture. If so, stop immediately. As I will stress throughout the book, you must learn to reject the language of your enemy because language frames the debate. If you concede to their terms, you are already maneuvering from a position of disadvantage.

Why 'liberals' aren't liberal at all

To win the war, you must understand your opponents. Even conservative activists often erroneously refer to them as "liberals," to which I typically respond: "*I'm* a liberal. *They* are fascists." But as you will see, even that is not entirely accurate. Let's look at the players, shall we?

Liberalism

Says the Mises Institute:

> "'Classical liberalism' is the term used to designate the ideology advocating private property, an unhampered market economy, the rule of law, constitutional guarantees of freedom of religion and of the press, and international peace based on free trade. Up until around 1900, this ideology was generally known simply as liberalism. The qualifying "classical" is now usually necessary, in English-speaking countries ... because liberalism has come to be associated with wide-ranging interferences with private property and the market on behalf of egalitarian goals."[1]

True liberals promote diversity of viewpoint. The radicals you face do not, nor do they respect individual property or freedom of religion, speech, or the press. Despite being far from "liberal," your opponents have effectively co-opted the label.

Progressivism

After Democrats lost the 2000 elections and "liberal" became a dirty word, the left mysteriously morphed into "progressives." It's a clever moniker which implies that you, the opponent of "progressives," must by definition be *re*-gressive.

But are your opponents truly progressive? American progressivism got its start in the late 19th Century – the era of robber barons and sweat shops. Definitions vary widely, but most center on advocating social and economic change to reduce inequalities in society. In their view, progress is stifled by vast economic inequality between the rich and the poor and inadequately regulated capitalism.

Your generous Aunt Nellie, who donates to the poor and (mistakenly) votes Democrat because she cares about the plight of minorities and the dispossessed is likely a "progressive." Your opponents are not. As I explain below, despite protestations to the contrary, your opponents seek not to *reduce* economic and social inequality, but instead to *exploit* it in their pursuit of power.

Fascism

A fascist is "...a dictator having complete power, forcibly suppressing opposition and criticism, regimenting all industry, commerce, etc., and emphasizing an aggressive nationalism and often racism."[2] Are your opponents fascists? Close, but no cigar. They meet all the definitions here (including racism) except nationalism, since they clearly want to abolish not only borders, but the entire concept of the nation-state.

Leftism

Here we are on to something. I'll hold with Wikipedia's definition:

> *"Leftist economic beliefs range from Keynesian economics and the welfare state ... to nationalization of the economy and central planning, to ... self-managed anarchist communism ... Other leftists believe in Marxian economics ... Some distinguish Marx's economic theories from his political philosophy, arguing that Marx's approach to understanding the economy is independent of his advocacy of revolutionary socialism or his belief in the inevitability of proletarian revolution ... The dictatorship of the proletariat or workers' state are terms used by some Marxists, particularly Leninists and Marxist–Leninists, to describe what they see as a temporary state between the capitalist state of affairs and a communist society."[3]*

In sum, leftists are characterized by advocating a welfare state, nationalized economic planning, and varying degrees of Marxist socialism. What they seek is *control*.

So who are we dealing with?

Let's take a look at the qualities of today's radicals – those the media misnames "mostly peaceful protestors," who riot, loot, and demand the abolition of police, as well as their supporters in government, academia, and the media:

❑ **Economic freedom?** Nope. From Alexandria Ocasio-Cortez' calls for punitive taxation of those she deems "wealthy" to "Medicare for All", free college, and universal guaranteed income, nobody can seriously argue that today's radicals are not socialist, which falls neatly under the definition of leftism. They aren't "liberals" because they most certainly do not align with classic liberalism's respect for private property.

❏ **Tolerance of intellectual diversity?** Hardly. Take, for example, "cancel culture." If you dare disagree with them on race, history, or a wide variety of other topics, they will boycott your company, viciously defame you on social media, even assault you physically. Behind the facade of "tolerance" lies only censorship. There is nothing "liberal" or "progressive" about such behavior, but it most certainly fits the "dictatorship of the proletariat" which leftists falsely insist is a "temporary" step toward their promise of socialist utopia.

❏ **Reducing social and economic inequality?** Not by a long shot. If anything, President Lyndon B. Johnson's "Great Society" has cemented inequality by making minorities dependent on social welfare programs and, in many cases, government housing. That subservience is by design, as evidenced by Johnson reportedly saying, "I'll have those ni@@ers voting Democratic for 200 years."[4] Again, your opponents don't *minimize* inequality, they exploit it – even *promote* it – as a pathway to power.

❏ **Racial equality?** Even barring anti-white quotes and proposals from radical leadership, a 2017 poll by the Public Religion Research Institute determined that, "Nearly half (48%) of all Americans—and a majority (54%) of white Americans—believe that discrimination against whites has become as big of a problem as discrimination against blacks and other minorities."[5] Radicals even argue that only whites can be "racist." Does that sound like racial equality to you?

It's all about *power* – leftist power

By any measure, 21st Century radicals fail to meet the criteria of either liberalism or progressivism. Some may be Marxist, most are socialist, and a few are undoubtedly anarchists, but only one moniker fits their narrowly dogmatic approach: *leftist*.

Under camouflage of promoting "democracy," leftists now pursue absolute control of society. They are willing to sacrifice lawful citizens' lives to crime; open borders to illegal immigrants; defy voters' will by using leftist judges to redraw political districts; rig elections by suing to overturn voter ID laws; and even admit the District of Columbia as a 51st state (and the Constitution be damned) if that is what it takes to secure a permanent lock on power.

The bright line between progressives and leftists

Two things differentiate leftists from progressives: First, leftists feel that as intellectuals they are "enlightened" and therefore entitled to plan society's future. Second, they seek to control you: what you say, what you earn, what you own, and how you worship. So if Aunt Nellie shakes her head and laments "gun violence," she is likely a progressive. If she starts expounding on the reasons guns need to be confiscated, she's a leftist.

When I was less experienced, I classified "liberals" as split between the stupid but well-intentioned, and the manipulators of the stupid but well-intentioned. Properly defined, the former are progressive, the latter are leftist. Often, your opponents might start out progressive but gradually morph into vicious leftists, the classic example being former President Jimmy Carter, whose Carter Center saw fourteen advisors quit over anti-Israel partisanship in his book *Palestine: Peace Not Apartheid*.[6]

Leftism spreads to America

I'll spare you a lecture on the intellectual basis of communism, the role of Karl Marx and Friedrich Engels, and the Communist Manifesto. Let's skip ahead to the man who engineered how communism would control the world by quietly insinuating itself into western culture and institutions: Antonio Gramsci (1891-1937).

Unique among European Marxists of the early 20th Century, Gramsci engineered the multi-generational effort to take over our society, writing, "Socialism is precisely the *religion* that must overwhelm Christianity … In the new order, Socialism will triumph by first capturing the culture via *infiltration* of schools, universities, churches, and the media by transforming the consciousness of society." [Emphasis added.][7]

Does any of that sound familiar?

Gramsci's tactics take over America

Breaking with Marx, Gramsci sought to take over society from within. Remember when I said that whether you recognize it or not, you are at war? "Gramsci used war metaphors to distinguish between a political 'war of position' – which he compared to trench warfare – and the 'war of movement (or maneuver)' which would be a sudden full-frontal assault resulting in complete social upheaval."[8]

Arguing that the Russian Revolution succeeded only because the conditions were ripe for revolt, "Gramsci argued that a 'frontal attack' on established institutions like governments in Western societies may face significant resistance and thus need greater preparation—with the main groundwork being the development of a collective will among the people and a takeover of leadership among civil society and key political positions."[9]

For generations, leftists have infiltrated our culture using Gramsci's "war of position." But it wasn't until the 1960s that German radical Rudi Dutschke stole a page from Chinese history to dub their multi-generational effort "the long march through the institutions." The "institutions" in question are (see if this rings a bell) *our cultural institutions, our media, and our schools.*

Having now secured control of academia and the media, and with leftists installed in governmental positions of power such as the city governments of Chicago, Minneapolis, New York, Portland, and Seattle, Gramsci's toadies now feel they are adequately positioned for their "war of maneuver" – namely, the full frontal attack which we experience as rioting in major urban areas controlled by Democrat governments. Their goal, of course, is to spread it throughout the country.

This is not conspiracy

I am not a conspiracy theorist. But as one of the founding board members of my organization once put it, "You don't have to be a member of the choir to sing from the same piece of sheet music."

Rather than conspiracy, what we're experiencing today is the result of ideology that spread like cancer into a receptive intellectual body, Columbia University, via carcinogens of Marxist theory advocated by intellectuals of Germany's Frankfurt School and its Institute for Social Research, and transmitted through a partnership forged with Columbia in 1933.

That cancer metastasized slowly until the 1960s when its progeny, "critical theory," became the darling of the "new left." Says *The New Republic*, "It would be hard to overstate the importance of the Frankfurt School in recent American thought."[10]

Why you should care about 'critical theory'

Without wading too deeply into political science, Max Horkheimer, philosopher and creator of critical theory for the Frankfort School in 1937, defined it as "social critique meant to effect sociologic change and realize intellectual emancipation, by way of enlightenment that is not dogmatic in its assumptions."[11] (I would argue that it has become quite dogmatic, but we'll save that for another day.)

Critical theory has now invaded our universities, promoting a "social critique" conveniently structured to rip down American culture and government. Incidentally, its offspring, "critical *race* theory," is now tearing apart both law enforcement and our common understanding of American history with its claims of "systemic racism" and demands to defund police.

In sum, nothing we are experiencing today is random, but neither is it the result of grand conspiracy. It is an insidious program designed in the 1930s, spread through our universities, and practiced by devotees who now occupy governmental positions of power.

The goal is mayhem

The death of George Floyd at the hands of police on May 25, 2020 created the rationalization for mass riots across the U.S. If you are like most Americans, you've probably pondered what rioters and looters stand to gain. You've probably said, "Don't they know that if the police disengage, more people will be victimized by criminals?"

To answer that question, let me quote Alinsky: "The first step in community organization is community disorganization. The disruption of the present organization is the first step toward community organization. Present arrangements must be disorganized if they are to be displaced by new patterns ... All change means disorganization of the old and organization of the new."[12] Translated, in order to create the great socialist utopia they dream of, they must first destroy the existing society.

The implication is that, at a minimum, the puppet-masters behind the protests know perfectly well that urban shop owners' lives will be destroyed by looting and, worse, that black children will die in gang violence as police withdraw and anarchy reigns.

The vilification of police with fraudulent claims of "systemic racism" has been particularly effective in degrading performance of law enforcement institutions, both from police withdrawal in the face of malicious prosecution for justifiable shootings, and in providing rationalization for leftist city governments to cut funding for local police.

Some leftists might care that they are causing death and destruction, but they have decided that death is a necessary price in order to destroy our republican system of government and replace it with the socialist autocracy they believe will create universal equality.

Thus is the nature of your enemy. To defeat them, you must understand them.

References:

1. Bruce Frohnen, Jeremy Beer, Jeffrey O. Nelson, "What Is Classical Liberalism?", *American Conservatism: An Encyclopedia*, ISI Books, 2006, https://mises.org/library/what-classical-liberalism

2. Dictionary.com: https://www.dictionary.com/browse/fascism

3. Wikipedia: https://en.wikipedia.org/wiki/Left-wing_politics

4. Some will claim LBJ never said this. But nobody can call it inconsistent with his references to minorities, and even left-leaning Snopes cannot discredit the claim.

5. Daniel Cox, Robert P. Jones, Ph.D., "Attitudes on Child and Family Wellbeing: National and Southeast/Southwest Perspectives," September 18, 2017, Public Religion Research Institute, https://www.prri.org/research/poll-child-welfare-poverty-race-relations-government-trust-policy/?gclid=Cj0KCQjwjer4BRCZA

RIsABK4QeUGVBngKWxFM-ub6NFRe4nKob4a0KMImON2HSGnj0DZlimB-TfTkkK8aAmjQEALw_wcB

6. Brenda Goodman, "Carter Center Advisers Quit to Protest Book," tuscaloosanews.com, January 11, 2007, https://www.tuscaloosanews.com/story/news/2007/01/12/carter-center-advisers-quit-to-protest-book/27697042007/

7. Roger Kiska, "Antonio Gramsci's long march through history," December 12, 2019, Acton Institute, https://www.acton.org/religion-liberty/volume-29-number-3/antonio-gramscis-long-march-through-history

8. Bradley Thomas, "The Left's Long March Through The Institutions Is Now Pretty Much Complete, And It's A Disaster," May 19, 2019, Center for Individualism, https://centerforindividualism.org/the-lefts-long-march-through-the-institutions-is-now-pretty-much-complete-and-its-a-disaster/?gclid=Cj0KCQjwjer4BRCZARIsABK4QeXhUc7UiucQURCcNJ_zih2zNnbDm_5H1c4jTUfGy_7Tfm1yqxA7LAkaAl-3EALw_wcB

9. Bradley Thomas, "Antonio Gramsci: the Godfather of Cultural Marxism," Foundation for Economic Education, March 31, 2019, https://fee.org/articles/antonio-gramsci-the-godfather-of-cultural-marxism/

10. Adam Kirsch, "Frankfort on the Hudson," *The New Republic*, August 31, 2009, https://newrepublic.com/article/68842/frankfurt-the-hudson

11. "Frankfort School," https://en.wikipedia.org/wiki/Frankfurt_School

12. Saul Alinksy, *Rules for Radicals: A Pragmatic Primer for Realistic Radicals*, 1971, Vintage Books Edition, 1989, page 117.

Chapter 3
How Leftists Bludgeon You into Submission

*"If liberty means anything at all, it means the right to
tell people what they do not want to hear."*
– George Orwell from an unused preface to *Animal Farm*

*"Who controls the past controls the future.
Who controls the present controls the past."*
– George Orwell, *1984*

Leftist intolerance isn't confined to the political arena. Whether you realize it or not, you encounter it daily. A 2020 Cato Institute survey found that fully 62 percent of Americans were afraid to share their political views with others, up several percentage points from just three years prior. Most afflicted, of course, were conservatives, 77 percent of whom were afraid to share their beliefs.[1] They have, in effect, become "closet conservatives." Would we have felt that way even twenty years ago? Of course not. What you see is the impact of constant leftist speech suppression.

Bludgeoning you into compliance

So thoroughly have leftist demands been inculcated into our culture in the past fifty-odd years that you might not even be aware of all the ways in which freedom of expression is gradually being strangled. Before extricating yourself from the stranglehold, you must first identify exactly when and where it occurs. Some of the examples below might be familiar; of others, you might not be aware.

'Newspeak' is not just fiction anymore

In the novel *1984*, George Orwell created "Newspeak," a fictional, forced change of language intended to change thinking. But "Newspeak" is no longer fiction. As part of the effort to hijack your language – and by consequence, your underlying thoughts – to conform with their political agenda, leftists routinely make additions to the long list of words and phrases we are prohibited from using.

A friend recently asked what was wrong with the demand to remove "plantation" from our lexicon as "racist." I replied, "I don't give a damn about the word. What I care about is their motive, which is to control how you think."

As we will discuss at length later in the book, attempts to brand your language as evidence of "racism" or "microaggression" have nothing to do with the underlying topics, and everything to do with silencing you and molding how both you and society regard the world.

Bias in language extends to the ostensibly "mainstream" media, which in recent decades have begun inserting carefully nuanced language into what purport to be objective news reports with the goal of changing public perception of events.

'Canceling' their way to censorship

Particularly virulent has been the spread of "cancel culture" wherein most of the methods below are applied to public figures and corporations to silence any with whom the left disagrees. The practice has become so extreme that even some on the left have referred to it as a "reign of terror," particularly when levied against other leftists. (I love it when the left eats its own.)

❑ **Accusations of racism**: The epithet "racism" is applied both to silence mainstream Americans and to marginalize those who dare speak. Most recently, leftists have banned as racist not only "illegal alien" but even benign words like "master" and "blacklist." A Massachusetts appellate court is now refusing to use the word "grandfathered" due to supposedly racist origins.[2] Other attempts to marginalize you as racist include claims of "white privilege" and the ever-expanding definition of "white supremacy."

❑ **Accusations of "microaggression"**: Although theoretically defined as "a term used for brief and commonplace daily verbal, behavioral, or environmental indignities, whether intentional or unintentional, that communicate hostile, derogatory, or negative prejudicial slights and insults toward any group, particularly culturally marginalized groups," the term actually means anything a leftist finds objectionable at any time. It is used to silence opposing opinions.

❏ **Media bias**: Although overt bias is commonly acknowledged by conservatives (and denied by leftists) as "fake news," media bias can be subtle enough to elude detection. In searching articles on media bias, for example, I came across one purporting to examine bias from both the left and right. Yet it featured a section on "Reading for Conservative Bias" with no corresponding section on reading for liberal bias.

Beyond slant in selection of topics the media chooses to cover and the spin placed on articles, look carefully for subtle shading of language. I once received a written apology from the news director of *The New York Times* (or as close to an apology as the *Times* would ever give), after I complained about a news article referencing black Republican Congressman J.C. Watts' "notions" of conservatism. That was years ago. Now, of course, that level of bias is child's play compared to falsehoods routinely propagated by the *Times*.

In television media, CNN satellite uplink technician and whistleblower Cary Poarch recorded a series of conference calls for Project Veritas in which CNN president Jeff Zucker can be heard demanding the network focus on "moves toward impeachment" of President Trump, while other CNN employees in secret videos describe Zucker's "personal vendetta" against Trump.[3]

❏ **Speaker bans**: University campus speakers "disinvited" have included not only conservative pundits such as Ann Coulter, Ben Shapiro, and Dennis Prager, but also public officials such as HUD Secretary Ben Carson and even Vice President Mike Pence. Universities did so despite hosting engagements by terrorists Angela Davis of the Black Panthers and Bill Ayers of the Weather Underground.

❏ **Politically biased euphemisms**: "Sanctuary city," for example, is a euphemism for state and local defiance of federal law. "Illegal aliens" have become "undocumented immigrants." The word "homosexual" has, of course, long been replaced with shifting acronyms wherein even "LGBTQ" is no longer adequate, having now been replaced with "LGBTQIA" (lesbian, gay, bisexual, transgender, queer or questioning, intersex, and asexual or allied) or, if even that isn't enough, "LGBTQIA+". And God help you if, in a public forum, you ever refer to "the two genders," which got comedian Dave Chappelle "cancelled."

❏ **Search engine bias:** When attempting searches using Google, there are certain search results you simply won't get. When I searched "liberals ban words," I got only results for liberals whose words were supposedly banned. Because it denies you access to entire categories of information, this is perhaps the most insidious and dangerous form of leftist censorship. Dr. Robert Epstein, senior research psychologist at the American Institute for Behavioral Research and Technology, found dramatic bias favoring Hillary Clinton in the 2016 election, saying, "I looked at politically oriented searches that these people were conducting on Google, Bing, and Yahoo. I was able to preserve more than 13,000 searches and 98,000 web pages, and I found very dramatic bias in Google's search results ... favoring Hillary Clinton – whom I supported strongly."[4] Personally speaking, anytime I do a politically-charged search, I now use DuckDuckGo.

❏ **Blocked email:** In a recent hearing of "big tech" executives before Congress, Representative Greg Steube (R-Florida) grilled Google executives, saying that after being elected to Congress, he discovered that campaign emails for Republicans were being routed to spam folders by Gmail. My organization has experienced similar problems in sending email action alerts, with delivery rates varying dramatically depending on email provider. Many of our supporters are switching to ProtonMail, which also offers encryption.

❏ **Social media censorship:** If you still harbor any doubt that Twitter engenders left-wing bias, consider how they flagged tweets by President Donald Trump for promising that anarchists would be met with federal law enforcement, while leaving untouched the tweets of Iran's Ayatollah Ali Khamenei when he quite literally called for genocide of all Israelis. And what was Twitter's excuse for flagging

POTUS while leaving unmolested the leader of the world's most prolific state sponsor of international terrorism? "Because the Iranian dictator's tweets [are] 'commentary on political issues of the day' while Trump's could 'inspire harm.'"[5] (Trump was eventually "permanently suspended" by Twitter.)

Similarly, Facebook routinely removes conservative items for failure to meet "community standards" while leaving violently leftist posts in place. Indeed, a Project Veritas undercover video recorded a Facebook content moderator saying, "If someone is wearing a MAGA hat, I am going to delete them for terrorism." A Facebook whistleblower also provided documents to Project Veritas showing how conservative content is suppressed in Facebook code using a process called "deboosting.[6]

❏ **Boycotts**: Boycotts have become a popular weapon for radicals bent on pressuring corporations to comply with their agenda. Where they once went after corporations over exploitative policies (e.g. child labor in Third World countries), leftists now ignore those abuses in favor of attacking corporations over choice of clients and products, or the speech of their executives. For example:

- Goya Foods CEO Robert Unanue found himself on the receiving end of a boycott for merely praising President Trump
- Walmart was pressured into curtailing gun sales
- SoulCycle and Equinox faced boycotts over news their billionaire owner Stephen Ross hosted a fundraiser for President Trump
- Wayfair faced employee walkouts and boycotts when it sold mattresses and bunk beds to a charity group that manages illegal alien detention camps
- Chick-fil-A capitulated to LGBTQ(IA?) activists by ceasing donations to religious organizations ostensibly opposed to the LGBTQ (or whatever the acronym is today) agenda

❏ **Loss of jobs or other opportunities**: As exemplified in the sidebar below, people are now afraid to speak out or to have their name associated with conservative causes for fear of getting fired from the jobs. In recruiting plaintiffs for a recent gun permit lawsuit against

a county sheriff, I recently had two individuals decline to participate for fear of just such repercussions.

Intimidation through violence

The only thing more outrageous than the increasing violence by leftists
against conservatives is media silence on the issue. In a particularly
egregious case described below, I had to rely on BBC news articles because U.S. media refused to cover it.

❑ **"Harvard graduate threatens to 'stab' anyone who says 'all lives
matter'"**, said a *New York Post* article, continuing, "Claira Janover,
who graduated in May with a degree in government and psychology, went viral after posting a short clip in which she attacked anyone with 'the nerve, the sheer entitled caucasity to say "all lives
matter." ... 'I'ma stab you,' the Connecticut native said, zooming
in close on her face ... 'I'ma stab you, and while you're struggling
and bleeding out, I'ma show you my paper cut and say "'My cut
matters too,"' she added."[7]

❑ **"Texas man arrested for attack on boy wearing Trump hat,"** said
the BBC, which went on to describe an unprovoked attack on a
16-year-old who got his MAGA hat ripped off his head with enough
violence to tear out hair.[8]

❑ **"New York City gallery owner says he was attacked for wearing
'Make America Great Again' hat,"** said ABC News, describing the
beating of Jahangir Turan. The beating apparently had the intended
effect: "Turan, who suffered from broken bones under his eyeball,
wasn't planning on wearing it [again] because 'I think it's dangerous to wear a hat like this in New York City.'"[9]

❑ **"Conservative speaker who was assaulted by protester: 'This was
a warning shot to conservatives'"**, reported Fox News in a clear
case of speech suppression. And what was the controversial topic?
That men and women are different. Rather than getting an apology
for the assault, the speaker, Michael Knowles, was smeared as a
bigot.[10]

❏ **"Michelle Malkin beaten by BLM thugs and prevented from speaking at Denver pro-police rally,"** said the "American Thinker," continuing, "Conservative author and activist Michelle Malkin was brutally assaulted and prevented from speaking as she made her way to the speaker's platform at a pro-police public rally in downtown Denver on Sunday."[11] Incidentally, I've met Michelle Malkin. She is barely over five feet tall.

Extorting society into compliance

While you, in the interest of civility, try to keep politics *out* of unrelated parts of your life, leftists do exactly the opposite. Perhaps they were inspired by Alinsky, who said: "All of life is partisan. There is no dispassionate objectivity."[12] Hence, leftists purge the mention of God from any public arena while leftist football players kneel to disrespect the National Anthem. Nothing in your life is safe from ideologically motivated attack.

Violent riots

Even the violence perpetrated against individuals described above pales by comparison to the killing, looting, rioting, arson, and miscellaneous destruction wrought on American cities such as Atlanta, Chicago, New York, Portland, and Seattle (among many others) by the leftists of Antifa and Black Lives Matter – a subject too lengthy to fully detail here.

I will, however, note one significant trend: What makes these riots different than those during our last period of civil unrest, the 1960s, is that enough leftists have now been installed into urban governments that rioters are actually receiving local governmental support from mayors and city councils who hamstring police and oppose intervention of federal law enforcement, even falsely alleging that federal "storm troopers" are assaulting "peaceful protestors." This has caused some observers to describe the rioting as "insurgency."

As but one example, when federal law enforcement agencies built a protective fence around the federal Mark O. Hatfield U.S. Courthouse in Portland, Oregon to prevent rioters from burning it down (a job Portland should have done), the Portland City Council not only passed a resolution prohibiting Portland police from cooperating with the "federal occupiers," but also levied a nearly $200,000 fine ($500 for every 15 minutes) against the federal government for erecting the fence.[13]

'Cancelling' American culture

If moderates thought leftists decrying "racism" would be satisfied with tearing down statues commemorating Civil War Confederates, they were quickly disabused of the notion when desecration immediately spread to all American historical figures, including Christopher Columbus and, ironically enough, Abraham Lincoln and abolitionist Frederick Douglass.

The effort has nothing to do with "racism" and everything to do with eradicating American history and culture in the interest of replacing it with a socialist model. Said George Orwell, "The most effective way to destroy people is to deny and obliterate their own understanding of their history."

As I write this, Democrat D.C. Mayor Muriel Bowser and her "District of Columbia Facilities and Commemorative Expressions Working Group ("DCFACES," which should more properly be called "DEFACES"), is contemplating how best to "remove, relocate, or contextualize" monuments such as the Washington and Lincoln memorials.

Propagandizing children

In Chapter 2, I detailed how Marxist intellectuals infected America with critical theory, and how they have perpetrated a "long march" through our cultural institutions, media and schools. No longer satisfied to merely indoctrinate your children in school, however, leftists now apply "cancel culture" to purge cartoon characters like Dumbo and Peter Pan, even leveling crosshairs at Dr. Seuss.

Lest you assume leftist censorship of children's programming actually has anything to do with "racism," an in-depth look at what is being "canceled" and what they replace it with demonstrates how censored material is actually that which teaches independent thought, responsibility, and self-reliance. The doctrine replacing it teaches identity politics, victimhood and loathing of American culture and institutions.

False narratives

Apparently channeling propaganda master Joseph Goebbels, who said, "If you tell a lie big enough and keep repeating it, people will eventually come to believe it," leftists now completely ignore truth in favor of bold and politically expedient lies.

As one example among many, let's consider the narrative being pushed on the American public by both the media and Democrat politicians regarding multi-week riots in Portland, Oregon. Here is what I recently wrote for an international news source:

> *"We have apparently reached a point in American political debate where facts don't matter. Ironically, our left-leaning media, which normally argues* **for** *federal intervention on virtually any topic, is arguing* **against** *federal intervention being made by President Trump on behalf of citizens essentially held hostage by leftist local governments as their civil rights under 18 U.S.C., Section 241 are repeatedly violated by the very people purporting to be their leaders.*

> *"Among the falsehoods being propagated is that 'peaceful' protestors are being targeted by 'anonymous' federal law enforcement officers. In truth, those arrested are far from peaceful, instead repeatedly attacking federal property. And as expressed by acting DHS Secretary Chad Wolf and substantiated in video footage, federal law enforcement personnel are clearly identified on their uniforms."*

How the left justifies its behavior

As a reasonable, law-abiding citizen, you are doubtless asking how leftists can justify bullying, lying, threatening and assaulting all who stand in their way. In an exercise of pure "Alinskyism," the answer has three components:

1. **As leftists, they are "The Enlightened"**: Because they are smarter and better educated than you are, they alone are entitled to chart your future. What they know that you don't, says Alinsky, is that, "We now live in a world where no man can have a loaf of bread

while his neighbor has none. If he does not share his bread, he dare not sleep, for his neighbor will kill him. To eat and sleep in safety a man must do the right thing ... and be in practice his brother's keeper."[14] Translation: "share" your property with the socialist state ... or else.

2. **Their utopian ends justify any means, however deceptive**: Indeed, Alinsky regarded the question of whether ends justify means as "meaningless," instead advocating flexible ethics that shift with both perspective and the potential for reward. So malleable are his ethics that he maintains the only relevant question is, "Does this *particular* end justify this *particular* means?"[15]

3. **Nothing is inherently evil**: Says Alinsky: "The grasp of the duality of all phenomena is vital in our understanding of politics. It frees one from *the myth that one approach is positive and another negative* ... The description of any procedure as 'positive' or 'negative' is the mark of a political illiterate."[16]

Among Alinsky's "rules of the ethics of means and ends" is a rule that goals must be sold to the unwashed in flowery terms like "Liberty, Equality and Fraternity." Remember that the next time you hear leftists promote gun bans or open borders "for the children."

Death by cancel culture...

The leftist jackal pack finally dragged down conservative University of North Carolina Wilmington professor and columnist Mike Adams, who had long stood for conservative principles. After years of Adams surviving calls for his firing, leftist reaction to his Tweet about Democrat North Carolina Governor Roy Cooper's refusal to release the state from coronavirus restrictions apparently did him in. The Tweet said he "felt like a free man who was not living in the slave state of North Carolina" before adding "Massa Cooper, let my people go!" and was related not to race, but to Cooper's COVID-19 proclamation. Immediately, Change.org started a petition for his firing which garnered 57,000 signatures plus support from Hollywood celebrities Orlando Jones, Sophia Bush and Hillary Burton Morgan, with the latter demanding a boycott of the school until Adams was fired.[17] Adams reached a $500,000 settlement with UNC for the resulting forced retirement, but allegedly committed suicide not long after.[18] The left doubtless celebrated.

(continued on next page)

(continued from previous page)

...elsewhere, a happy ending

In a video that went viral in 2019, Nick Sandmann and other students from Kentucky's Covington High School were in the District of Columbia for the March of Life. Using a maliciously edited version of the video and with the apparent intent to destroy his life, numerous news outlets claimed the youth, who was wearing a MAGA hat in the video, was harassing a Native American activist. But when the unedited video showed Sandmann was actually smiling and remaining calm despite harassment by the Native American, Sandmann filed libel suits against CNN for $275 million and the *Washington Post* for $250 million, eventually reaching undisclosed settlements with both. As of this writing, Sandmann has remaining lawsuits against NBC, the *New York Times*, CBS News, ABC News, Gannett, and *Rolling Stone*.[19]

References:

1. Emily Ekins, "Poll: 62% of Americans Say They Have Political Views They're Afraid to Share," July 22, 2020, Cato Institute, https://www.cato.org/publications/survey-reports/poll-62-americans-say-they-have-political-views-theyre-afraid-share

2. Lucas Manfredi, "'Grandfathering' to no longer be used due to 'racist origins', says Massachusetts appeal court," August 3, 2020, Fox News, https://www.foxnews.com/us/grandfather-clause-racist-origins

3. "PART 1: CNN Insider Blows Whistle on Network President Jeff Zucker's Personal Vendetta Against POTUS," October 14, 2019, Project Veritas, https://www.projectveritas.com/video/part-1-cnn-insider-blows-whistle-on-network-president-jeff-zuckers-personal/

4. Charles Creitz, "Dr. Robert Epstein: Study claims Google reflected 'very dramatic bias' in 2016 election search results," September 8, 2019, Fox News, https://www.foxnews.com/media/google-bias-search-results-trump-clinton-epstein-levin

5. Ebony Bowden, "Twitter defends blocking Trump tweets but not Iran's Ayatollah Khamenei," July 29, 2020, *New York Post*, https://nypost.com/2020/07/29/twitter-defends-blocking-trump-tweets-but-not-irans-ayatollah-khamenei/

6. Lucas Nolan, "Facebook Whistleblower: Staff 'Deboost' Unwanted Content – and I Saw Same Code Used on Conservatives," February 7, 2019, Breitbart News, https://www.breitbart.com/tech/2019/02/27/facebook-whistleblower-staff-deboost-unwanted-content-and-i-saw-same-code-used-on-conservatives/?fbclid=IwAR1cOLkgpS6K2LmxKsdN2q9hcT_rRvSIayOGTaGaCRqIwJYVWTl3tXG7uO0

7. Lee Brown, "Harvard graduate threatens to 'stab' anyone who says 'all lives matter'", *New York Post*, July 1, 2020, https://nypost.com/2020/07/01/harvard-grad-threatens-to-stab-anyone-who-says-all-lives-matter/

8. "Texas man arrested for attack on boy wearing Trump hat," BBC News, July 6, 2018, https://www.bbc.com/news/world-us-canada-44745676

9. Ella Torres, "New York City gallery owner says he was attacked for wearing 'Make America Great Again' hat," ABC News, August 2, 2019, https://abcnews.go.com/US/york-city-gallery-owner-attacked-wearing-make-america/story?id=64731770

10. Victor Garcia, "Conservative speaker who was assaulted by protester: 'This was a warning shot to conservatives'," Fox News, April 13, 2019, https://www.foxnews.com/politics/conservative-speaker-who-was-assaulted-by-protester-this-was-a-warning-shot-to-conservatives

11 Peter Barry Chowka, "Michelle Malkin beaten by BLM thugs and prevented from speaking at Denver pro-police rally," *American Thinker*, July 20, 2020, https://www.americanthinker.com/blog/2020/07/michelle_malkin_beaten_by_blm_thugs_and_prevented_from_speaking_at_denver_propolice_rally.html

12. Saul Alinksy, *Rules for Radicals: A Pragmatic Primer for Realistic Radicals*, 1971, Vintage Books Edition, 1989, page 10.

13. "Commissioner Eudaly's Statement on the Status of Portland's Federal Occupation," City of Portland, Oregon, July 28, 2020, https://www.portland.gov/eudaly/news/2020/7/28/commissioner-eudalys-statement-status-portlands-federal-occupation

14. Op. cit. note 12, page 23.

15. Op. cit. note 11, page 47.

16. Op. cit. note 11, page 17.

17. "'One Tree Hill' stars ask fans to help fire North Carolina professor," June 11, 2020, Associated Press, https://pagesix.com/2020/06/11/one-tree-hill-stars-ask-fans-to-help-fire-north-carolina-professor/?_ga=2.134946481.1555622036.1596128125-229377256.1595969090

18. Joshua Rhett Miller, "UNC Wilmington professor Mike Adams died by suicide: cops," July 28, 2020, *New York Post*, https://nypost.com/2020/07/28/unc-wilmington-professor-mike-adams-died-by-suicide-deputies/

19. Jack Phillips, "Washington Post Settles Defamation Lawsuit With Nick Sandmann Over Viral Video Claims," July 24, 2020, *The Epoch Times*, https://www.theepochtimes.com/washington-post-settles-defamation-lawsuit-with-nick-sandmann-over-viral-video-claims_3437075.html

Chapter 4
Beating Leftists at Their Own Game

"Political tags - such as royalist, communist, democrat, populist, fascist, liberal, conservative, and so forth - are never basic criteria. The human race divides politically into those who want people to be controlled and those who have no such desire." – Robert A. Heinlein

As expressed by Robert Heinlein above, political opposition on any issue can be reduced to control of others – who wants it and who doesn't.

In most cases, you will be fighting collectivists, for whom control is essential to enforce the will of the collective (or more precisely, those *claiming* to represent the collective), rather than individualists, for whom control is, if not an anathema, at least a necessary evil. Although I prefer the label of "leftist" to describe your political opposition, even that is only a subset of the "controllers" Heinlein describes above, since control can extend beyond politics.

Why you must engage the enemy

In *Waking the Sleeping Giant: How Mainstream Americans Can Beat Liberals at Their Own Game,* authors Timothy Daughtry and Gary Casselman detail why conservatives have consistently *won* the intellectual debate while simultaneously *losing* our republic. "Mainstream Americans play by the rules," say the authors, "But it has become obvious that we have put too much faith in elections and not enough in what happens between elections."[1] They go on to discuss why we win elections (e.g. 1994, 2000, 2010, and 2016), but continue to lose control of the culture which underpins our government and society.

Donald Trump was targeted for defeat primarily due to his effort to dismantle what has been called "the deep state" (leftists in bureaucratic positions of power thanks to the multi-generational power-grab described in Chapter 2) which continues to hamstring conservatives elected to office.

Waking the Sleeping Giant points out that because mainstream Americans simply want to "live and let live," we are prone to dominating an election and then, assuming we have won and that the people we elected will take care of everything, go back to mowing the lawn and watching football.

Not so, the left. Because their objective is control, regardless of whether they win or lose an election they continue to plot their next moves. That is why, despite national election victories listed above, we find ourselves on the precipice of defeat. After each loss, the left quietly continues to organize the incremental takeover of our republic.

To reclaim our society, *you* must fight socialism, not just in Congress, but in your children's school, on your city council, in local public forums, and in your state legislature.

Confronting leftists is probably something you would prefer to avoid. As *Waking the Sleeping Giant* points out, mainstream Americans respond with deep discomfort to the emotional blackmail levied against us by the left. Your opponents count on and manipulate that discomfort.

The basic differences between you and your opponents:

❏ *You* prioritize the individual; *they* prioritize the collective.

❏ *You* value individual rights and freedoms; *they* regard individual freedom as dangerous to the collective.

❏ *You* value individual achievement; *they* demand group collaboration.

❏ *You* believe building wealth benefits all, that "a rising tide lifts all boats"; *they* regard wealth as a zero sum game in which whatever you have is something someone else doesn't.

- ❏ *You* value private property; *they* think in terms of "stakeholders."

- ❏ *You* value independent thought; *they* demand adherence to dogma.

- ❏ *You* think rationally; *they* think emotionally. (This is more than just an observation. A 2014 study published in *Society for Personality and Social Psychology*[2] confirms it.)

- ❏ *You* believe success should be rewarded by rise in social hierarchy; whether they admit it or not, *they* want immutable social strata.

- ❏ *You* see individuals as they are; *they* see them in terms of "identity" (i.e. which ethnic or racial role they occupy).

Leftist lexicon

To debate a leftist, you must understand their language. Below are a few common phrases you will hear from the left, and what they really mean.

- ❏ **Cisgendered:** A term for the increasingly rare individuals in society whose "gender identity" matches the bits and pieces they were born with. If you want to get a group of leftists in a tizzy, refer to such people as "heterosexual" or as members of the "two genders."

- ❏ **Cultural appropriation:** Anything once considered humorous, if it refers to any culture other than Western European. To leftists, humor is forbidden.

- ❏ **Deplatforming:** Shutting down free speech by anybody who disagrees with the left … all in the name of tolerance and "Democracy," of course. Can originate from either left-wing activists or left-wing social media platforms.

- ❏ **Diversity**: People who look different but think in exactly the same way. Although leftists treasure diversity in things like sexual preference, diversity of thought is unacceptable and will be punished.

- ❏ **Hater:** Epithet used against people who make leftists unhappy.

Rules for Anti-RADICALS

- **Homophobe:** Anyone who still believes there are two genders.

- **Inclusiveness:** *Ex*clusiveness, particularly of opposing viewpoints.

- **Mansplaining:** Derogatory term for any rational explanation offered by someone so backward that he still thinks of himself as "male."

- **Offensive:** Anything that makes a leftist unhappy.

- **Racist:** You, if you are white.

- **Sexist:** You, if you are male.

- **Social justice:** The left's primary engine for redistribution of wealth and power.

- **Stakeholder:** A clever phrase used by leftists to create the impression of ownership in things they do not own.

- **Tolerance:** *In*tolerance, particularly of opposing viewpoints.

- **Toxic:** As added to "masculinity" or other concepts (e.g. Senator Josh Hawley's "toxic populism"), it means anything the left doesn't like. (Are you sensing a theme yet?)

- **Toxic masculinity:** A quality "[d]emonstrated by men who think masculinity is a virtue rather than a vice. Alas, toxic males can still be found in places like police forces, the military, and high school football fields. It is especially reviled by the kind of men who always got picked last for dodgeball in grade school."[3]

- **White privilege:** Claimed advantage held by a Caucasian, however handicapped, underprivileged, or impoverished he or she may be.

- **White supremacist (aka "white nationalist"):** An ever-expanding definition which now apparently includes all Caucasians, particularly any Caucasian with the audacity to defend American culture.

❏ **Woke:** Conforming to the leftist ideology of the day, however insane it may be.

❏ **Wokeness:** A unique form of hypocrisy in which ostensibly "moral" standards, often completely bereft of truth and logic, are applied only against conservatives, leaving the left free to lie, rob, cheat, and steal as it sees fit.

Debating leftists (if you must)[4]

I don't mean "debate" solely in the formal sense. The "debate" could be with a Third Grade teacher instructing your child on the evils of America; it could be over the American flag in your front yard which your leftist neighbor finds "offensive;" or it could be formally such as on a university stage, radio program or television forum. As a conservative, you start from a position of disadvantage because, unlike your opposition, you debate honestly.

Never forget that *when debating a leftist, you are unlikely to convert them*. No amount of rationality will win them over to your viewpoint. As a rational thinker, this will be hard for you to accept, but you must. As Mark Twain has been credited with saying, "No amount of evidence will persuade an idiot."

Accordingly, you can realistically expect to secure only two objectives. First, you can use the forum to win over *other* people who are not devout leftists. Second, you can impose your agenda on unwilling opponents. That much is achievable. Winning the hearts and minds of leftists is not. You must understand that while winning over a centrist is possible, doctrinaire leftists can be beaten but rarely converted.

Top 10 things to understand in dealing with leftists:

1. *Everything* **is political**: *You* just want to watch football; leftist football players politicize the sport by kneeling to protest our national anthem. The propensity of the left to regard everything in life as politics is why large corporations are now "woke," and why supposedly "beloved" talk show host and (gay) comedian Ellen DeGeneres instantly became, in the words of one tabloid, "the most hated woman in Hollywood" when she had the audacity to befriend for-

mer President George W. Bush. Absolutely everything you do will be seen by leftists through a political lens. Act accordingly. That doesn't mean changing your behavior to placate them; it simply means being prepared for their faux outrage.

2. **Language controls the debate**: Leftist lexicon is a battle tactic. The left creates phrases which are deliberately flavored to achieve political objectives. "Gun violence" isn't about violence, it's about guns. Gun "safety" really means gun *ban*, "Inclusiveness" means *exclud ing* anyone with competing views. Their goal is to insert their politically charged lexicon into common experience as a Trojan Horse for their intended objectives. *If you adopt their language, you cede the battle before it has begun.* I routinely say, "I reject the phrase 'gun violence' because it implies that death by stabbing, bludgeoning or improvised explosive device is somehow better than death by gun. If you were really interested in saving lives, you would be working to stop *all* types of violence."

3. **To leftists, words are merely bludgeons to secure obedience**: Just as leftists use flexible ethics (see Chapter 1), so, too, they use "flexible words" without fixed definitions. Theirs is a world in which "racist" can be levied at Abraham Lincoln and "offensive" is something *you* say, even when a leftist freely uses exactly the same word. Because they regard every means at their disposal as a potential weapon for securing your compliance with their agenda, words become bludgeons for obedience. That's why words like "racist," "hater," and "sexist" are so popular with leftists. They have no fixed meaning and, when levied, force you to defend yourself instead of pressing home a rational argument for which the leftist has no answer.

Said Daughtry and Casselman (and yes, I object to their description of opponents as "liberal"):

- "'Racist' is liberal for 'You're not making me happy and I hate you.'
- "'Sexist' is liberal for 'You're not making me happy and I hate you.'
- "'Hatemonger' is liberal for 'You're not making me happy and I hate you.'

- "'Greedy' is liberal for 'You're not making me happy and I hate you.'"[5]

4. **Expect name-calling:** When they lack a cogent argument (which is most of the time), leftists respond by calling you "racist," "sexist," a "hater," a "misogynist," or some other brand. The intent is two-fold: to hide the lack of grounding for their argument, and to turn the argument around by putting *you* on the defensive. Item eleven under "Top 20 debate tactics" below contains a simple retort that will stop them cold.

5. **Expressions of altruism are rarely altruistic:** You routinely hear leftists profess their benevolent goal to "save the planet," "end racism," or "minimize our carbon footprint." Unfortunately, when they say, "I want to save the planet," what they really mean is: "I am a better person than you are. Give me more power."

6. **To the left, ends justify any means:** Straight from the Alinsky handbook, their lofty goals, to them, justify any crime. For example, as demonstrated not only by rioters but also by Democrat local governments in the 2020 riots, there is no life they will not destroy and no city they will not render uninhabitable in their quest for The Great Socialist Utopia. Similarly, opposition to voter ID and advocating massive mail-in voting cannot be viewed by any reasonable person as anything more than an effort to increase voter fraud by groups that support Democrats.

7. **Cognitive dissonance is alive and well:** Because leftists think emotionally rather than rationally, they are able to simultaneously entertain utterly contradictory beliefs to a far greater degree than others. That is what enabled leftists to insist that businesses must remain closed during the coronavirus pandemic while simultaneously blaming Donald Trump for high unemployment. It allowed leftist Portland Mayor Ted Wheeler to blame federal government presence in defending the Mark O. Hatfield federal courthouse for riots which stretched for months after federal law enforcement vacated the site.

8. **Double standards rule the day:** Hypocrisy is a leftist's stock in trade. Some of it results from cognitive dissonance, as described in

#7 above, but most often it is an exercise of "ends justify means" as described in #6. That's what allows Barack Obama, engineer of both "Fast and Furious" gun smuggling to Mexico and possibly the Russia collusion hoax, to keep a straight face while calling Donald Trump "lawless." It is what enables leftists to attack conservative Supreme Court Justice Brett Kavanaugh for ancient, unsubstantiated, and transparently false claims of sexual assault while defending Democrat Governor Andrew Cuomo against eleven (at last count) credible women alleging sexual harassment. [Note: Cuomo eventually resigned.]

9. **Expect "preemptive accusation":** In psychological "projection," one unconsciously ascribes one's own fears, anger, anxiety, or duplicity to another person. With the left, it is quite conscious and was probably learned from the Soviet Union, which during the Cold War made art of accusing the U.S. of doing exactly what it was. Being the first to make an accusation insulates the accuser who is actually doing acts of which he accuses others. In 2020, for example, Democrats worked hard to steal the election while simultaneously accusing Donald Trump of planning to steal the election.

10. **Contrary to popular opinion, you and your opponents do *not* have common goals:** Everybody wants a better America, right? Wrong. *Your* goal is to improve the society in which your children live; *theirs* is to tear down our existing society to create The Great Socialist Utopia they envision.

Remember that Alinsky said:

> *"The first step in community organization is community disorganization. The disruption of the present organization is the first step toward community organization. Present arrangements must be disorganized if they are to be displaced by new patterns ... All change means disorganization of the old and organization of the new."*[6]

Therefore, in yet another exercise of Alinskyism, the only way to achieve their societal goal is to destroy existing society – *your* society. In the 2020 riots, Antifa actually cheered the death of innocents and BLM had nothing to say about gang violence in Chicago killing black children. Why? Because in their eyes, both were acceptable prices to pay for creating The Great Socialist Utopia.

Four general rules in debating the left

Said Daughtry and Casselman: "Leftists cannot defend the indefensible, so one of their tactics is to get their way by bullying. Accusations, name-calling, lies, demands, threats of lawsuits, and even intimations of violence – from left-wing race hustlers to union thugs, leftists all too often resemble those of the schoolyard bully."[7] The following debate rules will help you defend against them.

1. **"If you're explaining, you're losing"**: Invariably, a leftist will make an accusation which you will feel compelled to explain. As expressed above by Ronald Reagan, if you allow yourself to be put on the defensive, you will lose. Example of losing argument: "The Tea Party is *not* racist. Lots of black conservatives support the Tea Party." For effective opposing tactics, see below.

2. **Nothing good comes from a conversation starting with "you people"**: As an example, "*You people* selfishly think you can use your property any way you want without consideration for other '*stakeholders*.'" Anybody who uses "you people" is not your friend.

3. **Your opponent's claims of support always have a "but"**: Your opponent might claim to support your position before introducing a "but" which will negate the entire claim. Example: "I support the Second Amendment, *but* I think all gun owners should be licensed and all guns registered."

4. **Do not appease your opposition and do not "compromise"**: Said Alinsky, "To the organizer, compromise is a key and beautiful word. It is always present in the pragmatics of operation... *If you start with nothing, demand 100 percent, then compromise for 30 percent, you're 30 percent ahead.*" To leftists, "compromise" is a process in which you lose slightly less than you would have lost under their original proposal, but *you still lose*. In what Daughtry and Casselman call "the appeasement cycle,"[8] civil people, faced with accusations from the left, will typically offer something to appease them. The left will take it, and then start the cycle all over again, taking

more and more until they seize all of the power they originally intended.

Top 20 debate tactics

If you want a model for debate, watch videos of White House Press Secretary Kayleigh McEnany and observe how calmly and precisely she derailed the obscenely hostile press corps. The other perfect example was Vice President Mike Pence, who dominated Kamala Harris during the 2020 vice presidential debate. Some of the techniques below are shared in common with media interview techniques described later in the book, particularly with hostile media.

The hard truth is that most formal debates are sponsored by leftists and are therefore stacked against you. Suck it up and participate anyway. I once declined to participate in a forum heavily loaded against me on the grounds that I would deny them legitimacy. It didn't work. They got their media soundbites anyway and my plan to skewer them using plants in the audience failed. My policy now is to take all comers (and beat the crap out of them).

1. **Control the forum:** At "The Great Gun Debate," a televised forum hosted by the Southeastern Center for the Contemporary Arts, I was told by the organizer that I didn't need to put out a call for sympathetic attendees. Fortunately, I ignored that recommendation, because what I found when I arrived was a hostile cabal of limousine liberals and Birkenstock-wearing, leftover Hippies. At another televised gun debate, I arrived early and pulled the signs off the five front-and-center seats reserved for Michael Bloomberg's gun control organization, Moms Demand Action, then sat my people in them.

    • **Items to consider when participating in a debate:**

        o Who is moderating and what is the format?
        o Who are the other participants? Are they evenly balanced, or designed to outnumber you?
        o Who is in the audience, if any?
        o Does the format satisfy your preference for seating, table or lectern? Camera angles?

2. **Present yourself as a serious person on serious business:** Depending on circumstances, in the modern era this might or might not involve a jacket and tie. However, remember that the legislative arena is the last definite bastion of formal attire. I prefer a jacket and tie for media and debates, but that is just my style. What is *not* acceptable is a T-shirt displaying "I don't dial 9-1-1" or similar inflammatory slogans. Ditto for camouflage or ball caps.

3. **Prepare, prepare, prepare:** Too often, activists hem and haw, hunting for the right words when responding to questions. Prior to any debate or media interview, type up a list of potential questions and snappy, soundbite answers, particularly if the debate or interview will be a short format. The goal is not to read from the outline, which looks stupid, but to glance at highlighted phrases you have already rehearsed. Anticipate your opponent's debating points and have rebuttals ready.

4. **Practice by video:** This is particularly helpful for neophyte debaters. When I first started doing this, I discovered distracting mannerisms and expressions I didn't even know I had.

5. **Speak slowly, clearly, and charismatically:** In the heat of the debate, this might be more difficult than you think. Breath and think before speaking. Additionally, avoid jargon, abbreviations, and large words. Your intent is to make yourself as clear to the audience as possible. While practicing your talking points (preferably by video), try to boost your charisma while speaking. However ugly it gets, try to smile and not look angry.

6. **Present structured arguments:** Have a central thesis for your debate points. Return to the point periodically, using the debate points to shore up the central argument. Take, for example, a debate on the pros and cons of concealed handgun permit laws. If your opponent claims that permit-holders are wanton criminals, you can't just defensively rebut that argument with stats showing how law-abiding permit-holders are; you must instead go on offense with a central argument that concealed handgun permit laws deter violent crime and save lives.

7. **Don't let your opponent change the subject:** When skewered in a

debate, leftists love to change the subject. For example, Fox News reporter Peter Doocy pointed out to White House Press Secretary Jan Psaki that in Joe Biden's "press conference," he answered only pre-screened questions from a list, and never Fox News questions. Psaki answered, "Well, I would say that I'm always happy to have this conversation with you, even about your awesome socks you're having on today…"

When my organization ran Facebook ads in the 2020 election high-lighting Joe Biden's Sinohawk Holdings influence-peddling, leftists came unglued, demonstrating we had struck a nerve. In comments, they tried to change the subject to Donald Trump. I continued to bore into the topic they avoided: "I know you would love to change the subject since, after all, you don't have a rebuttal. But was the laptop Hunter Biden's or not? And if not, why not?" Don't allow yourself to be deflected from your point, not by your opponent, not by the moderator, and not by yourself.

8. **Consider your audience:** If the 2020 elections demonstrated anything, it is that in modern political debate, facts don't necessarily win the day. Structure your arguments to appeal emotionally to your target audience. That said, there is no point to trying to win over leftists. They don't operate on facts, and they don't have open minds. After the above-mentioned free-for-all passing itself off as "The Great Gun Debate" finished, various Birkenstock-wearing long-hairs in the studio audience came up to tell me why my hardball refusal to get rolled by my four opponents (whom I debated pretty much single-handedly) hadn't persuaded them. My answer? "Of course not. Only an idiot would expend time and energy trying to convince you. I was appealing to the television audience."

9. **Be the voice of rationality:** No gesticulating, excessive facial expressions or raised voices. In fact, if possible, speak softly (although not so softly that your opposition talks over you). *You* are the voice of reason; *they* are the radical nutcases. For a perfect example, watch a video of Vice President Mike Pence in the 2020 vice presidential debate. He was the quiet voice of rationality while Kamala Harris spent the debate smirking and scoffing. Moreover, he appears to figure out her "tell" – a nasty, sarcastic laugh when skewered on

a debating point – and exploits it by drawing it from her nearly at will.

10. **Use bullet-pointed notes with key phrases highlighted**: On a talking head television show, I once debated a woman named Kit Gruell (yes, that was her real name), whose "Coalition Against Domestic Violence," had decided to dip a toe into gun control. Gruell sat down and spread out reams of articles and pictures. In front of me, I placed a single sheet of paper with bullet points rehearsed and highlighted. When she would shuffle through papers looking for her point, I would fill the gap with mine. She went down in flames.

11. **Reject any label used against you**: Remember this retort: *"Isn't that just like a leftist."* Say it not as a question, but as a statement, preferably dripping with contempt. Use it whenever a leftist calls you a "hater," a "sexist," a "racist," etc. At the virtually unmoderated television "Great Gun Debate," which devolved into four leftists against me, we weren't five minutes into the free-for-all when one of them whined, "You're a hater." Had I responded with "No, I'm not," I would have lost. Instead, I shut him down with, "Isn't that just like a leftist: you don't have a cogent argument, so you start slinging names." The tactic shifts the focus back to the questioner, exactly like Ronald Reagan in his 1980 debate with Jimmy Carter. When Carter tried to pigeonhole Reagan on Medicare, Reagan used an exasperated line that resonates to this day: *"There you go again."* Not only did he avoid defense and make Carter look like a liar, it was all anyone remembered of the debate.

12. **Reject the premise**: Opponents love to use loaded questions for which there simply is no good answer. Following the Portland riots in which a conservative activist was shot by an Antifa type, an interviewer asked me, "Do you think it was a good idea for a right-wing militia to stir up trouble in downtown Portland?" My answer was, "That's kind of a loaded question, don't you think? The real question is 'Do I think a conservative should be able to exercise his rights under the First Amendment without getting shot?' and the answer is unequivocally yes." For examples of rejecting a false premise, check out videos of Attorney General William Barr's July 28, 2020 testimony before a ridiculously hostile and partisan House

of Representatives. Later, in the 2020 vice presidential debate, Mike Pence raised this to an art form by rejecting the premise without even appearing to do so.

13. **Don't answer the question you are asked; answer the question you *want* to answer**: This is a media tactic easily adapted to debate. Feel free to camouflage it by starting with, "That's an excellent question..." before moving on to the point you intended to make all along. Better yet, use the tactic Pence used to great effect by taking notes while your opponent is speaking and then using at least part of the time allotted to shoot down your opponent's last debating point.

14. **Speak in soundbites with crisp finishes**: Make your remarks memorable using remarks which are:

   - **Clean:** Clearly spoken.
   - **Well-articulated:** Minimize "uh"s and repetitive spacer words or phrases. (I have to fight the tendency to use "The bottom line is...")
   - **Plain:** No fancy words. The goal is not to show everyone how smart you are; it is to convey a point to people of all educational levels.
   - **Memorable:** It could be something clever or something relatively graphic (within the bounds of the law and decency), but make them remember it.

15. **Prepare "zingers"**: Memorable put-downs will be the thing most remembered from your debate. Analyze your opponent's weak points and have the zingers ready for delivery. In the 2020 vice presidential debate, VP Mike Pence nailed Kamala Harris with an old line from U.S. Senator Daniel Patrick Moynihan (D-NY): "You're entitled to your own opinion, you're not entitled to your own facts." Better still was Lloyd Bentsen's riposte to Dan Quayle who, during the 1988 vice presidential debate, had compared himself to John F. Kennedy: "Senator, I served with Jack Kennedy. I knew Jack Kennedy. Jack Kennedy was a friend of mine. Senator, you're no Jack Kennedy." (Ouch.) Incidentally, neither of those zingers was original. Feel free to lift one from previous debaters *provided* it hasn't become cliché.

16. **Call "B.S." on phony stats**: Leftists love to make up statistics, either from "whole cloth" or from biased research and polls. It is up to you to be prepared with not only the truth, but also with the fallacy behind their stats. Not only should you call your opponent a liar, you should do so with ridicule. In a debate with Peter Ambler of Gabby Giffords' gun control group, at that time calling itself "Americans for Responsible Solutions," Ambler claimed his organization had "one million" members. I replied, "In truth, you count everybody who surfs through your website as a 'member.' It should disturb you greatly to know that *I* am one of your so-called 'members.'" He was so busted that even he had to laugh.

17. **Cite your stats accurately and with sources:** Point out frequently that effective public policy should rest on facts, not feelings. Without becoming dry and pedantic, have the facts at your fingertips, including who did the study or compiled the statistics. Wherever possible, use unassailable sources such as the U.S. Department of Justice rather than talking points from advocacy groups. Summarize them in a few memorable words, giving just enough numbers to illustrate your point and demonstrate your credibility.

18. **Call out "straw man" arguments:** "Straw man" arguments involve deliberately misinterpreting, distorting, or even inventing something you supposedly said, and then attacking it. Democrats and the media routinely lambasted Donald Trump for things he never said. For example, misrepresenting his sarcasm about the hacking of state secrets from Hillary Clinton's private server, Democrats claimed "Donald Trump called on the Russians to hack the DNC." If your opponent does it to you, immediately come back with: "We both know I didn't say that, which makes you a liar."

19. **Interject, but don't allow interruptions:** Leftists love to talk over other people. I once watched James Carville make what could best be described as animal noises in his quest to drown out his opponent. Be prepared to talk over someone who attempts to talk over you. If interrupted, one tactic is to continue to repeat your point until the leftist finally relents. You can also call your opponent on his or her interruptions with something like, "Stop interrupting me." That said, you can interject short remarks when required. "That's nonsense," or "Not true" would be typical short interjections.

20. **Get the last word:** In debating, I prefer to dominate the forum from beginning to end. But if that isn't possible, make sure to get in the last point, and do it in a crisp and memorable fashion.

Dirty Debate Tricks

This was derived from "10 Bullying Debate Techniques from Ben Shapiro," featured on "thepowermoves.com".[9] It was not published by Ben Shapiro and likely wouldn't be acknowledged by him. It is, however, an excellent summary of dirty tricks leftists commonly use and which you, depending on your comfort level, can use yourself.

1. Get under your opponent's skin

2. Strike when they overreact (i.e. "gaslighting")

    a. Manipulate the victim into overreacting ("getting under their skin")
    b. Remain calm as they overreact
    c. Point out to the victim that they are overreacting and/or acting crazy and aggressive

3. Convey authority by talking like you're speaking the gospel

4. Ridicule your opponent (subtly)

5. Use (or bend) data & statistics to increase your authority

6. Play the victim

7. Hide your power source

8. Accuse your opponent of your own faults (I call this "projection," and it is commonly used by leftists. If you accuse your opponent of doing something you, yourself are guilty of, it sounds like "copy-catting" when he finally points it out in your behavior.)

9. Frame the interaction (the way it serves you): Whoever gets to frame the interaction holds a huge advantage in debates.

10. Seek peace (only) when they're on their knees: If debating aggressively, offering an olive branch once you have trounced them will make you look magnanimous.

Beating Leftists at Their Own Game

References:

1. Timothy C. Daughtry, PhD and Gary R. Casselman PhD, *Waking the Sleeping Giant: How Mainstream Americans Can Beat Liberals at Their Own Game*, Beaufort Books, 2012.

2. Ruthie Pliskin, Daniel Bar-Tal, Gal Sheppes, Eran Halperin. "Are leftists more emotion-driven than rightists? The interactive influence of ideology and emotions on support for policies." *Personality and Social Psychology Bulletin*, 2014, https://www.sciencedaily.com/releases/2014/11/141107091559.htm

3. Bradley R. Gitz, "The leftist lexicon," *The Arkansas Gazette*, August 5, 2019, https://www.arkansasonline.com/news/2019/aug/05/the-leftist-lexicon-20190805-1/

4. Ann Coulter's book, *How to Talk to a Liberal (If You Must): The World According to Ann Coulter*, Crown Publishing Group, Random House, Inc., 2004.

5. Op. cit. note 1, page 54.

6. Saul D. Alinsky, *Rules for Radicals: A Pragmatic Primer for Realistic Radicals*, 1971, Vintage Books, Random House, Inc., 1989, page 116.

7. Op. cit. note 1, page 13.

8. Op. cit. note 1, page 47.

9. Lucio Buffalmano , "10 Bullying Debate Techniques from Ben Shapiro," Power University, https://thepowermoves.com/ben-shapiro-debate-techniques/

PART TWO
Activist Tools & Tactics
(The Basics)

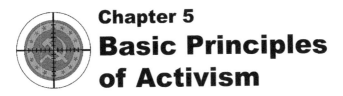

Chapter 5
Basic Principles of Activism

*"Identify the problem, find who can solve it,
and motivate them to do so.
That is what an activist does."* – FPV

I'm tired of seeing pro-freedom organizations run by hacks. Worse than the incompetent, however, are the compromisers. I don't mean activists who compromise tactically, but rather those willing to compromise their principles, often to assuage their own egos.

The tactics below and in following chapters will make you more effective in defending our constitutionally guaranteed freedoms. First and foremost, *you must vow never to compromise on principle.* And if you spend a significant portion of your time and effort telling your followers what they must accept rather than telling politicians what they must do, compromising your principles might be exactly what you are doing.

What is "grassroots" activism?

First, let's discuss what grassroots activism is not. It is not bussing in agitators – paid or otherwise – to create the illusion of popular support, as do Antifa and Michael Bloomberg's Everytown for Gun Safety. The political term of art for that practice is "astroturfing," as in *phony grass,* and you should denounce it for what it is whenever you encounter it.

Merriam-Webster's most pertinent definition for grassroots is: "…the basic level of society or of an organization especially as viewed in relation to higher or more centralized positions of power."

The "grassroots" is comprised of the people Patrick Buchannan once called "peasants with pitchforks." They are the average, everyday folks – not the movers and shakers – who are, to steal from the movie *Network*, "as mad as hell and not going to take it anymore."

And as a grassroots organizer, it is *your* job to feed that anger, collect it, and channel it to relevant decision-makers. To paraphrase the late Senator Everett Dirksen, "When they feel the heat, they see the light." Everything you are about to read is intended to make that possible.

At a basic level, your goal is to make a "demand" from a "target" which is capable of fulfilling the demand. Demands may be "substantive" (e.g. a bill passed or a company action stopped) or "procedural" (e.g. passing a bill out of committee). In some cases, your demand might contain a "fallback demand" to which you can negotiate without compromising your principles.

Are you an "activist"?

When your car is awaiting service at a dealership for ten days and the service underwriter shrugs, "The parts aren't in yet," do you just say, "Okay"? If so, you aren't an activist. At least, not yet.

Screw the Serenity Prayer ("God grant me the serenity to accept the things I cannot change…"). As an activist, your job is not "acceptance," it is to move heaven and earth to find a way to solve the problem. If you aren't willing to do that, get out of the way.

As an activist, your life will not be "serene," because you will refuse to operate using other people's definition of "that which you must accept." Instead, you will identify three simple things:

1. The problem;
2. Who has the capability to solve the problem; and
3. What will motivate the person (or persons) to solve it.

You won't be a "get along guy." You won't be popular. (In fact, I routinely say my goal is "to be reviled in all the right places" and I'm happy to be hated equally by both Democrats and Republicans). And very few people will describe you by that epithet given to beautiful losers everywhere: "nice."

Incidentally, the auto repair example above isn't hypothetical. It happened to me. I called for the service manager and ravaged his various excuses like COVID, staffing shortages, and parts "lost in the mail." When he whined that he "hadn't seen it like this since he got into the business in 1984," my response was simple. *That's. Not. My. Problem."*

Although I used words like "please," I used them not for pleading, but for cold civility. I didn't bluster. I didn't shout, instead raising my voice just enough for other customers and employees to hear. I didn't call him names, and I didn't debate. Instead, I explained in excruciating detail what would happen if my car wasn't ready the following day, and that if he didn't believe I was capable of doing it, he should Google my name. When he said I was "threatening" him, I shrugged indifferently. "Call it what you want. I call it getting the service I'm owed." Then I walked out.

Twelve minutes after I left, the service manager called to say he had located the part at another dealer and that my car would be ready the next day.

Identify the problem, find who can solve it, and motivate them to do so. *That* is what an activist does. Incidentally, at my next visit to the dealership, the service manager was my best buddy, which is what you can typically expect *if* you greet your opponent's capitulation with grace and civility.

Getting involved

This is the point where you have to decide whether you want to remain a "concerned citizen" (i.e. alarmed but less effective), or whether you want to go out and kick some tail. The investment of time, effort, and perhaps a little money by either creating or joining a grassroots organization is by far the best way to impact public policy.

"...but I don't have time..."

Potential recruits often tell me they "don't have time" to defend their freedoms. My response? "Do what you can, of course, but you need to prioritize. The next time you start watching a football game, ask whether that time might not be better spent making sure your kids have a world in which they can grow up and thrive."

"It seems a little overwhelming…"

Yes, the "how do I get involved" part can be a little intimidating. The easiest way is to find a local organization which seems both active on your issue and effective, then call them up to say, "How can I help?" If they are worth a damn, they will snap you up and show you the ropes.

The four types of action

Activism divides into four basic categories: economic action, political action, legal action, and a broad category I call "non-legislative operations" which includes tactics and techniques which can be used to support the first three. In addition to the short synopsis of each below, each is covered by separate chapters.

The flow chart in Fig. 5B describes the decision-making process you should use in addressing problems. You will note that economic action should be your first avenue of recourse. If that doesn't work, move to political action. Only if both of those fail or can't be applied should you move to legal action. If that doesn't work … well … the illustration should give you a general idea.

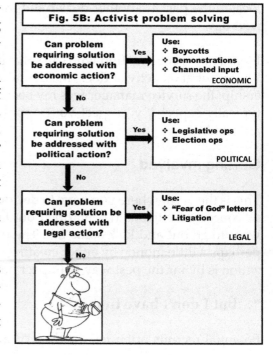

Fig. 5B: Activist problem solving

- ❏ **Economic action:** This is your tactic of first recourse because it is relatively cheap and easy. It involves using boycotts, demonstrations, and channeled input to force compliance from your target. It is usually but not always levied at corporate targets and is easiest because with the exception of small, privately held companies, corporations traditionally value profits above ideology. That makes it relatively easy to change corporate behavior. Unfortunately, in recent decades the left has picked up on this and now dominates the field. Meanwhile, corporations have learned to hunker down and wait out the storm. (See Chapter 6 for details on economic action.)

❑ **Political action:** This battlefield divides further into legislative operations and election operations, which are generally directed toward governmental targets, and represents the most commonly used type of activism. Although activist organizations are often legislatively active, most make the mistake of either not being active in elections, or in limiting election operations to throwing money at a few candidates. (See Chapters 8, 9, and 10 for legislative operations, and Chapter 11 for election operations.)

❑ **Legal action:** As the option of last recourse, you should use legal action only if economic and political action have failed or are not applicable to the problem to be solved. It is the last option because it requires highly specialized expertise (lawyers), is the most expensive, and is most uncertain in outcome, often failing to solve your problem even if your legal case is sound. (See Chapter 12 for details on legal action.)

❑ **Non-legislative operations**: Typically used to support the first three categories, options in this category range from rallies and demonstrations to physical intimidation, civil disobedience, and even violence. Many of the more extreme are suitable only to leftists, who typically have less to lose than mainstream Americans. (See Chapter 13 for details.)

The real nature of politics & politicians

One of my early mentors, Mike Rothfeld, is fond of saying, "America's system works, but not the way you think it does." He goes on to write:

"Simply put, politics is not about the common good, appealing to men's better angels, nor serving our Lord. These may be your motivations. Occasionally, they will be a politician's motivation. Politics is the adjudication of power. It is the process by which people everywhere determine who rules whom.

"In America, through a brilliant system of rewards and punishments, checks and balances, and diffusion of authority, we have acquired a habit and history of politics mostly without violence and excessive corruption.

"The good news for you and me is that the system works. The bad news is it is hard, and sometimes dirty work, for us to succeed in enacting policy.

"There is absolutely no reason for you to spend your time, talent, and money in politics except for this: If you do not, laws will be written and regulations enforced by folks with little or no interest in your well-being." [1]

Politicians, not education and not public opinion, make policy

Rothfeld goes on to elucidate why most activists get it wrong:

"The first mistake most folks make when they set out on a good-faith crusade to do good is to completely misunderstand their targets.

"Sometimes, activists make the local newspaper or media the target. The thinking goes, 'If we can just get them to understand the problem, things will change.' It is fortunate that this is not correct, because the media in the U.S. is overwhelmingly committed to big government, gun control, and the supremacy of state-controlled education over parent-controlled education.

"The fact is newspapers cast no votes. Dan Rather controls no elections. If this were not true, Ronald Reagan would never have been President.

"An even more common mistake is to believe that the key to victory is education. The 'education is the key to political victory' theory goes that if we educate people as to the problem and the solution, then the elected officials will fall in line. Wrong."[2]

Rothfeld explains that rather than responding to education, politicians who make public policy respond to the application of votes, money, and power, or the withholding thereof; that the making of policy does not directly follow public opinion; and that it is, in fact, a small group of people who ultimately drive policy.

Predicting political motivation

If a member of the political class – a politician, staffer, consultant or lobbyist – tells you how to behave or how politics works, ask yourself, "If I believe them and do what they say, how does it benefit them?" What you will find is that advice is designed not to benefit you, but to benefit *them*, often to your detriment.

The corollary of this rule is, when predicting a politician or opponent's next move, ask: "Which action will most benefit them?" If you ask that simple question, you will be able to predict both politicians' and opponents' actions with considerable accuracy.

Confrontational politics

Said Alinsky: "Conflict is the essential core of a free and open society. If one were to project the democratic way of life in the form of a musical score, its major theme would be the harmony of dissonance."[3]

As you will read throughout this book, politics is not the "art of compromise." Politics is the art of conflict. Said Senator H.L. Richardson in his book *Confrontational Politics*:

"So, what happens politically when one raised with traditional American values comes into contact with a fellow American adhering to contemporary humanist dogma? In politics, it is obvious that confrontation is the inevitable result, often desired and manipulated by the radical liberals and disliked and misunderstood by traditional Americans."[4]

As a civilized human being, you are taught to avoid conflict: forgive, accept, walk away, turn the other cheek. And while that might be good policy in personal relationships or to avoid potentially deadly physical confrontation, in formulating public policy, conflict avoidance is not only exploited by the left, but places you at a serious disadvantage.

Three rules of confrontational politics:

1. **Embrace conflict in politics**: Expect it, use it, and enjoy it. Rather than taking things personally, think of it like playing rugby. Politics is a blood sport. Treat it as such.

2. **Avoid compromise**: Alinsky loved compromise, saying: "If you start with nothing, demand 100 per cent, then compromise for 30 per cent, you're 30 per cent ahead."[5] Generally speaking, "compromise," as your opposition defines it, is a process in which you might lose less than under their original proposal, but *you still lose*.

3. **Never compromise principle**: As discussed below, your opposition might force you into tactical compromise, but it should be hard fought and not result in you willingly accepting an outcome at odds with your operating philosophy.

The corrupting nature of politics

Understand that like holding office, participation in politics even as an activist means swimming in a sea of corruption. The *process* is inherently corrupting. However, corruption for activists and politicians takes different forms, sometimes for different reasons, and you need to know it when you see it – not just in others, but also in yourself.

Corruption of politicians

As we will discuss later, politics is all about votes, money, and power. For politicians – who, incidentally, typically have about two good terms in them before starting to believe that they truly are "The Honorable" – corruption usually comes giftwrapped in money and power.

Of all the potential motivations for a politician, holding on to that money and power comes first. Usually (but not always), the pathway to money and power lies in getting votes. Once secure in their districts,

60

however, politicians' focus shifts to currying favor with party leadership in order to get plum positions in terms of committee assignments and leadership positions (which, of course, translate to more votes, money, and power).

A few legislators (I refuse to call them "politicians") remain true to their mission to represent the people. They are trustworthy. And unfortunately, they rarely make it far in politics precisely because they are trustworthy. One such state senator routinely angered his own leadership as often as the Democrats because he refused to compromise his principles. When the legislature convened one year, I went to his office only to find he'd been consigned to a windowless closet. My greeting to him was, "Okay, Hugh. Who did you piss off this time?" He served for five terms, targeted in each election by *both* sides, before they finally got him.

Corrupting influences on politicians

Below are a few potentially corrupting influences on politicians. It is by no means an exhaustive list. You must always remember that with a very few exceptions, politicians are not your friends, especially when they profess to be.

Top four corrupting influences for politicians:

❏ **Money:** Although individual and political action committee (PAC) donations to candidate committees are limited by law, there are all sorts of shadowy channels for things like lobbyist donation bundling or soft money donations to parties rather than politicians which then find their way to individual party favorites. How these "public servants" enrich themselves from their relatively paltry salaries is never entirely clear, but they definitely get rich, with a significant percentage going to jail.

❏ **Primaries (or the absence thereof):** Because politicians like being secure in their districts (and because they hate spending money for re-election), they avoid getting embroiled in primary elections – primaries which might be orchestrated either by their own party, by other candidates, or by *you*. Primaries are my favorite tool for keeping politicians honest.

- ❏ **Committee/leadership assignments:** Watching a politician climb the leadership ladder can be enlightening. One Republican freshman senator gave me pretty much carte blanche access to his office and legislative assistant. This continued for as long as Republicans were in the minority, even as he became Senate Minority Leader. But when we finally wrested control of the chamber from the Democrats and he became President Pro Tempore (effectively running the Senate), his attitude suddenly became, "Paul who?" We eventually came to an arms-length understanding, but the relationship was never again the same. This is why committee chairs and party leaders make poor bill sponsors: you can never trust them not to sell you out to (or for) leadership.

- ❏ **Miscellaneous ego massaging:** This could take the form of higher-ups in the party hosting or attending his fundraisers, positive press, earmarks for his district, roads or bridges named after him or her, etc.

Corruption of activists

Politicians will try to corrupt you because it is in their best interest to do so. The longer an activist plays the game, the more prone he is to being corrupted.

Equally dangerous are coalitions with inherently compromised organizations. In 2013, I helped forge the Coalition to Stop the Ban, which was largely responsible for killing S. 649, the so-called "universal background checks" (read that "universal gun registration") bill. We put together thirty-nine organizations, but there were a few I didn't ask to join, because either their motives or their tactics were incompatible with our "no compromise" mission. One of them with good intentions but a history of "preemptive concession" eventually crafted the "Toomey-Manchin compromise" which nearly saddled us with what could only be called "gun registration lite."

Corrupting influences for activists

Here the pacts with the Devil are sometimes less blatant but just as dangerous. If you are an organizational volunteer, look for them in your leadership. If you are a leader, look for them in your volunteers.

Basic Principles of Activism

Top five corrupting influences for activists:

❏ **Money:** Funny how this always tops the list. To avoid potential conflicts of interest, I prefer to keep my organizations all-volunteer. Everybody has a "day job." I don't even pay myself a salary. For the ultimate example of money corrupting political activists, think Wayne LaPierre of the NRA, who one year got a reported $5.1 million in salary and "deferred compensation" and who ultimately ended up on the receiving end of an investigation by the State of New York which continues as I write this.

❏ **Access:** Because professional lobbyists have inherent conflicts of interest due to their need to cultivate access to politicians, what I advocate instead is a grassroots mobilization model, which we will discuss at greater length elsewhere. But don't think that grassroots activists can't be corrupted by access each time a legislator invites them into his office while others wait outside, invites them to dine in the legislators' lunchroom, or otherwise rewards them with perks and ego strokes. When a politician introduces you to others as a "patriot," your inner voice should scream, "Danger!"

❏ **"Big brothers":** Beware any state-level organization which has a large national organization as its "big brother." The classic examples are state-level affiliates of the National Rifle Association, which are beholden to the NRA for money and shooting sports certification, and rarely speak for themselves. Lest you assume this is a conservative disease, fear not: the left suffers from the same affliction (e.g. Sierra Club state chapters).

❏ **Big organizations:** The larger the organization, the more prone it is to corruption, often in the interest of telling potential donors how "successful" it is, and generally to the betterment of its officers. Examples include trade unions in general and the International Brotherhood of Teamsters in particular.

❏ **Need for "success":** Large and small organizations alike are under constant pressure to produce, lest their donors go elsewhere. As a consequence, they will sometimes accept "compromises" which allow them to declare "success."

Basic principles of activism

The chapters which follow will deal, respectively, with economic action, political action (including legislative and election operations), legal action, and civil disobedience. Underlying each, however, are the following basic principles applicable to all. Ignore them at your own peril.

Never compromise on principle

When playing defense, you might be forced into tactical compromise, but it must never sacrifice your underlying principles. In the 2013 debate over S. 649 for "universal background checks" (aka universal gun registration), if we had accepted the "Toomey-Manchin compromise" which can only be described as "gun registration lite," we would have been conceding their point that adding additional data to the computerized National Instant Background Check System is a worthy goal. Once you have conceded the point, it is only a matter of how much you will lose and when. For that reason, it is generally bad strategy to give the opposition even "half a loaf" when playing defense.

When on offense, however, grabbing what you can get, if the whole thing isn't possible, is not a compromise of principle and moves the ball downfield toward your objective. Paraphrasing wisdom commonly attributed to Voltaire, don't allow the perfect to be the enemy of the good.

Pursue concrete, achievable goals

As an example, my organization spearheaded passage of a concealed handgun law. Legislators who knew they lacked the votes to defeat the bill weakened it by adding "no concealed carry" zones designed to ensure that although citizens could obtain permits, they couldn't actually carry firearms anywhere. In particular, they encouraged merchants to post signs in their stores prohibiting concealed firearms.

In response, we once ran a "Don't Buy" project against merchants who posted signs prohibiting permit-holders from carrying concealed firearms. We didn't target businesses with *policies* prohibiting concealed carry, only those with *signs* which subjected permit-holders to criminal prosecution. Nor did we target professional offices (nobody will boycott their kidney dialysis unit due to its gun policies), but rather *retail merchants* whose livelihoods depended on our supporters. The result? Not only did dozens of retail chains comply with our demands, a vice president of one popular home improvement chain told me our people sent him receipts for entire home additions purchased at a competitor who was not posted. Their signs came down immediately. By pursuing realistic goals, we broke the trend toward posting.

Surround yourself with simpatico people

As you gather supporters to help fight your battle, you will probably encounter well-intentioned, energetic people who are, for one reason or another, contentious. Perhaps they have a different "take" on your issue; perhaps they've developed a negative reputation on other issues; perhaps they don't play well with other children. Before recruiting them, bear in mind that as difficult as it may be to find talented volunteers, these people might cost you more than they bring to the fight. In battles with opponents you will enjoy more than enough controversy without having to simultaneously quell infighting.

You frame the issue, not your opposition

As I will repeatedly hammer into your brain, the "problem" is what you want to solve. The "issue" is how you frame the debate to solve the problem. Frame your issue to maximize your core constituency of supporters. (See also "issue management" in Chapter 10.)

❑ **Terminology controls the debate:** The left learned this long ago. They aren't "pro-abortion," they are "pro-choice." They aren't *for* "gun control," they are *against* "gun violence." Each phrase implies a unique set of motivations and goals, and each should be salable to the target demographic. Do you want the opposition, via phraseology, telling the world what you want?

❑ **"Bill branding":** When debating proposed legislation, the struggle over terminology extends to the name of the bill itself ... or the language you use to describe the bill. We once killed a mandatory gun storage bill by re-branding it the "Rapist Protection Act." This so un-nerved the radical sponsor that she actually stood before the chamber to whine, "I would *never* introduce a 'Rapist Protection Act!'"

Hold the highest ranking *elected* official responsible

In the "Medical Records Disclosure Act" debate described in Chapter 10, we didn't blame the sponsors of the bill, nor the bureaucrats who endorsed it. We found a plausible reason to blame *the governor*, making his life just a little bit miserable. By so doing, we motivated him to make us go away by suppressing committee hearings on the bill. Given his lack of popularity and unrelated legal woes, he just didn't need the hassle. The bottom line is this: don't waste time with bureaucrats. They answer not to you, but to their elected masters. Got a problem with a police chief? Don't bother with him; blame the mayor and the city council.

Concentrate fire

I often say that I am but a lightning rod whose job is to gather energy and channel it to particular legislators and corporations. Knowing supporters' attention span will last only for a finite number of phone calls or emails, your goal is to focus input from as many people as possible onto as few targets as possible in order to maximize the number of contacts received by each.

Unions often boycott hostile companies, generally with dismal results. Why? Because they publish the names of anti-union merchants—without contact information—in a newsletter sent to a limited number of union members and are then pretty much done. Contrast that with a "don't buy" project which channels hundreds or thousands of contacts directly into one or two businesses at a time, encouraging respondents to tell the merchant why they won't be patronizing them.

Let's say you have three retail companies making donations to an organization pushing Marxism to teenagers. If you launch on all three simultaneously, you will dilute your impact. Instead, target only the most economically vulnerable company. Once it capitulates, rotate to the next target. After one or two capitulate, others may relent without you having to lift a finger.

Ditto for legislative targets. Assume, for a moment, you want to kill a bill in committee. Of fifteen committee members, five oppose you, five support you, and five are undecided. Instead of wasting resources on opponents or friends, concentrate fire on the fence-sitters. (We will discuss how to identify those fence-sitters in Chapter 11.)

Cultivate a persona of power

Not coincidentally, the legislative process is intimidating to people unfamiliar with its complexities. Consequently, activists thrust into the arena tend to be overly deferential to politicians and easily manipulated. Politicians will use this intimidation factor against you. They tell you how they really support you ... despite having minutes ago voted against you. They flatter you, saying things like: "We really need a patriot like you to tell it like it is at our Republican Woman's Club meeting." Failing that, they bluster: "You're hurting your own cause. If you keep pressuring me, I'll vote against you."

Most activists back off. Instead of securing the politician's vote, they end up acting as *his* apologist to others. By contrast, politicians become genuinely unnerved when they encounter an activist who *likes* the fight. I make it a point to let them know (politely, of course) that win, lose or draw, I *enjoy* beating up my opposition. I cultivate a reputation not simply of fighting for a just cause, but treating it like a blood sport – what another (unsuccessful) activist once called "full body contact politics."

To enhance my reputation as a bad-ass, after our organization shuts down a legislator's office with constituent emails and phone calls, I send a volunteer (preferably female) to play good cop. "I absolutely sympathize with you, Senator," explains the volunteer. "I think Paul is being very unreasonable. But we need your vote on this bill, Senator. And without it, I really don't think I can dissuade him from sending twenty thousand pieces of hit mail into your district."

That, of course, is *my* persona. Yours will likely be different. Use the "strong and vigilant" character, perhaps "the deal-maker" (be very careful of that one), or whatever comes naturally to you. The key is to let politicians know you aren't prey.

As for the opposition, I prefer to demoralize them. While Niccolo Machiavelli, the father of modern power politics, noted the drawbacks of being despised by your opposition, I can't count the number of my opposing activists who've simply disappeared after getting their noses smeared in excrement a few times.

Prove four things to politicians

Unless you are taken seriously, you will be ignored. Accordingly, you must demonstrate four things:

1. That you are a serious person on serious business;
2. That you have numbers to back you up;
3. That you will inflict pain in the election season for transgressions committed in the legislative season; and
4. That absent satisfactory resolution of your problem, you will never, ever go away.

Control the perceived threat level of supporters

Bill Clinton was the best thing for conservatism in the 20th century and Joe Biden is the best in the 21st. Why? Because the threat they create molds conservatives into a unified front.

Conversely, winning an election is often the worst thing for your cause. When Trump won in 2016, for example, the gun rights community went to sleep. I called it the "Trump Slump" because gun rights supporters, believing they had done their bit by electing him, went back to mowing the lawn and watching football, as conservatives tend to do when we win.

Top three principles in motivating supporters:

❑ **Defense is easier than offense:** The inherent inertia of political leadership works to your advantage when killing hostile legislation, but against you when passing friendly legislation.

❑ **Alerts must convey clear and present dangers:** Legitimate threats must be expressed in clear, imperative language which resonates with the target audience. Rather than saying, "H. 666 could present a danger to the Second Amendment," say: "H. 666 threatens *your* gun rights!"

❏ **Never hype a non-existent threat:** Some groups use what I call "predatory fundraising" by graphically alarming potential supporters with either hyperbolic descriptions of actual legislation or legitimate threats they are actually in no position to do anything about.

One particular gun rights group raised tens (if not hundreds) of thousands of dollars hyping the supposed threat from HR 45, the "Blair Holt Act." Although the bill was legitimately bad, in truth it was going nowhere. What the organization neglected to tell supporters was that bills intended to fail are introduced in every session of Congress, typically to appease supporters. It doesn't mean they will even get committee hearings, much less become law.

The same organization also fundraised off then-Secretary of State Hillary Clinton and United Nations gun control. What they didn't say is that because they didn't have a non-governmental organization (NGO) with consultative status to the UN, they couldn't do a damned thing about the issue they fundraised on.

Predatory fundraising might raise funds in the short term, but you will ultimately lose credibility with your core constituency of supporters, just as did the group mentioned above – a group now uniformly reviled as a fraud among the gun rights community.

When losing is winning

Developed by free market policy analyst Joseph P. Overton, the "Overton Window" refers to the range of policies politically palatable to the mainstream population at a given time. By this theory, the Overton Window frames the range of policies that a politician can recommend without appearing too extreme to win and retain public office given the climate of public opinion.

Your goal is to move the Overton Window toward your side. For example, gun rights activists have spent three decades normalizing the carry of concealed handguns by gradually passing laws in most states across the U.S., and then expanding them to include permitless or "constitutional" carry.

But it is the left which has proven itself the true master of the Overton Window, typically by bringing up something repeatedly, even when it loses, and framing the debate by staking out an extreme position. For example, Hillary Clinton went down in flames when she first pushed socialized medicine in the early 1990s. But she also began normalizing the position, and socialized medicine was partially enacted as Obamacare in 2010.

References:

1. Michael I. Rothfeld, "The Real Nature of Politics and Politicians: America's System Works, But Not Why You Think!", Foundation for Applied Conservative Leadership, https://facl-training.org/

2. Ibid.

3. Saul D. Alinsky, *Rules for Radicals: A Pragmatic Primer for Realistic Radicals*, Vintage Books, Random House, Inc., New York, 1971, page 62.

4. Sen. H.L. Richardson, Ret., *Confrontational Politics*, Gun Owners Foundation, Springfield, VA, 1998, page ix.

5. Op. Cit. note 3, page 59.

Chapter 6
Economic Action

"Politics is downstream from culture, and the liberal shareholders have been dominating the corporate proxy vote to advance policies they otherwise could not achieve through the legislative or political process." – Justin Danof[1]

Economic action refers to the use of economic measures to impact the behavior of a target. Boycotts represent the most common and visible tactic, but economic action includes an arsenal of possible weapons. Potential targets include not only corporations, but also cities, states, and even whole countries.

When conducting economic action, your goal is to make a demand and force the target to capitulate either to the demand or a fallback demand that gives you more than you had to begin with. It is the purest exercise of Alinsky's Rule 3: "Wherever possible go outside of the experience of the enemy. Here you want to cause confusion, fear, and retreat." You force the target to balance the cost of giving you what you want against the cost of not doing so.

Unfortunately, the left learned long ago the value of boycotting entities they find "offensive," and have increasingly used economic action to advantage over recent decades, particularly to bypass the legislative process for measures that lack popular support. Ask Kentucky Fried Chicken, which introduced recently vegan "Beyond Fried Chicken" nuggets (ugh) in an unsuccessful bid to get People for the Ethical Treatment of Animals (PETA) off its back.

Thanks to increasing left-wing economic action and its sibling, "cancel culture," we have reached a point at which corporations reflexively capitulate to leftist threats. That is why major companies have signed on to support the Marxist/terrorist organization known as Black Lives Matter.

Types of economic action

Although boycotts are what most people think of when targeting corporations, they are only one in a broad array of available tactics, including proxy campaigns, demonstrations, employee slowdowns, and social media shaming. Which tactic or tactics you use depends on the nature of the target.

Outside vs. inside operations

Some methods of economic action work from outside the target organization (e.g. boycotts, demonstrations), some from inside (slowdowns, proxy campaigns), with the latter almost uniformly ignored by conservatives. In order to stop "wokeism" in corporate America, conservatives have serious catching up to do with respect to inside operations.

Boycotts

As an activist manual put it, "A boycott, like a strike, is similar to a revolver with one bullet in the chamber. The threat of using it is more powerful than the weapon itself. But don't make the threat unless you are prepared to carry it out."[2]

As the most visible type of economic action, boycotts are the obvious choice for activists looking to change corporate behavior. Using the tactics described above, boycotts can be effective, particularly when combined with social ostracizing and pickets or demonstrations. On the downside, over the past couple of decades, corporations have become somewhat hardened to boycotts and often tend to hunker down and wait out the storm, so be prepared to turn up the heat.

A particularly effective tactic is to send business to a competitor of the target which is not engaged in the egregious behavior you seek to change. Years back, Lowe's Home Improvement Centers made a big mistake when they posted against concealed carry because their customers heavily overlap our supporters – contractors and handymen tend to own guns. I actually got friendly with Lowe's vice president of loss prevention, who told me people were sending him receipts for entire home additions purchased at Home Depot because they were not posted. Lowe's signs came down in short order.

Corporate proxy campaigns

Hats off to Saul Alinsky, who started using shareholder proxy fights to twist arms at corporations such as Eastman Kodak decades before the Internet made it easier. (Because they have to be done internally, proxy campaigns are still the most complex type of economic action.)

At its most basic level, here is how proxy campaigns work: (1) Decide what corporate behavior you want to change; (2) Get lots of shareholders to give you their proxies; (3) Go to the annual meeting of the corporation and make your demand (err, "proposal"), voting the proxies for your demand if necessary. Even proposals that get as little as ten percent support can shape corporate behavior. The tactic is especially well-suited to targets for which you can't significantly impact profits through boycott.

Alinsky claimed to have invented "Proxies for People," the use of shareholder proxy campaigns to impact the behavior of corporations. How effective has it been? Given that we now have "woke," "green," "fair trade," and "socially responsible" corporations pushing "diversity" and "equity" even when it negatively impacts corporate earnings, and that we even have "socially responsible" mutual funds, it is clear that leftists dominate corporate America. In fact, I would argue that conservatives have all but ceded the use of corporate proxy campaigns to the left.

Writing in *The Hill*, Justin Danof, director of the Free Enterprise Project, said: "The left dominates the shareholder proposal space, annually filing 95 percent of Environmental, Social and Governance (ESG) proposals. With 400 to 500 ESG proposals filed per year, that's a lot of opportunities to influence corporate behavior. Compounding this is the fact that the organizations that advise investors on how to vote for these ballot initiatives have become fully 'woke.'"[3]

As a result, says Danof, dozens of corporations are donating to Planned Parenthood, banks are cutting off services to Second Amendment organizations, and major corporations have donated massive sums to the leftist (and arguably fraudulent[4]) Southern Poverty Law Center. Moreover, Danof's article was published before 23 major companies donated to Black Lives Matter, including Cicso, Comcast, IBM, Microsoft, Paypal, and Uber.[5]

Until I researched this book, even I didn't realize how pervasive the tactic had become, but it quickly made sense to me why so many companies have become "woke." So pervasive is the left's control over corporate boardrooms that companies have developed "ESG" ("Environmental, Social and Governance") procedures, even hiring consulting firms to do "ESG analysis" to placate leftists.

Fortunately, conservative proxy campaigns are finally starting to recapture lost ground. As a resource, consider the conservative National Center for Public Policy Research and its "Free Enterprise Project" (FEP)[6], which describes itself as "the conservative movement's only full-service shareholder activism and education program". Corporations the FEP has gone after include AT&T, CVS Caremark. Pfizer, and The North Face, among others.

Particularly interesting is the FEP annual "Investor Value Voter Guide."[7] Described by FEP director Justin Danof as "the antidote to stop the woke train in its tracks," Danof goes on to say: "Conservatives have been ignoring corporate proxy ballot votes for decades, and it's to our own peril. Politics is downstream from culture, and the liberal shareholders have been dominating the corporate proxy vote to advance policies they otherwise could not achieve through the legislative or political process." I urge anyone embarking on activism against a corporation to contact the FEP.

As a final aside, I would recommend anyone who wants to start gathering proxies to use a tool Alinsky didn't have available to him: Facebook. To kick off a proxy campaign, I would start a Facebook group and associated Twitter campaign specifically addressing my proposal and do my best to send it viral.

Demonstrations and picketing

For economic action, public demonstrations and picketing are best if used in support of other tactics. Used alone (i.e. without boycott, proxy campaign or other measures), they are relatively ineffective in changing targets' behavior because they are generally too short in duration, allowing the target to hunker down and wait you out. Note that in the Southwest Airlines employee action against mandatory vaccination described below, the demonstration was used *in conjunction with* a slowdown.

Theoretically, you could try to prolong the demonstrations. But as Alinsky put it, "A tactic that drags on too long becomes a drag." If you intend to use demonstrations, make sure to do press releases to draw attention to the effort. (For information on conducting demonstrations, see Chapter 13. For press releases, see Chapter 17.)

Economic sanctions

Sanctions describe commercial and financial penalties applied by one or more countries or other governmental entities against a targeted self-governing state, group, or individual. As an individual activist, this tool is generally not available to you but could easily be directed *at* you.

Employee slowdowns

This form of internal action is risky because it you get caught, you get fired. Similarly, unions sometimes end up on the wrong end of multi-million dollar penalties imposed by courts. That said, however, slowdowns can be tremendously effective if surreptitious. With respect to Joe Biden's COVID vaccine mandate, which encompassed airlines because airlines operate under federal contracts, the following series of *Epoch Times* headlines on Southwest Airlines and its threat in 2021 to fire unvaccinated workers pretty much say it all:

❑ **October 4:** "Southwest Airlines Requires Its US Employees Get COVID-19 Vaccine, Citing Federal Mandate"

❑ **October 11:** "Southwest Airlines Cancels Hundreds More Flights on Monday Amid Widespread Disruptions"

❑ **October 12:** "Southwest Airlines Apologizes as Shares Tumble Amid Mass Flight Cancellations"

❑ **October 13:** "Southwest Airlines' Pilots Warn Fatigue, Future Problems Could Arise Following Series of Flight Cancellations"

❏ **October 18:** "Hundreds of Southwest Workers Protest COVID-19 Vaccination Mandates at Airline's Headquarters"

❏ **October 19:** "Southwest Airlines Backs Off Plan to Put Unvaccinated Employees on Unpaid Leave"

❏ **October 22:** "'Makes No Sense': Southwest Airlines Says It Won't Fire Workers Who Don't Get COVID Vaccine"

Service cutoffs

This form of economic action will more likely be directed *at* you than *by* you, particularly if you run a Second Amendment organization. Starting with "Operation Chokepoint," when Barrack Obama's Department of Justice began "investigating" business dealings between banks and firearms companies in 2013, financial companies began putting the squeeze on even gun rights organizations. Although "Chokepoint" got shut down in 2017, PayPal, Square, and Apple Pay banned firearms sales and transactions through their systems. Citibank, Bank of America, and Berkshire Bank then imposed limits on firearms companies or dried up lending altogether. Thus far, Wells Fargo has resisted the trend.[8] Fortunately, Second Amendment-friendly lenders have at least partially filled the gap. If faced with a service cutoff, immediately double down by calling out the provider on social media platforms and conducting a nationwide boycott on the company as described above.

Social media shaming

Otherwise known as "cancel culture," social media shaming is best for impacting the behavior of targets which might not directly depend on your supporters for income (e.g. celebrities or politicians). Yes, it is most commonly used by the sort of leftists whom actor Rowan Atkinson ("Mr. Bean") described as "medieval mob[s] looking for someone to burn." However, that doesn't mean you shouldn't use the tactic as well.

Although Twitter is the most common tool for attacking individuals, Facebook is good for embarrassing local government officials. For example, early in the COVID pandemic, the Wake County Commission decided to shut down gun shops as "non-essential businesses." Before we could even get out an email alert, members started a weekend Facebook campaign against the chairman of the commission, who did an about-face on Monday morning, deciding that gun shops were, after all, essential businesses.

Social media shaming can also be used to good effect against corporations. Ask Quaker Oats Company, forced to discontinue its Aunt Jemima branding of breakfast, pancake, and syrup products after 131 years; or Land O' Lakes, forced to rebrand by removing its iconic 1928 photo of a Native American woman; or on the conservative side, Dick's Sporting Goods, after it not only stopped selling AR-15s, but actually destroyed its inventory and tasked lobbyists with pursuing gun control. When the dust finally settled, CEO Ed Stack told CBS the decision cost Dicks $250 million. Dicks eventually sold off its Field and Stream stores.[9]

Economic action to change public policy

Economic action can also be levied to impact public policy. Not unlike acts of terrorism, the goal is to hurt the businesses of a particular area with the goal of turning them against the politicians who created the objectionable policy.

Among leftist examples, in 2017 the National Basketball Association pulled its All-Star game out of Charlotte in response to "radical" legislation requiring men to use men's bathrooms (perish the thought!), costing local merchants millions of dollars and putting pressure on state legislators to change the law. Similarly, Major League Baseball moved its All-Star game out of Atlanta in response to fallacious claims about Georgia's voter integrity legislation. In the latter case, Delta Airlines and Coca-Cola Co., both based in Atlanta, were forced to denounce the law for fear that they themselves might face boycotts.

Although those examples are writ large, economic action for political goals is best applied in microcosm such as against merchants in a particular mall or shopping center or a small community. For example, faced with malls posting against concealed handguns, we didn't target the mall management companies, we targeted retail stores *within* the malls.

Incidentally, although some activists have occasionally advocated boycotting elections, any tactic that so effectively hands power to the opposition goes beyond stupid.

Commonalities across different types of economic action

Examples of pitifully applied economic action abound. In fact, although I got the idea from my union for the "GRNC Don't Buy List," which targeted merchants who posted against concealed carry, the project as originally applied by the union was utterly worthless. When I modified the program to correct their mistakes, however, it was responsible for getting merchants to remove concealed handgun postings from literally hundreds of businesses across the state.

Effective vs. ineffective economic action

Everybody wants to boycott a business they don't like, but most aren't willing to do what it takes to conduct an effective boycott. Frankly, it can be a time-consuming pain in the ass. In one of its usual diatribes against Donald Trump, *The Washington Post* got one thing at least partly right when it said, "It's the spasmodic nature of the Trump/Republican boycotts that makes them generally impotent. As any organizer can tell you, boycotts don't work simply by calling for them to happen. They work only when there's repeated pressure for the boycotts to be upheld — a slow, tedious process that depends on the public seeing a real motive for the boycott and on a willingness to do without the product."[10]

In the gun rights movement, I've seen all manner of economic action, almost all of it ineffective. Whether it's a list of "anti-gun" businesses on a website or a mobile app to run on smartphones, they usually lack the attributes below.

Another example of ineffective economic action involves boycotting things people cannot or will not do without – things like medical providers or other essential services or, for that matter, any popular business without competition. In *Rules for Radicals*, Alinsky talks about the failure of a Christmas boycott directed at downtown merchants selling things people wanted for Christmas. Today, the project would likely succeed because the Internet has provided competitive alternatives.

By contrast, the GRNC Don't Buy List succeeded because it carefully did *not* target, among other things, medical providers that posted against concealed carry. Why? because people will not boycott their doctors. Our one area of suboptimal performance was shopping malls, whose owners did not derive their income from our people, but instead from their tenants.

Target assessment

As previously noted, your first objective in economic action (particularly boycotts) is to *not fail*. Accordingly, before sighting in a target, take a cold, hard look your chances of success, then do a Red Fox 4 analysis of potential gains or losses. (See Chapter 14.)

Before undertaking economic action (particularly a boycott), ask the following:

❏ **Will your supporters boycott the target?** There are certain things people value more highly than your cause. As noted previously, even a devoted follower won't boycott his kidney dialysis unit. Schools, churches, and companies without convenient competitors are equally resistant to boycott.

❏ **Does the target make money from your supporters?** Mall and office building management companies don't. The more tenuous your connection to the target's bottom line, the less effective you will be.

❏ **Is the target vulnerable to negative media?** It is almost always a plus when your target is getting beaten on for other reasons, since they will have an incentive to make you go away.

❏ **Will other groups pile on?** Obviously, the more, the merrier.

❏ **Is the company otherwise vulnerable?** Bonus points if the target is losing money, undergoing bankruptcy or embroiled in scandal.

Attributes of effective economic action

Done properly, boycotts or other types of economic action share certain commonalities, regardless of the type of target or method of action. Below are the top three requirements for effective economic action and methods for implementing them.

Rules for Anti-RADICALS

Top three requirements for effective economic action:

1. **The target must be acutely aware they are being targeted:** One of the things that rendered impotent the union "don't buy" list I plagiarized in creating the "GRNC Don't Buy List" was its practice of publishing the names of anti-union businesses in its own magazine and then calling it a day. The union didn't list contact information for the businesses and didn't tell supporters to contact them and say why they wouldn't be patronizing them. To make your target acutely aware of its plight:

   - **Make one person responsible:** Find contact information for the highest level corporate or governmental representative and disseminate it to your supporters. I have gotten contact information for high level corporate executives simply by calling their headquarters and asking for it (without revealing my motives, obviously).
   - **Tell your supporters to contact them:** By phone or by email (preferably both), have your supporters contact the person whose life you will make sheer, living hell, and tell them why they won't be patronizing their business.
   - **Go public early, using press releases:** Media, particularly local media, love a conflict. For example, when you tell them you're boycotting the local grocery chain for hiring exclusively "LGBTQIA+" grocery clerks, they will carry the story, and there is little a retail chain hates more than negative publicity.
   - **Be unfailingly polite and professional:** Overt threats are a no-no. To garner positive press and demonstrate competence, advise your supporters to deliver the message with civility.

2. **Impact on the target must be tangible:** Although you must activate as many potential supporters as possible, the fallacy in *The Washington Post* quote above is their claim that you need "public" support. You don't. What matters is not how many people stop patronizing the business, it's the target's *perception* of how many people stop patronizing the business.

   - **Use mass distribution of information:** You must reach supporters beyond your immediate membership using social media and gatherings of like-minded people (e.g. conservative conferences, gun shows, rallies, speeches, etc.). Accordingly, recruit groups of people sympathetic to your cause. Among those groups, prioritize those most likely to take action. At gatherings, distribute fliers with the target's contact information.

- **Give good contact information:** Ideally, get a phone number and email address for a representative as high as possible in the company.
- **Prioritize and concentrate fire:** The more targets you hit simultaneously, the fewer contacts each will receive. Accordingly, find one offender (preferably the weakest) and nail it first. Only once the first target capitulates do you move to the next. Because retail and restaurant chains are generally run by bean-counters, they are more vulnerable than other types of businesses. When you demonstrate that you dole out the beans, they capitulate. Next come smaller merchants, which are sometimes less vulnerable because private owners may be ideologically rather than financially motivated. Least vulnerable are professional services and companies that don't depend on retail customer bases, including mall and commercial real estate management companies.
- **Use "feedback days":** To better concentrate fire, distribute thousands of fliers over a weekend event (e.g. a gun show or conservative conference) advising supporters to contact the target on Monday morning between 9 AM and 11 AM, thereby shutting down its office. I did this to the headquarters of A.T. Williams Oil Company, which then operated Wilco convenience stores which it posted against concealed carry. At 10:30 AM, *Williams called me* and agreed to remove "no firearms" signs. At 11:00 AM (the scheduled ending time), the calls magically stopped, making it look like I turned off the spigot.

3. **Target compliance must be both possible and attractive:** By "attractive," I don't mean they need to support your cause; I mean that you must offer incentives to comply. In media interviews on our "Don't Buy List" project, I routinely said: "We don't want to boycott businesses, we want to welcome them back. When they remove signs prohibiting concealed carry, we will send business their way." I told merchants that their *policy* was irrelevant to us. What mattered was whether they posted *signs* which would subject concealed handgun permit-holders to potential prosecution. We also

sold signs which allowed them to prohibit all firearms *except* lawfully carried concealed firearms. (I also told merchants the signs were a waste of money, but that if they wanted to post something, it would at least get us off their back.) Both measures gave merchants face-saving means of complying with our demands without feeling like they were being forced to comply.

GRNC Don't Buy List

After we passed concealed carry, the governor printed up "No Firearms" signs and started handing them out. In response, our "don't buy list" worked as follows: First, we sold two-part wallet cards to supporters. When they encountered a business posted against concealed carry, they tore off half the card to give to the store manager, and filled out contact info on the remainder to be sent to us. (To our later "Safe Restaurants" project, we added online reporting capability.)

When we got the report, we sent the merchant notification they were being added to the list, giving them a chance to either report errors or to tell us signs would come down. Failing that, we added them to the don't buy list.

The list contained full contact information and advised supporters to email or call them to say why they would no longer patronize the business. Beyond putting it on our website, we printed thousands of copies for distribution at gun shows, usually scheduling a "feedback day" to shut down a selected merchant on Monday morning following the show.

As a result, hundreds of stores removed postings, including chains such as Lowe's, Wilco Convenience, Walmart, McDonalds, Kroger, West Marine, and many more. It broke the trend toward posting which remains infrequent in our state even decades later.

Risks of economic action

When subjected to economic action, your target may threaten to sue you. Although, as the saying goes, "anybody can sue anybody over anything," their chances of success are slim. In NAACP v. Claiborne Hardware Co., (1982)[11], SCOTUS held that political expressions in support of a boycott constitute protected speech and that individuals and associations exercising their rights cannot be penalized for lawful conduct. Furthermore, when acts of violence are committed in conjunction with lawful economic action, prosecution must be sufficiently precise to impose damages only upon those guilty of unlawful conduct rather than the entire entity conducting economic action.

Although political speech via boycott is protected under the First Amendment, boycott for economic gain is not. (Federal Trade Commission v. Superior Court Trial Lawyers Association, 1990.[12]) Similarly, economic action such as a slowdown against your employer can be risky, particularly if in violation of a union contract, as one of the airline unions representing me in my "day job" discovered when it ended up on the receiving end of a permanent injunction (with financial settlement) over what was billed as "The Summer of Safety."

By far, however, the biggest risk of economic action is failure, because failure demonstrates weakness to your opposition – something you must never, ever do. Consequently, you should never start economic action unless you have at least a reasonable chance of success, and, once initiated, you must dedicate whatever resources are necessary to win. Half-hearted efforts need not apply.

How *not* to do economic action

"Do you eat at Chipotle, Shake Shack, Panera, Burger King, or Subway, or have a meal delivered by Door Dash?

"Do you wear clothes from Levi Strauss, the Gap, or Gucci?

"Do you watch CNN, MTV, NBC, HBO, MSNBC, or Showtime?

"Do you browse Tinder, Yelp, eBay, or Pinterest on a Microsoft computer with Comcast internet?

"Do you shop at Costco?

"If you answered yes to any of these questions, you have financially supported companies that want to strip us of our God-given constitutional rights."

So began a piece in Ammoland.com[13] that linked to a list of nearly 200 "anti-gun businesses" gun rights supporters were advised not to patronize. Beyond the fact that the recommendations would make it nearly impossible to watch TV, meaning potential supporters won't comply, it's unlikely any of the businesses even knew they were on the list because it provided no links or other contact information for listed business, nor did it advise gun owners to let the companies know why they wouldn't buy from them. The net result will be no change in corporate behavior.

References:

1. National Center for Public Policy Research Free Enterprise Project "2021 Investment Value Voter Guide," https://nationalcenter.org/wp-content/uploads/2021/04/2021_Investor_Value_Voter_Guide.pdf

2. Kim Bobo, Jackie Kendall, Steve Max, *Organizing for Social Change: Midwest Academy Manual for Activists,* Seven Locks Press, 2001, p.14.

3. Justin Danof, "Conservatives, take back the franchise with proxy voting," *The Hill,* May 14, 2020, https://thehill.com/opinion/finance/497271-conservatives-take-back-the-franchise-with-proxy-voting

4. Kyle Smith, "Essentially a Fraud," *National Review,* August 23, 2018, https://www.nationalreview.com/magazine/2018/09/10/southern-poverty-law-center-essentially-a-fraud/

5. Tatum Hunter, "23 Companies That Support Black Lives Matter (BLM) in 2021," "Built In," October 20, 2021, https://builtin.com/diversity-inclusion/companies-that-support-black-lives-matter-social-justice

6. National Center for Public Policy Research "Free Enterprise Project," https://nationalcenter.org/programs/free-enterprise-project/

7. Ibid., note 1.

8. Hollie McKay, "US banks and financial institutions have been slowly severing ties with the gun industry," Fox News, July 22, 2020, https://www.foxnews.com/us/us-banks-financial-institutions-severing-ties-gun-industry

9. Rachael Siegel, "Dick's Sporting Goods CEO says overhauled gun policies cost the company a quarter of a billion dollars," October 8, 2019, *The Philadelphia Inquirer,* https://www.inquirer.com/business/dicks-sporting-goods-gun-sales-20191008.html

10. Philip Bump, "Why half-hearted conservative boycotts rarely take root," *The Washington Post,* April 6, 2021, https://www.washingtonpost.com/politics/2021/04/06/why-half-hearted-conservative-boycotts-rarely-take-root/

11. Richard Parker, "NAACP v. Claiborne Hardware Co. (1982)," *The First Amendment Encyclopedia: Presented by The John Seigenthaler Chair Of Excellence In First Amendment Studies,* https://mtsu.edu/first-amendment/article/288/naacp-v-claiborne-hardware-co

12. Dara E. Purvis, "Boycotts," *The First Amendment Encyclopedia: Presented by The John Seigenthaler Chair Of Excellence In First Amendment Studies,* https://www.mtsu.edu/first-amendment/article/987/boycotts

13. Lee Williams, "Current List of Anti-Gun Businesses You Should Avoid Giving Your Money," October 21, 2021, Ammoland.com, https://www.ammoland.com/2021/10/list-anti-gun-business-avoid-giving-your-money/#ixzz7AVUa9X9b

Chapter 7
Overview to
Political Action

"Politics is the adjudication of power. It is the process by
which people everywhere determine who rules whom."
– Mike Rothfeld, Foundation for Applied
Conservative Leadership[1]

As noted previously, political action is second to economic action as the preferred option to solve a problem. Because it requires a higher level of skill and resources, apply it primarily to problems that cannot be solved by economic action. (See Fig. 5B: Activist Problem Solving.) Political action comprises two parts:

❏ **Legislative operations**: This includes the actual tactics involved in passing or killing bills, initiatives, referendums, or resolutions by influencing the legislative process.

❏ **Election operations**: Here we prepare the battlefield to maximize our chances of legislative success. Rather than a physical battlefield as a military force might define it, however, the legislative battlefield is the chamber you plan to influence, including its leadership, committees, and members. Election action involves manipulating elections to send people to the legislative body who will benefit you, of course. But equally important is delivering a message to *all* members of the body that you are capable of effectively organizing to help or hurt them.

To varying degrees, many small organizations do a credible job of legislative action. What they often avoid, however, are the ardors of election action, which allows you to motivate politicians by delivering pain or pleasure at the ballot box.

Without the certain knowledge that you can back up your demands with political pain, politicians will be less likely to support you and, consequently, your effectiveness will be degraded. You will be limited to *asking* for your agenda rather than *demanding* it. What follows are the tactics involved in motivating legislative players to follow your agenda. Those tactics might not be pretty, but they are brutally effective. Following chapters will expand on the two categories of political action.

The two pathways to power

There are two pathways to political power. On the direct path, you run for office. On the indirect path, you work to influence those on the direct path.

Direct path

Players on the direct path to power include officeholders, staff, and other "insiders" such as lobbyists. Direct exercise of power motivates politicians to spend exorbitant sums of even their own money getting elected to jobs paying (in theory) relatively little.

Unfortunately, the citizen-legislator is an endangered species. Due to resources required, holding office higher than town council or county commission may require you to be independently wealthy, retired, self-employed, or (ugh) a professional politician.

If you run for office to solve a specific problem, be prepared to expend significant time, effort, expertise and money. Half-assed, underfunded campaigns need not apply. (Libertarians: heed this.) Even if successful, it will be years – if ever – before you can effect meaningful change. Moreover, once elected, you will be forced to deal with issues unconnected to those that motivate you (unless, of course, you enjoy the prospect of voting on the Official State Rodent).

It the direct path interests you, there are books, seminars and boot camps for aspiring politicians. For our purposes, we will assume you are unwilling or unable to pursue this route.

Indirect path

Players on the indirect path to power include unions, the media, and political organizations from across the political spectrum. The indirect pathway to power lies in motivating politicians to dance to your tune by voting how you want them to, sponsoring legislation, or otherwise furthering or hindering specific proposals. It requires you to become, in essence, a "lobbyist" (a title which, given its connotations, I prefer to avoid).

Advantages of indirect path to power

The advantages of indirect application of power are many. It generally requires less time and money. Because you don't need the financial or logistical support of a political party, you don't have to toe a party line. And metaphorically speaking, it's generally a whole lot more fun beating up politicians than getting beaten up. (Or maybe that's just me. As a group, I don't like politicians very much. To quote Rothfeld, "There are those I dislike, and those I merely distrust.")

Disadvantages of indirect path to power

The disadvantage, of course, is that you aren't the one casting the vote. No matter how you implore, cajole or threaten, Joe Pol might blow you off. The likelihood of being disobeyed varies directly with not only your effectiveness, but also with the politician's ideology, personality, seniority, party stature, and vulnerability in his or her district.

Even sympathetic politicians may shun you if you ask them to do something politically unhealthy. For example, one House representative had been helpful when bills that concerned us were in a subcommittee on which he served. Our political action committee even gave him money (something I eventually learned to avoid). We were best buddies ... until I asked him to sponsor a certain bill. He exploded, "Are you nuts? If I sponsor that in my district, it'll cost me $50,000 in mailings during the next election!"

Why you are ill-prepared for political action

As I say in my legislative tactics seminars, "Lest you believe the political system is designed to exclude you, let me assure you that it is." Believing in the high principles of democracy, people tend to be wholly unprepared for its gritty application. The reason, unfortunately, is that you are honest.

Neophyte advocates tend to assume that if politicians actually understood the issue, they couldn't possibly disagree with the advocates' position. If, for example, Senator Karl Marx actually **understood** why the Framers drafted the Second Amendment, he couldn't possibly support infringements, could he?

Being the professional parasites they are, politicians feed off that naivety. "Why, thank you for your input, Mr. Constitutionalist. I'll be sure to consider your opinion when the Second Amendment Evisceration Act comes up in my committee," says Senator Marx, roughly three minutes before forgetting you exist.

He knows perfectly well he can ignore you because you probably won't attend the committee meeting to watch what he does. Even if you are savvy enough to track the bill, he and his cohorts will blindside you by putting it on the calendar at 11:00 PM on the night before its hearing, almost certainly on a day and time when normal people earn a living.

Whenever possible, these con artists will avoid the gold standard used to judge politicians' actions: the recorded vote. They will use procedural tricks to hide their subterfuge. They might play a shell game in which they strip whole bills, replacing their guts with entirely new, unrelated – often insidious – language. It is entirely plausible they will adjourn a chamber floor session for ten minutes to convene an ad hoc committee meeting – even holding it on the chamber floor – to give a hearing to the brand new monster born just moments ago, reporting it out of committee and back to the floor for a vote ten minutes later.

Power vs. access

When using the indirect path to power, it is important not to confuse power with access. When using access to influence politicians, as lobbyists do, it is the politician who controls the relationship and can cut off access at any time. When using power to influence politicians, you may be feared and even hated; you might not have as much insider's knowledge of behind-the-scenes politicking. But it is you, not the politician, who controls the relationship.

Education vs. grassroots mobilization

In exercising indirect power, you can rely on either education (of politicians or the public) or grassroots mobilization. The Foundation for Applied Conservative Leadership (FACL) preaches that education is ineffective, particularly when directed at the public, since vast amounts of money can be spent to change very little. Members of the public, after all, aren't the ones formulating public policy.

Grassroots mobilization, by contrast, is more efficient. You can use it to *immediately* change the environment of decision-makers by applying or withholding what they most want: votes, money, power, and public accolades.

I would add only that if you don't do some level of "education," you will eventually find yourself unable to swing the "3% + 1" of voters required to win elections (see Chapter 11), and you will ultimately lose. That is why I advise using op-eds, letters to the editor, social media, and comments to online articles, wherever possible, as cheap ways to augment grassroots mobilization.

Objectives of political action

In college, I earned spending money by gambling at backgammon, which I regard as a better metaphor for battle than chess because its outcomes depend, in part, on chance – in this case, the roll of dice.

Those who lost to me in backgammon often whined that I was "lucky." What they failed to realize is that I courted Lady Luck by preparing the battlefield: setting up the board so the maximum number of rolls of the dice would benefit me. That is precisely what you will do with political action.

Legislative vs. election objectives:

❏ **Objectives of legislative operations**: To manipulate the political process—whether in a city council, state assembly, Congress, or other body—to achieve your desired outcome by influencing the target, either to change laws or regulations (or the interpretation or enforcement thereof) or to prevent change.

❏ **Objectives of election operations:** First, to prepare the legislative battlefield by manipulating elections to elect favorable representatives and thereby maximize your chances of legislative success. Second, to demonstrate to politicians your ability to impact elections, thereby motivating susceptible players – through either fear or greed – to support you.

Politics as the adjudication of power

It's nice to be nice, and it's good to be right; but alas, political effectiveness depends on neither. Politics is the adjudication of power: who wields it, how, and at whom. By "adjudication," I mean the formalizing of how power is applied, be it by legislative body, court or commission. However politely it is wielded, what you are witnessing is the raw application of power by one human being (or group) over another.

"But," you insist, "this is a Democracy!" (Actually, ours is a constitutional republic, not a democracy, but we will save that discussion for another time.) What you need to understand is that even our republic, as intended by the Framers, does not eschew the application of power. Rather, it creates a relatively just and (usually) non-violent *means* for applying power.

Machiavellian power politics is alive and well

Niccolò di Bernardo dei Machiavelli (1469-1527), Florentine diplomat, political philosopher and author of *The Prince,* is often considered the father of modern political science. Although sometimes denounced for advocating deception and treachery, he recognized that man's basest instincts generally drive his quest to control others. In a Machiavellian world, altruism, if it exists at all, is rare indeed.

Machiavellian power politics dominate *all* political systems, however democratic (or autocratic) such systems may be. What differentiates ours is that, at least in theory, we settle power struggles with elections and courts rather than bullet-riddled automobiles.

For that, you can thank the Framers, who designed a republican system of government which, like Machiavelli, acknowledges man's innate quest for power. Accordingly, they created an intricate set of checks and balances between competing branches of government in order to prevent any single entity from gaining complete control. It is precisely that system of checks and balances which leftists seek to undermine in order to consolidate power.

While Saul Alinsky earns justifiable condemnation for arguing that his ends justify almost any means, he correctly treats means and ends as different, entirely independent factors. As an activist, you must learn to separate the application of power from the (hopefully) high-minded goals for which you intend to apply it.

What politics is <u>not</u>

Politics is not the "art of compromise." In fact, compromise, as your opposition defines it, is a process in which you might lose less than under their original proposal, but *you still lose.*

Saul Alinsky made clear the left's use of "compromise" when he said: "To the organizer, compromise is a key and beautiful word. It is always present in the pragmatics of operation ... If you start with nothing, demand 100 percent, then compromise for 30 percent, you're 30 percent ahead."[2]

What Alinsky neglects mentioning is that having "settled" for 30 percent, his minions will soon be back for the rest, typically under the guise of "closing loopholes" in what they didn't get the first time. They will repeat this until you are left with nothing.

That is why "preemptive compromise" (aka "preemptive concession"), as a political tactic, invariably fails. In 2013, for example, Obama et al. wanted S. 649 for "universal background checks" on gun purchases – a bill actually intended to turn the computerized "National Instant Background Check System" (NICS) into a defacto gun registry. While some admittedly well-meaning gun rights leaders pushed the so-called "Toomey-Manchin compromise," We put together a 39-member "Stop the Ban" coalition which refused to compromise, accepting nothing less than death of the bill.

We won and S. 649 died. Nine years later, the left has still made no significant inroads on expanding NICS. Had the "Toomey-Manchin compromise" prevailed, however, we would still be fighting for increasingly smaller exemptions from universal gun registration. What advocates of preemptive compromise seemingly fail to understand is that once they concede to *part* of the opposition's agenda, they concede the need for *all* of it.

What politics is

In truth, politics is the art of conflict: vectors of political force applied by a small minority (Fig. 7A). Unfortunately for conservatives, the left has long understood this and applied it to your disadvantage. It is why eighty percent of Americans support voter ID laws[3], but only thirty-six states have them.

Morton Blackwell, founder of the Leadership Institute, has been quoted as saying, "Political success is determined by the number and effectiveness of the political activists on either side." Your goal should be to use your activists to create conflict, forcing the center of debate toward the right and toward what has always been the mainstream of American political opinion. And you will do so not through "compromise" or "education," but via the application of political force. Your goal, quite frankly, is to impose your will on the opposition.

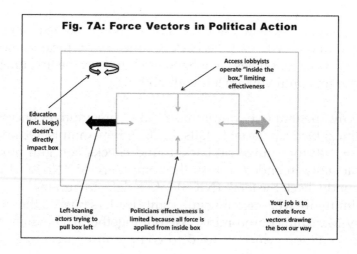

Fig. 7A: Force Vectors in Political Action

Politicians and rats (but I repeat myself)

Your first instinct will be to educate the politician. That instinct is usually wrong. A few neutral legislators might be swayed to your position after being made aware of its merits, and friendly legislators will need talking points to argue your position in committee or on the floor. But by and large, politicians respond not to education, but to pleasure and pain in the form of votes, money, power, and public accolades.

In the first half of the 20th Century, psychologist B.F. Skinner developed a school of psychology called "operant conditioning" in which he shaped behavior using a combination of reward ("positive reinforcement") and punishment. A "Skinner box," for example, might offer a rat two alleys, one containing a lever which, when pressed, delivers a food pellet. The other features an electrified floor grid, delivering a shock if the rat chooses that alley. The rat quickly learns to avoid the shock and press the lever for food.

Although ostensible intellectuals often eschew Skinner's theories as oversimplified, I would argue that any failure of operant conditioning to change behavior results entirely from failure to correctly identify and manipulate what motivates the subject.

Think of politicians as rats in a Skinner box (which should be easy enough). The reward and punishment you deliver come in the form of votes, money, power, and accolades … or the denial thereof.

Effective political action lies in manipulating the politician's environment. As we will examine in the next chapter, access-based lobbyists rely almost exclusively on pleasure. Grassroots mobilization, by contrast, combines pleasure and pain, often with emphasis on the latter. Indeed, Rothfeld has been heard to say, "If you can't say something bad about a politician, don't say anything at all."

Things that provide pleasure & pain for pols:

❏ **Pleasure:** Money, good press, endorsements, volunteers (surrogates for money), no primary challenge, earmarks (schools, roads, etc.), committee chairmanships, public praise.

❏ **Pain:** No money, primary challenge, denouncement, angry voters (a strong motivator), public ridicule (more effective than attacks), having bills killed in committee or on the floor (leadership does this to party members who don't play ball), loss of money, opposition from within his party (e.g. by RINOs[4]).

How pols respond to pain

When pressured, a politician will try to make you go away, preferably while doing as little as possible to placate you. First, they will try to ignore you, which may lead you to incorrectly conclude that your actions aren't having the intended effect. Failing that, below are the things you will hear from politicians or their minions to make you go away. Rather than backing down when you face them, double down and increase the pressure.

In response to pressure, expect three things from pols:

1. **Deflection:** They will try to deflect you using the following tactics.
   - **Rationalization:** "I'm really on your side, but we need to wait until ["we have a bigger majority"] ["after the election"] ["we get the support of XX"].
   - **Condescension:** "I've already explained to you why we can't move that bill."
   - **Compromise:** "Half a loaf is better than nothing."
   - **Fatalism:** Here, the politician will act as your "friend," trying to convince you of the error of your ways.
     o "It's inevitable: There's nothing we can do."
     o "If we did what you want, we'd get something worse."
     o "But we'll lose." (This may come from the pol, his staff – who operate to shield the pol and thereby protect their own jobs – access lobbyists, or other operatives. Could be a "citizen lobbyist" from another organization.)
     o Note: The politician, a lobbyist, or a member of another organization (or even your own) may try to deliver one of the above messages to your board, donors, members or other key operatives within your organization in order to get to you.

2. **Threats:** Use of intimidation is a common tactic that can be difficult to resist.
   - **Political threats:**
     - o "If you do that, I'll vote against you."
     - o "I'll tell the media that you're a trouble-maker."
     - o "You're hurting your own cause."
     - o "That's not how we do things here."
     - o "The emails I've been receiving are threatening and offensive."
     - o "I'll make sure nobody will ever work with you again."
   - **Other threats:** Could be with violence (principally in other countries), could be legal ("you're threatening me"), or could be using litigation, audits or other bureaucratic bird-dogging.
   - **Your response:** Rather than backing off, *double down* – increase pressure. Understand that it is sometimes extremely difficult to stay the course.

3. **Enticements:** They might try to buy you off.
   - **Flattering you:** "I'd like you to serve on my advisory committee."
   - **Introducing you to powerful people:** "This is XX, he's a real patriot."
   - **Bribing you:**
     - o "Host a fundraising event, and we'll explain to them together why we just can't get it this year."
     - o "I think I have a place on my staff for someone just like you."

Safer to be feared than loved

In committee, a second term Republican played "CYA" by introducing weakening amendments to our concealed carry bill. As invariably happens with elected officials, he was starting to forget who "brung him to the dance." Tasked by the sponsor with getting him to withdraw the amendments, we lobbied him across the courtyard and into a crowded elevator. When he refused, in front of the crowd I said, "If you insist on the amendments, we will have to tell your constituents what you've done." As the doors closed, he said, "You do what you've gotta do."

(continued on next page)

> **(continued from previous page)**
>
> When his constituents started to object, he called me to complain, "You know, if this is how you treat your friends, I'm not sure I want to be your friend." When I allowed that this was not how friends behaved, he hung up on me. When one of my leadership threatened to leaflet his district, he tried to sic the NRA on me, only to find that I didn't answer to the NRA.
>
> But he ultimately complied. And after withdrawing his amendments, who do you suppose became our best buddy? Who do you suppose cosponsored our bills and forcefully argued our position in committee? Yep, you guessed it.

The two seasons of political action

Just as political action divides into the arenas of legislative operations and election operations, so too each arena has its own "season." In the former, the chamber is in session and actively legislating. In the latter, it generally adjourns to give politicians time to campaign. Although time frames for the two may occasionally overlap, treat them as distinct but closely related theaters of operation.

Objectives of the two seasons:

❑ **Objectives of legislative season:** To impact law-making by twisting the arms of politicians, particularly by deluging them in channeled input. Most grassroots organizations stop here, usually to their own detriment.

❑ **Objectives of election season:** To leverage your input during the legislative season by systematically awarding or withholding the votes, money, power, and public accolades politicians so love. You reward desirable and punish undesirable behavior. Without the threat of political action, pols will pay far less attention to your legislative action.

The value of payback

Says Mike Rothfeld, "Unless you are politically feared, you will not be politically respected."[5] Make that your mantra and do not deviate from it.

Again, the politician's goal is to convince you that the legislative and election seasons are unrelated, that you should forget, in the election season, what they did in the legislative season. When punished in elections for things done in legislation, they become indignant. They insist they are really your friend, that the seven votes they cast against you didn't really mean anything, that they *had* to do it. They will lie, whine, equivocate, rationalize and bluster, all to avoid answering for what they did.

Your goal, by contrast, is to make sure the legislative season and the election season are inexorably intertwined. You will punish or reward politicians in the election season for what they do in the legislative season … each time, *every* time.

Only by consistently linking behavior to reward or punishment will you be able to successfully apply the principles of operant conditioning; only then will you deliver the message to politicians that they must either toe the line or pay the price; and only when they get that message will they comply with your politely delivered demands.

The NRA has a bad habit of disconnecting actions and punishment by giving ostensibly "friendly" politicians a pass for bad behavior. Consequently, politicians know they can get away with dropped votes or, more frequently, less overt subterfuge such as procedural tricks.

By contrast, I make it a point that if a politician crosses me, I *always* deliver payback, even if the politician is secure in his or her district. (Obviously, if the chances of victory are slim, I don't spend as much precious PAC money against them.)

And yes, even friendly politicians get a slap on the wrist, and generally learn their lesson when they do. With our help, for example, a state house rep who had done much to help us got elected to Congress. Thanks to the inherently corrupting influence of political office, within a year he dropped a vote on a bill we opposed. I responded by sending an alert telling people to call him and ask why he had stabbed them in the back. Four hours later, I got a page (this was before common use of cell phones) asking to call his office. When I called, the Congressman immediately got on the line, asking: "Paul, is this how you treat your friends?" My response was the same one I have used repeatedly: "Robin, I'm not sure that's how 'friends' behave." Although he eventually became fully corrupt, he never again betrayed *me*.

The advantage of always delivering payback, regardless of chances of victory, is that it forces even your opponents to do a cost-benefit analysis for each opposing action. It forces them to say: "If I sponsor this bill, they will go after me in the next election and I'll have to spend $50,000 to defend myself. Is it really worth it?"

A tale of two paybacks

Payback #1: A Republican state house member voted against us and was later overheard screaming, "If the Second Amendment came before me today, I'd vote against it." He subsequently decided to run for an open state senate seat. In the primary race for that seat, we beat the crap out of him, sending thousands of pieces of mail into his district, plus robocalls and texts, emails, social media ads, and even radio spots. He lost, ending up out of power for two years, after which he ran for his old house seat. We once again beat him senseless, but thanks to name recognition in his old district (and spending boatloads of money), he won. When the subsequent legislative session convened, another legislator suggested we bury the hatchet, so I visited the wayward Republican's office, finding him deferential to the point of groveling, even rationalizing that he hadn't really meant what he said. What I heard in his voice was fear. I graciously accepted his apology, since which he has not yet voted against us. Lesson learned.

Payback #2: One of Michael Bloomberg's "Moms Demand Action" gun control leaders, Christy Clark, decided to run for state house. Thanks to Bloomberg's money, she beat a Republican incumbent, after which she and two other infamously leftist legislators introduced bills for *all* of the left's pet gun bans. (In the Republican-controlled chamber, all died for lack of committee hearings.) In the next election, we threw everything we had against her, even using a "dirty tricks PAC" to beat her up over her signing a national "defund police" petition. We focused on her rather than the other two because she was weakest in her district. As a result, she lost re-election to the previous Republican incumbent. So did her cohorts re-introduce their full gun control wish list in the next session? Nope. Too costly. Lesson learned.

References:

1. Michael I. Rothfeld, Foundation for Applied Conservative Leadership, https://facl-training.org/

2. Saul Alinsky, *Rules for Radicals: A Pragmatic Primer for Realistic Radicals*, Vintage Books, Random House, Inc., 1971, p. 59.

3. "Public Supports Both Early Voting and Requiring Photo ID to Vote," Monmouth University Polling Institute, June 21, 2021, https://www.monmouth.edu/polling-institute/reports/monmouthpoll_us_062121/

4. "RINO": Republican in Name Only.

5. Op. cit. note 1.

Chapter 8
Lobbying vs. Grassroots Mobilization

"...it is much safer to be feared than loved because ... love is preserved by the link of obligation which, owing to the baseness of men, is broken at every opportunity for their advantage; but fear preserves you by a dread of punishment which never fails." – Niccolo Machiavelli, *The Prince*[1]

"Authority has always attracted the lowest elements in the human race. All through history, mankind has been bullied by scum. Those who lord it over their fellows and toss commands in every direction and would boss the grass in the meadow about which way to bend in the wind are the most depraved kind of prostitutes. – P.J. O'Rourke[2]

Presuming you have chosen the indirect path to power as detailed in Chapter 7, there are two ways to go about it. First, you can buy access to a politician. Wine and dine him (if legal). Help him get things he wants. Donate to his campaign, or to his pet project. Kiss his ass. This is called "access-based lobbying," and is the premise on which professional lobbyists rest their influence.

The alternative is called "grassroots mobilization" and depends on motivating politicians from the position of being able to provide (or withhold) votes, money, power and public accolades. Rather than schmoozing politicians, as your people's representative you will literally speak truth to power. Ultimately, you may find the optimal solution involves adding a smattering of access-based methods to a strategy relying primarily on grassroots mobilization.

Access-based lobbying

The best characterization I can think of for access-based lobbying comes from the title of P.J. O'Rourke's book, *A Parliament of Whores*. Like a high-priced escort, in access-based lobbying the politician controls the relationship, taking money directly or indirectly from the "john" (the lobbyist) and, in return, doling out the occasional favor.

While the days of overt bribery are (mostly) past, access-based lobbyists curry favor by "bundling" campaign donations, using political action committees to support candidates, and brokering deals to help the politician pass other legislation he or she wants—even if unrelated to the lobbyist's goals.

Access-based lobbyists are often former politicians or political staffers—insiders who have made the connections necessary to influence legislators. Unlike ordinary people espousing causes, they are very much the "in" crowd.

Given that you probably don't want to make a profession of lobbying (although if you do, I'd suggest taking your first lessons in a bordello), the following discussion assumes you are contemplating hiring one, as many political organizations do, often to their own detriment.

Pros & cons of access-based lobbying

Money is the primary lure used by access-based lobbyists. With money comes access. Although modern campaign laws limit the most extreme forms of corruption, politicians still get mysteriously rich in jobs paying meagre salaries.

Advantages of access-based lobbying:

❏ **The lobbyist is an "insider":** Good ones know where all the bones are buried. (Does Politician X have a potential kiddie porn charge hanging over his head? Perhaps a DUI in his history?) Power brokers take his calls. His relationships give him resources such as access to committee chairs to advocate (or suppress) hearings for bills, cooperation from party leadership in lining up votes, support from ex-officio committee members (see below), and logistical support such as bill drafting and research services. A good lobbyist is rarely seen, but often felt.

❏ **It's easier to line up sponsors:** Because grassroots mobilization often achieves its goal by arm twisting, getting politicians to introduce legislation can be problematic. You can pressure pols into voting with you, but short of outright blackmail you can't pressure them into sponsoring bills. By contrast, lobbyist largess may provide the needed inducement.

❏ **Hiring one saves you time and effort:** Learning the tricks of the legislative process isn't easy. You and your supporters will spend months, even years getting your butts kicked before you figure out how to kick back. Even then you can plan on spending twenty to forty hours a week staying on top of politicians' many feints and dodges.

Disadvantages of access-based lobbying:

❏ **The politician controls the relationship:** Rather than telling the politician what he must do for his constituents, access-based lobbyists become the politician's representative to his constituency, telling *them* what they must settle for.

❏ **Lobbyists can't afford controversy:** Most lobbyists represent multiple interests. Because their clients and livelihoods depend on access, they can't do anything which threatens that access. Even if they don't represent multiple interests, their dependence on access requires them to avoid displeasing the host politician.

❏ **Inherent conflicts of interest:** Because hired lobbyists often represent a variety of interests, you never know exactly who they are representing today. Let's say you chunk down $20,000 for a lobbyist. When he's whispering into the ear of Senator Pearlywhites during a relevant committee hearing, is he representing *you*, or is your own lobbyist selling you out in favor of another (more lucrative) interest he represents?

❏ **Exorbitant costs:** Should you choose to hire a lobbyist, be prepared to pony up big bucks. Figure that entry-level lobbying services for a state legislature will cost $10,000 (more likely $20,000) and up.

❏ **Vested interest in prolonging the process:** Rest assured that during the massive "education campaign" your lobbyist claims is essential to pass your bill, they will be racking up hefty fees.

❏ **Vested interest in selling "compromise":** Since the lobbyist may have little personal interest in your issue, any compromise that allows him to claim success is fine by him. Better yet, perhaps he will pass an imperfect bill that gives him a chance to try and "fix" it later … at your expense, of course.

Grassroots mobilization

As an entirely different school of political influence, competent grassroots mobilization genuinely alarms politicians. They look for a money trail and find none. They try to buy you, flatter you or threaten you, only to whack their heads against a brick wall.

In grassroots mobilization, *you* control the relationship. Rather than representing the pol to his constituency, as do access-based lobbyists, you represent *them* to *him*. Rather than currying his favor, you tell *him* what he needs to do. This technique requires organization and a decent dose of moxy. What it does *not* require is fame and fortune on your part. In fact, as an unknown, you have nothing to lose by being edgy and aggressive, as compared to prominent people whose reputations – and potentially, livelihoods – are at stake.

In grassroots mobilization, your goal is not *access* to the politician, but *power* over him. You provide votes, money, power and public acclaim … or their opposites. As noted previously, this is not fuzzy, warm "write-your-congressman" stuff. Success rests less on education than on arm-twisting. One of my early mentors described it as "political thuggery." Indeed, I was quite happy when Representative Don Munford, whom we were primarying as payback for his transgressions and who discovered our people distributing hit literature against him at polls, called us "a bunch of thugs."

Power vs. access

Power and access are very different things. Ironically, exercising power will likely deprive you of access.

❏ **Access:** This is exemplified by having your phone calls returned, "having a seat at the table" (a popular goal among compromised activists), and most important, *never being perceived as a threat.*

❑ **Power:** This implies both the ability and the willingness to apply pleasure or pain to politicians as the circumstances dictate, regardless of threats or consequences. It will not make you popular among politicians, and might also make you a pariah among other activists on your issue – specifically, lap-dog activists who rely on access.

Advantages of grassroots mobilization:

❑ **You control the relationship:** To steal from Machiavelli, it is better to be feared than loved. For use in legislative seminars, I still keep a fear-laden voicemail I received from a legislator after I pleasantly offered to unleash the peasants with pitchforks. By demonstrating the ability to deliver or withhold votes, money, and power, you become the voice of the people to the legislator, telling him what he must do. To this end, I generally refer to legislators by first name rather than "senator" or "representative," and I *never* use "the honorable" (except sarcastically).

❑ **It baffles the opposition:** Opposing politicians and professional lobbyists look for a money trail. In their eyes, anyone in the legislative arena must benefit financially from you being there. And when they can't find a money trail, it eventually dawns on them that you probably can't be bought ... and that *really* scares them.

❑ **You can afford to be controversial:** To win new clients, lobbyists need access. To maintain access, they must avoid controversy. When channeled input, rather than access, becomes the primary weapon, however, it reduces your need to be "the get-along guy." Depending on the activist persona you project, being nasty and controversial may actually enhance your effectiveness. I often say that my goal is to be "reviled in all the right places."

❑ **Reduction in corrupting influences:** Uncharacteristically, for politics, you can maintain relative purity of mission. Presuming your leadership are primarily volunteers, the absence of money from the equation dramatically reduces temptation to stray from the objective – not that corrupting influences are entirely absent, since even the "power" (actually access) of having politicians accept phone calls can be corrupting. But if "the love of money is the root of all evil," removing money from the equation reduces at least some of the attendant evil.

❏ **Fewer conflicts of interest:** Unlike a lobbyist who earns money from different, potentially competing clients, grassroots mobilization activists generally lobby for, if not a single cause, at least a limited range of less conflicted causes.

❏ **More "bang for the buck":** Compared to paying lobbyists and campaign consultants, grassroots mobilization is cheap. You can accomplish goals for less money than your opposition. Political organizations typically waste thousands or even millions of dollars as worthless lobbyists, campaign managers, and consultants siphon off hard-to-raise funds. By using volunteers and doing chores in-house – even when the product is slightly more crude than what professionals might produce – you can beat your opponents on a fraction of their budget. This is particularly true on certain issues (e.g. gun rights) where the left can't raise comparable grassroots support and is forced to "astroturf" (i.e. to create the false appearance of grassroots support).

❏ **Your followers will love you:** Attractive though this may sound, it is a mixed blessing. As a representative of the people on your issue, you will be their hero … until somebody with less-then-pure intentions decides to depict you otherwise (and rest assured you will encounter such people). Additionally, the moment you buy in to the hero worship, you neuter your effectiveness. Effective grassroots mobilization demands ego, not arrogance.

Disadvantages of grassroots mobilization:

❏ **You will need thick skin:** Count on being told that you are not only wrong, but stupid. "That's not how we do things here" will be the mantra not only from politicians, but from those who purport to be your allies. (My standard response to that mantra is, "I know. That's why you always lose.")

❏ **You are not an "insider":** Consequently, when your opposition drafts legislation, you will be among the last to know which committee it is assigned to and on what day it will be calendared for consideration even, occasionally, in a relatively friendly chamber. That said, if you cultivate a reputation for beating the daylights out of ideologically compromised legislation offered by other organizations purporting to be on your side, chances improve that friendly legislators will bring it to your attention before introduction, if for no other reason than to avoid conflict. On several occasions, I have had legislators approach me for our stance on legislation (usually hair-brained) that other organizations asked them to sponsor.

❑ **You are at the mercy of volunteers:** Our running joke is that in our organizations, we punish incompetence by promotion; the more you screw up, the more work you get (which explains why I am president). But seriously, some of your volunteers may be less than bright, less than motivated, and less than organized. And if you lean on them too heavily, they disappear. The corollary here is that one marginally talented volunteer who consistently gets the job done is worth three talented volunteers who don't. I'll take dedication over skill almost every time.

❑ **Volunteer organizations require a constant search for talent:** Because volunteers will generally be less dedicated than you are, they will drift off for issues of family, work or other interests. The most resolute might last years, but nearly all will eventually need replacement. Talented volunteers, who typically shoulder most of the burden, tend to burn out. Consequently, any time you find someone with talent, recruit them.

❑ **Activism can be (another) full-time job:** You will be replacing money with sweat. If you don't have the hours to spend, grassroots mobilization might not be for you. Frankly, if you can't prioritize to find time, you just might not be dedicated enough.

❑ **Your operation will be more crude:** Polished communications by consultants cost money. By contrast, your bare-bones grassroots organization will likely display some warts. I tell people that my organizations operate like the Israeli Defense Forces: what we do isn't necessarily pretty, but we get the job done.

❑ **Specialized tasks aren't suited to volunteerism:** That is why legal action is generally the mode of last resort for grassroots mobilization. You will have to hire lawyers, and lawyers rarely work for free. (And this is why you should recruit as many lawyers as possible to your cause.) Similarly, if you decide to run for office, you may have to hire a campaign manager. (I have no patience for mismanaged political campaigns.) The good news is that precludes an otherwise volunteer organization from occasionally contracting skilled help on an as-needed basis.

Serious people on serious business

Your overriding priority is to demonstrate to legislators you are serious people on serious business. Dress accordingly. Legislatures tend to be the last bastion of the suit and tie. Wear them.

For example, the Concerned Bikers Association for years tried to repeal my state's helmet law. God bless them, their dedication, and their use of the legislative process. Every year, they turned out in droves at the legislature. But how seriously do you suppose politicians took people sporting sleeveless denim jackets, Harley patches, and Death's Head tattoos? Don't get me wrong: You might have to turn out droves of volunteers yourself. Some of them might have gnarly beards and own one shirt. But your leaders should dress like leaders.

Exercise similar control over what your volunteers say. Subject to the constraints below, your leadership may be authorized to discuss with legislators the fine points of legislation you support or oppose. Not so, however, with your rank and file, who should receive short, simple bullet points with instructions to stick to them.

After a committee hearing at which a bill we opposed was tabled for later consideration, one of our well-intentioned volunteers tried to *educate* the opposing lobbyist by showing him how definitions in the bill were overbroad and could be construed to impact a huge number of people never mentioned. In response, the lobbyist showed up at the next committee meeting with an amendment omitting those people, denying us a potential coalition with other groups to defeat the bill. (Incidentally, this tactic, which I call "preemptive concession," usually doesn't work for reasons I will later outline.)

Lesson learned: I now strictly limit contact between volunteers and the opposition, particularly if the opposition has hired nice, friendly professional lobbyists.

Don't mistake being a serious person for being strident or boringly dogmatic. Religious conservatives, for example, sometimes take themselves entirely too seriously. When my leaders get outraged by the opposition, I tell them to lighten up, that this is just one battle among many, and that we are in it for the long haul. When targeting opposing politicians, the best way to destroy them is clever ridicule. (Alinsky's Rule 5: "Ridicule is man's most potent weapon.")

We once bestowed upon the mayor of Durham our "Fireplug Award"—a caricature of our mascot "Max" (fittingly enough, a pit bull with the Constitution clenched in his teeth, daring anyone to try and take it), with his leg held high against an offending fire hydrant. On Thursday, we sent the cartoon to our press list and placed it front-and-center on our home page.

On the evening news, most of the local television stations carried footage of our web site, forcing the mayor to do a little rug dance to explain his position. That was on Friday. On Monday, his phones lit up from thousands of alerts we distributed at a weekend gun show instructing respondents to call him on Monday morning.

Hazards of grassroots mobilization

You nasty ol' "special interest," you

Even ostensibly "friendly" access-based lobbyists will oppose you. Unlike you, they have a financial interest in prolonging the process, and if you are effective, they will view you as a threat that stands to marginalize them.

Consider these quotes from a book for access-based lobbyists, some of which are true, some patently false: "Single issue lobbies do not have to trade off gains for their cause against other political considerations; [true] in fact, they often have nothing to give [false]."[4]

Of how about this one: "In former years ... congressmen attempted to balance conflicting interests by voting for projects most or their constituents would like most of the time. This gave the members the freedom to take controversial stands on particular issues without fear of losing their seat [sic] because of one or two controversial votes. That freedom has been diminished by the special interest lobbies."[5]

Allow me to translate: Because Joe Lobbyist understands that grassroots mobilization activists do not compromise on principle, he wants you to believe they have nothing to offer a candidate, and he laments the present inability of pols to screw you behind your back with what he euphemistically calls "controversial votes."

The limits of volunteers

As we've discussed, the talent, training, and sophistication of volunteers may be limited. Your control over them is less direct, meaning grassroots mobilization is largely the realm of self-motivated people. Such people occasionally turn into loose cannons.

More hazardous still, activists eventually begin to seek the rewards brought by access. They *like* having Senator Circlejerk return their phone calls; it's *nice* having lunch in the legislators' private dining room. Eventually, they may begin responding to the subtle bribery more or less constantly offered by politicians and lobbyists.

Beware when a lobbyist (either friendly or not) starts giving your volunteers perks such as free hotel rooms and meals. Watch carefully when he offers special access to a politician. If you get sucked in by access, you will eventually find yourself in the position not of telling politicians what they must do, but of telling your constituency what they must accept.

References:

1. Niccolo Machiavelli (author), Harvey C. Mansfield (translator), *The Prince: Second Edition*, University of Chicago Press, 1998 (originally published 1532).

2. P.J. O'Rourke, *A Parliament of Whores: A Lone Humorist Attempts to Explain the Entire U.S. Government*, Grove Press, 2003.

3. Robert L. Guyler, *Guide to State Legislative Lobbying*, Engineering THE LAW, Inc., 2000.

4. Ibid.

5. Ibid.

Chapter 9
Navigating the Legislative Battlefield

"Our political system is anchored by two dominant parties, the Stupid Party and the Evil Party. And occasionally, in the spirit of bipartisanship, they produce legislation which is both stupid and evil." – Samuel Francis, syndicated columnist and adjunct scholar at the Ludwig von Mises Institute

Having outlined how grassroots mobilization addresses political bodies, let's discuss the political bodies to be addressed. Lest the tune from Schoolhouse Rock's "I'm Just a Bill" start dancing in your head, however, understand that beyond the basics, little on the legislative battlefield resembles anything you learned in high school civics class. Regardless of your level of knowledge, I suggest reading even the basics presented here, since they might contain wrinkles you haven't thought about. Chapter 10 covers tactics and treachery in greater depth.

Legislative bodies in a nutshell

As Civics 101 tells us, government in the United States generally divides into legislative, judicial, and executive branches. The federal government is, in theory (if not in practice) guided by the U.S. Constitution, a document which few politicians ever read and to which fewer still bother to adhere. Your state will have a similarly unheeded document. As to the structure and intent of the Constitution, I will leave that to better minds than mine, focusing instead on how to bend legislative bodies to your will.

General structure

Governmental bodies are generally bicameral (Nebraska excepted), being divided into an upper chamber (the senate) and a lower chamber (the house or assembly). Local government entities such as county commissions and city councils have only one chamber. With the exception of a few non-partisan boards, presiding over the bodies are the leaders of our two dominant political parties, the Stupid Party (Republicans) and the Evil Party (Democrats), plus executives such as the Governor.

Politicians' terms of office vary widely, typically ranging between two and six years. In some bodies, all pols run for reelection at the same time. In others, terms are staggered. Legislators in a given body generally represent a district which, given partisan motives in drawing political districts, may be positively bizarre in shape. (We had a congressional district, little more than 200 yards across at points, which became popularly known as "the I-85 district.") City and county legislative bodies typically have some (or occasionally all) members who run "at-large" in the entire area governed by the body rather than one of its subdivisions.

Although the majority party generally dictates who leaders will be for the full body, the minority party also elects its own leadership. In any given body, the majority and minority parties form their respective "caucuses," which meet outside the legislative chamber to plot strategy.

Congress

The United States Senate is the upper chamber of the U.S. Congress, with the House of Representatives being the lower chamber. Together they compose the national bicameral legislature of the United States as dictated by the U.S. Constitution.

U.S. Senate

The Senate currently comprises one hundred members (two per state). Senators serve staggered six-year terms with one-third coming up for re-election every two years. Although the vice president of the United States serves as president of the Senate, the president pro tempore is the constitutionally recognized officer who presides over the chamber in the absence of the vice president, is elected by the Senate and is, by custom, the senator of the majority party with the longest record of continuous service. In practice, the officer actually setting the agenda is the senate majority leader. Similarly, the minority party elects the minority party leader. Both parties also have "whips" whose job is to line up or "whip" votes on pending legislation within their caucus.

As the upper chamber of Congress, the Senate has powers of "advice and consent" to approve treaties, and to confirm cabinet secretaries, Supreme Court Justices, federal judges and other officials. As the supposedly "deliberative" body, closing debate and actually voting on a bill requires a "vote of cloture," currently a 3/5 super-majority (sixty votes).

Adopted in 1917 and reduced from 2/3 to 3/5 in 1975, the vote of cloture provides a means to end what previously was a potentially endless debate, called a "filibuster," in which a senator may speak continuously for hours (the current record being 24:18) in order to force the opposition to relent on taking a vote. (See *Mr. Smith Goes to Washington*.) Filibuster is threatened far more than done and is what leftists are trying to end in order to consolidate their power and foist their agenda on an unwilling citizenry.

U.S. House of Representatives

As the lower chamber, the U.S. House comprises representatives who sit in congressional districts allocated to each state on a basis of population as measured by the U.S. Census (including illegal aliens), with each district having one representative. Redistricting occurs every ten years, and its importance is routinely underestimated by conservatives. Rest assured that former Attorney General Eric Holder, his "National Democratic Redistricting Committee," and its "sue 'til their blue" campaign to nullify Republican-drawn districts take redistricting quite seriously.

As fixed by law, the number of voting representatives is 435 with a total number, including non-voting members, of 441. All members stand for re-election every two years. Non-voting members are from U.S. territories and the District of Columbia. Democrats are trying to add Puerto Rico and D.C. as states in order to secure additional leftist seats in Congress and, consequently, a permanent lock on power.

U.S. House majority leadership includes the speaker, majority leader, majority whip, assistant speaker, and the caucus chairman. Minority leadership is similar in structure.

State legislatures

What follows are generalities. Because state legislatures vary widely, you will have to research the structure and rules of the state legislature in which you plan to operate.

❏ **State senate:** As the upper chamber, the state senate's role is similar to that of the U.S. Senate. Leading the chamber is the president, who is either the lieutenant governor or elected by members of the senate. Next comes the senate president pro tempore ("pro tem"), who directs the senate in the president's absence. If the president is the lieutenant governor, as is the case in 25 states, the president pro tem often directs day-to-day senate operations. Caucus leadership structures vary, but are generally similar to the U.S. Senate.

❏ **State house (or "assembly"):** In the lower chamber, House members are more numerous and may serve shorter terms than their senate counterparts. Leading the house is the speaker, elected by members of the house, typically followed by a speaker pro tempore (who serves as speaker in the speaker's absence), majority leader, rules chair and majority "whip" (who lines up or "whips" votes in his caucus), majority caucus leader, and committee chairs. The minority party typically has a minority leader, minority whip, and minority caucus leader.

Legislative sessions

At present, forty-six state legislatures hold regular annual sessions. Four states—Montana, Nevada, North Dakota, and Texas—meet in odd-numbered years. Session length may be set by a state's constitution, a statute, or by the legislature and varies widely between states. According to the National Conference of State Legislatures (NCSL), eleven states do not place a limit on the length of regular session, while thirty-nine set limits by constitution, statute, chamber rule or other method.[2] Special or extraordinary sessions may also be called by a state's governor or legislature over a specific legislative item.

Nine state legislatures have full-time legislators, with the legislature meeting throughout the year. All other legislators are considered part-time, meeting for only a portion of the year. In my state, for example, the legislature meets for a two-year session, with the first year being the "long session" and the second year the "short session" in order to allow politicians more time to campaign.

Legislative leadership

The objective here is power. As such, the primary goal of legislative leadership is to remain within legislative leadership. The first priority of a leader is to get re-elected. The second priority is to ensure that members of his caucus get re-elected, thereby gaining or keeping a majority. A leader's constituency is not you, not the state, not even their district; it is his caucus. Even in a friendly chamber, your interests rank no higher than a distant fourth, and probably far lower than that.

Given those priorities, the easiest way for leadership to stay in power is not to piss anybody off. The easiest way to do that is to not do anything. When it comes to inertia in the legislative arena, the force is strong. Consequently, leadership acts as a bottleneck for bills – specifically, *your* bills. You will routinely hear leadership tell you what they cannot do because it might risk caucus members in marginal districts. When you hear this reasoning, politely ignore it.

Committees

Committees are graveyards for bills. If the majority leadership doesn't like your bill, they will deny it a hearing, inflicting upon it the dreaded "Death by Committee." Politicians would much rather kill your bill in committee than on the floor. First, it's easier. They face more legislation than time allows, so burying hostile or contentious bills in committee frees up their crowded calendar. More importantly, however, it spares them what they fear most: being on the wrong side of a recorded vote.

Typical "standing" (permanent) committees include appropriations, budget, environment, judiciary, transportation, etc. Gun bills typically go to judiciary or law enforcement committees, educational bills to education committees, climate bills to environment committees, and so forth. Assignment of your bill to the rules committee (technically, "Rules, Calendar, and Operations") is often the kiss of death, since the rules chair, in conjunction with the speaker, usually decides which bills move and which die, and taking it into his committee allows him to sit on it until dead. On the bright side, some chamber leaders shunt *all* bills to Rules, later re-referring those they plan to move to other committees. You will have to find out which approach majority leadership takes in the applicable chamber.

Floor sessions

Although most activity centers on committees, final passage occurs in sessions of the full chamber. To coordinate legislative action within the party and line up floor votes, each party appoints a majority or minority "whip," as appropriate.

At the beginning of its session, each body of the legislature adopts its own rules, ostensibly intended to facilitate orderly passage of bills. Get a copy of them from the legislative website or from the clerk or secretary of each chamber. It's also a good idea to keep handy a copy of *Robert's Rules of Order* for a general understanding, although most legislative bodies actually use variations of the slightly different *Mason's Manual of Legislative Procedure*, which is available from the National Council of State Legislatures (www.ncsl.org).

Passing and killing legislation

With apologies for repeating myself, any activist seeking to either enact or prevent change needs to know how to manipulate the legislative process to his advantage. Know the rules of the chamber. You will hear all manner of reasons why passing your proposals just isn't possible. For example, politicians will tell you reasons they can't sponsor it: that it's too controversial; that the rules prohibit it; or failing all else, "That's just not how we do things here." Most of the time you hear such excuses, they will either be lies or half-truths. My pat answer to "That's not how we do things here" is invariably, "I know. That's why you always lose."

Bills make the world go 'round

Bill drafting is less complicated than you might expect because you can modify existing laws from other states or boilerplate legislation from national organizations. Technical compliance, in the form of the final language to be introduced, will be handled by the legislature's bill drafting office, which will invariably try to hand you back something that accomplishes little or nothing of your original intent.

Believe it or not, the greater challenge lies in reading your opponent's bill. In fact, a cursory reading of the legislation may fail to reveal scores of unstated impacts, many of which are quite intentional. In reading a gun show bill, for example, I once skipped over a referenced statute I assumed was tax law. Only when a sharp member of my leadership said, "No, Chapter 14 is criminal law," did we discover that it would have shut down every gun show in the state. Thanks to him, we killed the bill with extreme prejudice.

Components of proposed legislation:

❏ **Bill titles:** Bill sponsors give their progeny some truly Orwellian titles. Consider, for example, the "For the People Act of 2021," which would have increased voter fraud, degraded the accuracy of voter registration lists, and banned voter ID laws. In addition to providing "spin," the title will indicate the status of the bill such as "draft" (not yet introduced), "proposed committee substitute" or "PCS" (a change not yet voted on in committee), "ratified" (passed by the legislature and sent to the governor), or "session law" (signed by the governor into law).

❏ **Time and date:** This stamp provides the best way to differentiate between versions of bills. Always, always, *always* make sure you are working with the latest version of the bill, which may bear little or no resemblance to earlier versions.

❏ **Sponsors and co-sponsors:** Check rules for timing in recruiting co-sponsors. At least in theory, the more sponsors a bill has, the more likely it is to move, particularly if sponsors hail from both parties. A bill with few sponsors is likely D.O.A.

❏ **Bill type:** For example, is it a "public" bill (i.e. one which organizations such as your own might draft), or from a study commission? Deadlines and rules for each may differ depending on how the chamber classifies the bill.

Rules for Anti-RADICALS

❑ **New or deleted language:** Although different legislatures use different methods, generally speaking, <u>underscored</u> phrases indicate new language, while words ~~struck through~~ are being deleted from law. Some legislatures may use different color fonts for new language, or occasionally all caps.

❑ **Line numbers:** Typically added on the left-hand margin, line numbers are the reference point by which legislators and staff verbally describe parts of the bill, particularly for floor amendments which refer to them when striking or adding language.

When reading bills:

❑ **Learn the shorthand:** Each legislature uses a template to denote sponsors and cosponsors, committee referrals, reports and other procedural items. Glean what you can from the legislature's web site, and by visiting each chamber's clerical office to get whatever pamphlets, information sheets, or books they might have.

❑ **Have several people read the bill:** If you have anyone with legal experience, so much the better. In any case, a second (or third) person might catch implications of the bill you missed. As a "big picture" guy, for example, I am terrible at catching small items that could be of help in killing hostile legislation.

❑ **Ensure you are using the most current version:** This sounds like a no-brainer, but is what you are looking at the original bill or the latest committee substitute? A bill could go through a dozen or more incarnations, and finding the latest isn't as easy as it sounds.

You may find, for example, that the legislative website won't display the latest "proposed committee substitute" (PCS) if the PCS has not yet received a hearing, even if the PCS has been referred to a subcommittee for action. Lest you think that a triviality, once when an NRA lobbyist tried to sell us out, the NRA claimed we were lying about their betrayal. To buttress their lie, they sent members to the legislative website, which didn't show the PCS which was the version of the bill actually being considered.

❑ **Check all the statutes it refers to:** Your opponent will try to sneak in some surprises, or might overlook an implication you can use to attack the bill. Unfortunately, this can be tedious. The good news is that while it once meant going to the legislature's library or another law library, state and federal statutes are now readily available via the Internet. Even city and county governments will have local ordinances on their sites.

❑ **Find the "gotchas":** It can be difficult to draft airtight bill language. Even when your opposition tries to craft the bill as narrowly as possible, it may accidentally regulate unintended groups or activities; it might reveal private information; it might allow certain groups to escape regulation. The list of potential technicalities is endless. Your job is to read the bill carefully and repeatedly, finding each little "gotcha," which you then use, one at a time, to attack the bill in what I call "layered defense" wherein you attack one – and only one – of the flaws you find at each stage of the bill's movement through the legislative chamber, thereby tying it up at *each stage* of its movement.

❑ **Read between the lines:** As mentioned above, our opposition introduced a gun show bill containing a long list of statutes with which gun show promoters would be required to comply. Given that most involved taxation, I failed to check each. Only when one of my leadership pointed out that the statutory chapter referred to involved *criminal* statutes rather than taxes did we realize that it would have rendered nearly every gun show promoter in the state ineligible for required gun show permits.

During the bill's committee hearing, we not only attacked the provision, but also painted the intentions of opposing lobbyists as deceitful. After the hearing, gun control lobbyist Bruce Thompson collared me, complaining, "Gee, Paul, I wish we were as clever as you claim we are." I replied, "Bruce, I figured you had to be either disingenuous or incompetent. I was giving you the benefit of the doubt." Plagued with our continuing effort to embarrass the lobbying firm, they eventually dropped their gun control client.

Drafting and introducing a bill

Don't be scared. Bill drafting isn't as hard as it sounds. Frankly, when the pols are done, the final draft won't look like what you wrote anyway. Your intention is to have a relatively polished first draft for your sponsor, sparing him work. (Whatever their flaws, politicians are busy devils.)

To draft a bill:

❑ **Do thorough research:** Know all of the ramifications of your topic. Your research can later be refined into talking points for distribution, particularly in committee. (For example, see Appendix VII.) Go to your state's web site and figure out which statutes you plan to amend. Search past sessions of the legislature to find out whether similar legislation has been previously introduced. If you find someone who personifies your bill (e.g. a crime victim) to be your poster child, introduce them to the sponsor.

❑ **Check other states and organizations:** Find out which other states have similar legislation, analyzing it for strengths and weaknesses and how well it works. You might be able to copy their language. You might also be able to modify "boilerplate" model legislation from a sympathetic national group. I wrote North Carolina's first "Castle Doctrine" bill by lifting it from Florida statutes.

❑ **Coordinate with appropriate agencies:** If a state agency will be administering whatever your bill does, try to coordinate the bill language with them, particularly if it will require a financial appropriation. This becomes more complicated if either the agency or the elected official overseeing it are hostile to you. Consider, for example, the Federal Flight Deck Officer program, under which airline pilots are trained and armed with handguns. The public wanted the program, Congress passed the program, and it became law as the "Arming Pilots Against Terrorism Act" ... after which the Transportation Security Administration slated to administer the program immediately tried to hamstring it.

❑ **Write an accurate draft:** Because bill formats vary between states, go to your legislature's website and pull down a few to serve as examples. Set up a template using your chosen word processing program. If you know any sympathetic lawyers who won't charge a fortune, run it by them.

Shopping for a sponsor

Ideally, your sponsor should be rock solid on your issue and willing to stand up to party leadership. The tougher, the better. Barring that, start with the lawmaker representing your district or that of someone in your organizational leadership. He has a vested interest in keeping constituents happy. If your representative is unsuitable, try finding one in a district whose constituents are sympathetic to your issue.

The "Personal Protection Act"

When we introduced a bill enabling lawful citizens to obtain concealed handgun permits, we not only had stats for the twenty-five-odd states that had already passed such laws, but also boilerplate legislation derived from those states. When the bill hit the more recalcitrant Senate, we had the victim of a robbery and shooting lined up to deliver emotional testimony to the Judiciary Committee that she wanted an opportunity to protect herself. Her testimony—and tearful photo—were prominently featured in several major newspapers.

The ideal sponsor is:

❑ Tough: can't be pushed around by media, opposition, or his own leadership;
❑ Knowledgeable on parliamentary procedure;
❑ A good spokesman;
❑ Sympatico on the issue you plan to address;
❑ Not a marginal character (e.g. out-of-control visionary);
❑ Hopefully conservative across the board; and
❑ Someone with a decent *but not excessively close* relationship to leadership.

When a potential sponsor pledges he is with you, don't take his word for it. To evaluate where a given politician stands, check with state and national organizations that generate candidate ratings. Project Vote Smart (www.justfacts.vote-smart.org), for example, is a non-partisan organization which publishes candidate ratings from a broad array of groups and issues representing both ends of the political spectrum. Understand, however, that voting right on your issue doesn't mean a politician will be willing to sponsor your bill. The majority fall into a mediocre category I call "votes right when squeezed." Even if you recruit a bill sponsor with a solid voting record, unless your bill holds his interest, it won't move.

In a perfect world, you would have primary sponsors from both parties. In the past, I had Democrats sponsor concealed handgun reciprocity legislation. In today's increasingly polarized political environment, however, you are unlikely to find Democrats who will vote with you, much less sponsor your bills. Even if you find a "Blue Dog" Democrat (e.g. West Virginia Senator Joe Manchin), he will invariably be drawn to the dark side by left-leaning party leaders who threaten to bury bills he sponsors, shelve economic projects for his district, even primary him if he doesn't toe the party line. Barring that, your ideal sponsor is from the majority party – and yes, I realize that might be impossible if you live in a "blue" state.

Don't make your sponsor work any harder than necessary. Be prepared to spoon-feed him with all the background information he needs, including talking points to defend the bill in committee and on the floor. Anticipate opposing arguments. Few things alienate friendly legislators faster than getting blind-sided by an unforeseen consequence of a bill.

To assess the quality of your sponsor, research the following questions:

❏ **Is he in the majority party?** If not, he won't get the time of day when it comes to securing a committee hearing. (Again, a majority party sponsor might be unattainable in a hostile chamber.) Is he a maverick within his own party? If so, you might get the same result, even if he's in the majority party. (This is one example of a "flawed sponsor.") On the other hand, if he is too ambitious, too much a team-player, he won't stick his neck out for you. Although it seems counter-intuitive, party leaders and committee chairs often make poor sponsors because being ambitious makes them risk-averse.

❏ **Is he on the likely committee of first reference?** Certain types of bills go to certain types of committees (e.g. gun bills generally go to judiciary committees). Having your sponsor on the committee likely to hear your bill enhances your probability of obtaining a hearing, as well as relieving you of having to recruit a "committee advocate" to argue your position in hearings.

❏ **How secure is he in his district?** If not and your bill is contentious, he is unlikely to stick his neck out. If he does, it could make him vulnerable. Don't squander sympatico legislators by exposing them to unnecessary risk.

❏ **Is his credibility "flawed?"** Look for nasty sex scandals, D.U.I.s, etc. One of our sponsors got censured by the entire House for licking the wrist of a nubile page. (Fortunately, our bill had already passed.) Another went to jail, later, after selling his party affiliation to the opposition for $60,000 and a used car. Another group's sponsor—a teacher by profession—was charged with exhibiting a certain fondness for adolescent boys.

Care & feeding of your sponsor:

1. Show him advantages of being a sponsor by highlighting him in membership communications and public events.

2. Legislators come and go; accept and assume it.

3. Form a symbiotic relationship:
    a. Create an I.O.U. (e.g. by introducing him to potential donors).
    b. Cash in the I.O.U. immediately. In politics, they have short shelf life.

4. Run news releases for bills in advance. Have them mention your organization.

5. Promote your sponsor via email and news releases.

6. Hold the sponsor's hand. Sponsors need frequent encouragement, particularly in the face of negative media.

7. Prepare him for adversity.

8. Be clear on expectations. Let him know what you want.

9. Make him a hero to your people.

10. Work hard to build bonds with him, but do so as equals, not with the legislator in a superior role.

11. Don't leave him hanging with an incomplete project.
    a. Back him up: Attend & testify for hearings.
    b. Have talking points ready.

12. Protect him in elections and elsewhere (e.g. on social media or talk shows) using independent expenditures for elections and supporters via either pre-staged phone calls for talk shows or comments for social media and online publications.

Which chamber?

If possible, introduce the bill in your weaker chamber (i.e. the chamber in which you have less support). That way, if your bill suffers weakening or hostile amendments (aka "the death of a thousand cuts"), you have a better opportunity to clean it up again once it gets to the chamber in which you have more support. It also enhances your ability to use recorded votes to later punish opposing lawmakers.

I say "if possible," because the weaker chamber might have few willing sponsors, or might deny your bill a committee hearing. In that case, introduce the bill in your stronger chamber, demonstrating to your members that you are doing something, creating inertia to help carry the bill through the weaker chamber, and allowing you to focus heat on hostile legislators.

Bearing in mind that bill passage is a time-limited game in which missed deadlines mean death, you might benefit from introducing "companion bills"—identical bills in both chambers of the legislature. If both bills remain identical, or if both chambers vote to concur on any differences, you'll save time over the tortured trail usually trekked through one chamber and then the other.

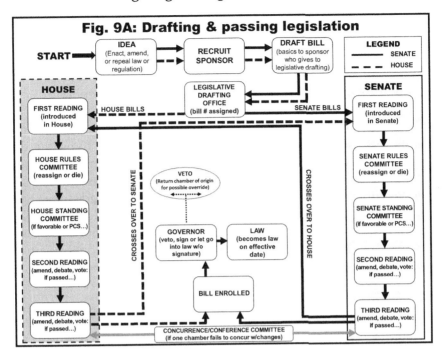

Fig. 9A: Drafting & passing legislation

Moving your bill

For the mechanics of how a bill becomes law, see the flow chart in Fig. 9A. In passing legislation, never underestimate the treachery of politicians. The steps are as follows:

❏ **First reading:** After being introduced by a sponsoring legislator, a bill gets its "first reading" on the chamber floor which, depending on your state, might or might not require a vote. Next it is referred to a committee (or two, three, maybe ten). Should it survive there—probably in some barely recognizable form—it advances for second and third readings on the floor.

❏ **Second reading:** Votes on second readings are generally (but not always) "recorded," allowing you to track whether or not a particular legislator supports your position. During the floor debate for second reading, the bill may undergo either friendly (or ostensibly friendly) or hostile amendments. Make sure to track votes on any that are relevant, including making your position on amendments known to legislators to prevent them from pleading ignorance while stabbing you in the back. I also recommend tracking votes on "procedural" motions (e.g. motions to table or to "divide the question"), since politicians routinely use procedural votes to avoid putting themselves on record on the substance of the bill.

❏ **Third reading:** On third reading, recorded votes and rules stipulating that second and third readings not occur on the same day may be dispensed with by unanimous consent to temporarily suspend the rules of the chamber. In such cases, objection by any single member requires the rule in question be followed rather than suspended. Like the rats they are, politicians often divine whether a bill will pass on the second reading, then switch to put themselves on the "right" side of the vote for third reading. Consequently, I avoid using third reading votes for candidate evaluation purposes unless, as occasionally happens, the bill is amended on third reading.

If the bill passes, it is referred to the other chamber, which repeats the process. If the two bodies pass slightly different versions of the bill, they may either vote to concur with the version that passed last, they may iron out differences in a "conference committee," or the bill might die for lack of action.

Presuming it passes both chambers, the "engrossed" or "enrolled" bill goes to the Governor, who may either sign it or veto it. Should he veto it, it may be sent back to the legislature, which may or may not override the veto, typically with a 3/5 or 2/3 vote, although in a few states it can be done by a simple majority. Inaction by the governor (i.e. neither signing not vetoing it) for a prescribed period of time may also allow the bill to become law.

The value of recorded votes

"Well, you know, Joe, I've always supported the God-given right to keep and bear arms," says Sen. Circlejerk.

"Then why did you vote for the 'Second Amendment Evisceration Act,' Senator?" demands the savvy constituent.

Here is a theme I will ram down your throat again and again and again. Recorded votes represent the measures by which you tell friends from enemies. They are the weapons by which you deliver pain to enemies (and occasionally, wayward "friends"). Moreover, the knowledge that you are tracking votes will bring you *more* votes ... even from politicians who hate you.

In defeating a mandatory gun storage bill, we once beat on the chamber so heavily that even co-sponsors of the bill didn't vote for it, instead whining to the sponsor, "I can't vote for it! Do you know how many gun owners live in my district?"

Floor votes

Depending on the state in question, floor votes are usually (but not always) recorded. The National Conference of State Legislatures (www. NCSL.org) publishes a handy list of which votes require roll calls in various states.[1]

However, tracking floor votes is not always straightforward. Be alert for what I call "mixed issues" in which legislators might have to weigh two or more disparate impacts of a given bill. When fighting a bill encouraging merchants to post signs prohibiting concealed carry, for example, I convinced a senator to offer an ostensibly "friendly" amendment which would neutralize the impact on concealed handgun permit-holders. Before offering it he made me promise that if the amendment failed, we would not hold Republicans responsible for voting for the final bill, since it was being run at the behest of another pro-Republican constituency, the state retail merchants' association. Happily, we won and the sponsor sent his own bill back to committee to die rather than pass it with our gun-neutral language.

Another question is whether to track procedural votes, such as motions to table (technically, to "lay on the table") or motions to "divide the question." The former suspends debate on a bill or motion (usually but not necessarily permanently), while the latter separates consideration of two different parts of a bill or motion. On another mixed issue, I had a senator offer a motion to divide the question, using that vote for candidate evaluation purposes rather than the final vote on the mixed bill.

Politicians use procedural tricks to avoid putting themselves on record for substantive votes (also called "up or down votes" or "clean votes"), which is why I advise them we usually track procedural votes. If you don't, you might never get politicians on record in a hostile chamber. That said, tracking procedural votes has complications. One conservative house rep refused on principle to vote for motions to table because he felt all legislators had the right to be heard. When the rules chair tabled twelve successive hostile amendments to our bill, the rep voted against each and every one despite being a stalwart supporter of the bill. Because our rules of engagement don't make exceptions, our objective candidate evaluation system made him what I dubbed "my favorite zero-star candidate." (After a certain amount of debate, we continued to work together and he eventually worked his way back up to our highest four-star evaluation.)

While we are on the topic of whether or not to give a "pass" by making exceptions for friendly legislators who drop votes, don't. Not ever. If the rats (pols) know that *sometimes*, when they choose the alley with electric floor grid (i.e. vote against you), they ***don't*** get a shock, the result is what behaviorists call "extinction," which is the gradual weakening of a conditioned response resulting in the desired behavior decreasing or disappearing.

Committee votes

Unlike roll calls on floor votes, committee votes are often unrecorded. Rules in some chambers *prohibit* roll call votes in committee, relying entirely on the chairman's determination of "yeas" and "nays." Depending on the rules of the chamber, a member of the committee may be able to call for "division," which typically results in a show of hands. Even here, recording who is for you and who is against you might require videotaping the committee hearing (if the chamber doesn't keep a videotape record). I've actually had volunteers ejected from committee hearings for videotaping them ... until we pointed out that doing so was a violation of the state's "open meetings" law.

Since committee votes are often unrecorded, opposing politicians (and some "friends") can more easily subvert you without getting caught. Recruit a legislator to act as your "committee advocate," equipping him with talking points to argue your bill and instructing him to call for division on relevant votes. On one bill, a call for division revealed three Republican defectors, whom I then featured, with pictures, as "The Gang of Three" on fliers distributed shortly thereafter at the state Republican convention. (See Fig. 9B.)

Fig. 9B: Holding your "friends" accountable

As the legislative season heats up, post "watchers" on committees, even on days when your opponent's bills are not on the calendar. Hostile committee chairs have a nasty habit of adding bills to the calendar at the last minute, when they think you aren't looking. Above all, ignore assurances about your opposition's bills such as: "*That* bill? Don't worry about that. It'll never get a hearing." I once had a subcommittee chair (hostile, of course) offer that assurance roughly five minutes before I ran into the chair of the full committee who, when queried, allowed that it would get a hearing in two days. The corollary to that rule is that when trying to divine what a committee will do with a given bill, feign ignorance and ask multiple legislators (and their staff) the same question. You will often get dramatically different answers.

As legislative deadlines approach, committee meetings come fast and furious, often at hastily scheduled times. We've actually had watchers simultaneously posted to several committees, communicating by cell phone to let us know where to dispatch the full legislative team, complete with a speaker, updated talking points, and tactics.

Know your enemies (and your 'friends')

Effective grassroots mobilization means gathering timely information (e.g. when a bill will move, which committee will hear it, etc.) and getting it to your members promptly. Start early by lining up sources of information in the first days of the legislative session. Unless you can cultivate a relationship with a staffer in leadership offices, however, do not rely on even friendly leadership to give you an early heads-up on bill progress. Chamber leaders are usually tight-lipped about which bills they intend to move and which they intend to kill by denying them committee hearings.

Sources of information:

- ❑ Chamber or legislature websites
- ❑ Legislative calendars (either printed or emailed)
- ❑ Chamber clerk's offices
- ❑ Friendly legislators (bearing in mind that many who claim to be "friends" are not)
- ❑ Legislative staffers or assistants (who often know more than their bosses)
- ❑ Friendly lobbyists (exercise extreme caution, since "friendly" is a relative term)

Prepare for upcoming legislative session:

- ❑ **Gather contact information for all elected officials:** From the chamber website get mailing addresses, phone numbers, email addresses and other relevant information, entering it into a spreadsheet which can be sorted by party affiliation, district number, name, or office number. Additionally, either the legislature or a commercial publisher may produce a book with photos and contact information for the full body. Keep photos handy to find out who is doing what during committee meetings and floor sessions, or to intercept politicians as they leave committee hearings or other functions.

- ❑ **Identify and visit party leaders and potential sponsors:** Analyze the support you are likely to get from each (bearing in mind that politicians have a pronounced tendency to say what you want to hear). In many cases you may be directed to staff, which is not ideal, but at a minimum try to develop contact information and a relationship with staffers responsible for your area of interest.

- ❑ **Analyze key committees:** Using Five Column Analysis (see below), determine the number of supporters, opponents, and swing voters on relevant committees. For at least swing voters, include the demographics of their districts and how they fared in the last election (available from boards of elections). Other questions: Where do they sit in the chamber? What occupations do they have? Do you have members in their districts? Do you have members who know them?

❑ **Subscribe to calendars:** Have all members of your legislative team sign up for emailed floor and committee calendars, if available. Tell them to check their email daily. It is *very* easy to miss activity for a bill.

❑ **Know where to find language:** Bills are available from the legislature's printed bills office or from the website. Remember, the bill you are reading might not be the latest version. Check the bill's latest activity on the chamber website or within the bill heading.

Legislative calendars

Your legislature will publish calendars, typically emailed, for both committee hearings and floor votes. Subscribe to them, but realize that calendars often change at the last minute. If you are smart, you will befriend a simpatico staffer who hears all the chamber rumors and can keep you abreast of last-minute changes.

Deadlines

Know what deadlines you (or your opposition) have to meet. When an activist starts demanding that legislators introduce something after the bill filing deadline has already passed, they will treat him like the rube he is. (I especially love it when gun control idiots waste money on expensive campaigns for their various pet gun bans *after* the applicable deadline has passed.) Note that different types of bills (e.g. public, study committee, or appropriations) may have different deadlines.

❑ **Bill drafting deadline:** The date and time by which your sponsor must submit your bill to the legislative drafting division. Ride herd on your sponsor to make sure he doesn't miss it.

❑ **Bill filing deadline:** The date and time by which the bill must be filed with the chamber for first reading.

❑ **Crossover deadline:** The date and time by which your bill must pass at least one chamber in order to remain alive for future consideration. Some types of bills (typically those with fiscal considerations) may be immune from crossover. Understand that crossover is intended as a barrier only for *you*, not for chamber leadership, who will manipulate the process by adding fiscal notes, stripping other bills and replacing their contents, or otherwise circumventing what they claim are the rules.

❑ **When deadlines don't apply:** Leadership uses legislative deadlines to hinder you, not politicians, who have various ways around them. Popular tricks include filing blank bills, stripping and replacing the guts of bills, and adding fiscal notes to make them immune to crossover deadlines. Your bill sponsor can use those tricks.

Committee assignments

To an extent, your bill's topic determines the committee to which it goes. Gun bills generally go to judiciary or, occasionally, law enforcement committees; bills to stop critical race theory would go to an education committee. Leadership may create multiple committees on a given topic in order to divide up workload, some of which might be friendlier than others.

If there is any latitude available on committee assignments (e.g. which judiciary committee if the chamber has several), work with your sponsor to get it assigned to the one most favorably disposed to your issue. How is the chair's voting record and history of sponsorship? How about the rest of the committee? Do a committee analysis, dividing members into allies, foes, and fence-sitters. It is the latter category that you will give the most "love" by channeling grassroots input to them.

The most sophisticated sponsor I've recruited kept flow charts on his office wall of committees, evaluating likely votes and factoring in "floaters"—members of the party leadership who may act as "ex officio" committee members, allowing them to vote on any standing committee.

If the available committees are weak, get your bill some "sunshine" by having it referred to a marginally-related but favorable committee first, after which it goes to the logical committee. For example, rather than sending a gun bill to the usual Judiciary Committee, I might run it first through a more favorable Law Enforcement Committee. Doing so creates inertia to carry it through less favorable committees beyond.

Bear in mind, however, that the more committee hearings you incur, the greater the chance you will fail to meet deadlines required by the chamber rules.

Dealing with your bill, the committee may:

❏ **Give it a favorable report:** Here it goes either to the next committee or to the full chamber for its second reading.

❏ **Give it an unfavorable report:** In this case it is dead unless they give an unfavorable report on the original but a favorable report on a "committee substitute" which changes the bill as described below.

❏ **Amend, markup, or substitute its language:** Lobbyist Robert Guyler[3] notes that rules often prohibit committees from actually amending bills, instead recommending amendments for the floor. Because such recommendations are nearly always followed, however, this is a distinction without a difference. In the U.S. House, committee amendments are called "markups."

The most popular way to change a bill in committee is the oft-dreaded "committee substitute," under which the bill that goes in and what comes out might bear as much resemblance to each other as Jekyll and Hyde. When your opposition suggests a committee substitute for either their bill or yours, *beware*.

❏ **Send it to a subcommittee:** This may be done to study changes to the bill, or it may be orchestrated by the bill's advocates to keep the bill alive by avoiding an unfavorable report. Like committee meetings, subcommittee meetings are subject to state open meetings laws designed to avoid lawmaking in secrecy. Because that protection sounds better than it works, however, it might require some persistence to get the calendar for subcommittee meetings, which are often not published on the chamber's main calendar.

❑ **Sit on it until dead:** As noted above, this is the preferred method of killing unpopular bills because it avoids subjecting legislators to a recorded vote.

Differentiating between friends and enemies

As we've already discussed, recorded votes tell you who your friends are, since politicians' unsubstantiated claims of support are nothing but window dressing. Because politicians do their best to camouflage themselves, however, accurate candidate evaluation is harder than it sounds. Chapter 11 will cover using not only recorded votes, but also survey scores, bill sponsorships, and a measure I call "bill support" to give you a more accurate picture of where candidates stand on your issue.

My original mentors at the Foundation for Applied Conservative Leadership advocate "Five Column Analysis" of legislative bodies, using their "best guess" to rank legislators as ++, +, 0, -, and --. Because I regard their system of analysis as too subjective, my organization created the "Remember in November" *objective* candidate evaluation system, using a zero- to four-star evaluation system which lends itself perfectly to five-column analysis as depicted in Fig. 9C. Do a Five Column Analysis for each committee to which your bills or your opponents' bills are referred, as well as the full legislative chamber for floor votes.

Fig. 9C: Five column analysis of legislative committee

NC HOUSE JUDICIARY 4 COMMITTEE ANALYSIS

NAME	TITLE	****	***	**	*	0
		STAR EVALUATION				
BLACKWELL, H	CHAIR	1				
ADAMS, J	VICE CHAIR	1				
ALSTON, V						1
BELK, M						1
EVERITT, T						1
HOWARD, J			1			
KIDWELL, K		1				
LOFTON, B						1
MCNEELY, J		1				
WILLIS, D			1			
ZENGER, J		1				
TOTAL:		5	2	0	0	4

Let's assume you've done candidate evaluations as recommended in

Chapter 11. The next question is on which category or categories to focus your channeled input. If you joined most neophytes in picking the 0-star (worst) column because, after all, they need "education," you would be wrong.

As we note elsewhere, to make the grassroots input you channel to targets as intense as possible, you should minimize the number of targets; the more targets you pick, the more diffuse will be your supporters' input to each, since your supporters have limited time, enthusiasm, and attention span.

Zero-star candidates are ideologues committed against you, for whom no amount of education is likely to help. Four-star candidates are already likely to support you. That leaves 1-, 2-, and 3-star candidates. Who first?

Order of priority in legislative targets:

1. **3-star candidates:** This is the most efficient use of your limited resources.

2. **2-star candidates:** These fence-sitters could go either way, so try to get at least some of them.

3. **1-star candidates:** Most will oppose you, but hit them on an as-available basis in hopes of getting some.

In Fig. 9D above, I would regard assignment to the House J-4 Committee as favorable because I have five extremely likely votes and two more probable, but only four in opposition. If my bill has been assigned to the committee, I would channel grassroots input to Howard and Willis, the two 3-star (***) committee members. Incidentally, note the polarization (i.e. lack of centrists) in committee member evaluations. This is typical of politicians in the current environment. Centrists have largely disappeared, particularly from the Democrat Party.

References:

1. "Mandatory roll call votes," National Conference of State Legislatures, https://www.ncsl.org/documents/legismgt/ILP/08Tab5Pt10.pdf

2.   "Legislative Session Length," National Conference of State Legislatures, https://www.ncsl.org/research/about-state-legislatures/legislative-session-length.aspx

3.   Robert L. Guyler, *Guide to State Legislative Lobbying*, Engineering THE LAW, Inc., 2000.

Chapter 10
Legislative Tools, Tactics & Treachery

"The 'problem' is what you want to solve; the 'issue' is how you frame the debate to solve the problem. Frame the issue to maximize your core constituency of support." – FPV

As noted previously, I open legislative tactics seminars by saying, "Lest you assume the political process is designed to exclude you, let me assure you that it is." Now let's focus on the corollary to that axiom: "Lest you assume any part of the political process is honest, let me assure you it is not."

Enemies profess to be friends; friends profess to be enemies (at least to other enemies). If the word "frenemy" wasn't invented for politics, it should have been. In political action, very little is what it seems. If treachery is used by friendly legislators to your benefit, so much the better. If used by your enemies, however...

Sportsmanship ... or not

I stole many of the following tactics from the left for use against them. (They hate that.) The tactics range from basic planning to the truly hard core. Some require chutzpah to execute. Some might not be for you. But before you discard them as "unfair," understand that the application of these tactics by the left got us where we are today, giving them a position of advantage. And it is likely that only through the application of such tactics can we rescue our republic. Years back, I took "Urban Rifle" from Clint Smith at Thunder Ranch. I took one of his axioms to heart, albeit perhaps more broadly than he intended: "Always cheat. Always win."

That might offend your sense of "sportsmanlike" behavior. If so, please allow me to use the same metaphor I gave the legislator who insisted on voting against motions to table hostile amendments out of "fairness." Because he had retired from the U.S. Marine Corps, I phrased it this way: "Michael, during your military career, did you ever say, 'We have the enemy in retreat. Let's allow them to regroup and resupply so we can have a *fair* fight'? I would guess the answer is never, and the reason you never said it is that battles for life and death, like battles for liberty, are for all the marbles. If we don't win, some small part of the world dies."

Issue management

Remember these words: *The "problem" is what you want to solve; the "issue" is how you frame the debate to solve the problem. Frame the issue to maximize your core constituency of support.*

I call this "issue management," and it is key to changing public policy. The cold truth is that most people don't care about the same issues you do. Getting them off their collective ass to take action means presenting them with something *they* – not you – care about. The trick lies in getting them to solve *your* "problem" by addressing *their* "issue."

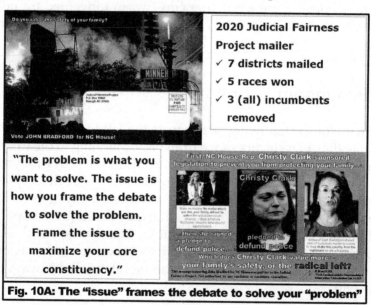

Fig. 10A: The "issue" frames the debate to solve your "problem"

Fig. 10A depicts a mailer we sent. Although the black and white image doesn't do it justice (the flames and card were "burning orange"), what you see is one of the most effective issue campaigns we ever conducted. Although I run gun rights organizations, you will notice that it is not a gun rights mailer. In fact, neither the card nor the name of the political action committee mention guns anywhere.

Happily, just before the election a number of Democrats in our state legislature were kind enough to sign a national "defund police" petition. The mailer you see took out Representative Christy Clark, one of Michael Bloomberg's "Moms Demand Action" astroturf gun control activists who previously beat a Republican incumbent to occupy a district that slightly favored Republicans.

Did I mail it just to gun owners? Nope. This mailer went to the much larger group of unaffiliated male voters who voted only in presidential elections – guys who didn't care much about gun rights or even politics in general, but want to protect their families. Thanks in large part to this mailer, Clark and four other "defund" petition signatories lost their races.

Issue management allows you to:

❑ **Frame the issue to maximize grassroots support:** In the case above, the people doing my heavy lifting might not have even been gun rights supporters;

❑ **Give cover to your supporters:** In this case, we returned previous office-holder John Bradford, who has a 100% pro-gun voting record, to the North Carolina House; and

❑ **Marginalize your opponents:** Christy Clark and four other "defund" leftists not only got exactly what they deserved, but helped set a precedent for other politicians.

In other issue campaigns, we passed the expansion of concealed carry into restaurants by compiling news accounts to create a brand new category of crime we dubbed "restaurant homicide." Before that, we killed a mandatory gun storage bill by discovering that such laws correlate with increases in rape, murder, and aggravated assault, then branding it as "the Rapist Protection Act."

On a different issue, in 2000 I directed "Concerned Citizens of Lake

Norman," a citizens' organization devoted to killing a sewage treatment plant planned by my county for the lake on which I lived. To raise money for litigation, I used a headline from the *Charlotte Observer* and did a carrier-route mailing around all 520 miles of shoreline lamenting the "Summer of Sewage on Lake Norman." It detailed recent sewage spills into the lake and made the case to homeowners that $1000 to our organization was cheaper than the hit they would take on their property values from lake pollution. In a single mailing, we raised $60,000 for litigation. Sparing you the details, suffice to say the land bought by the county for that sewage plant remains vacant to this day.

Keeping it honest ... unlike the left

Are these dirty tricks? Perhaps. I simply adapted a common tactic of the left. Do you think Black Lives Matter (BLM) was actually formed to save black lives? Of course not. BLM founder Patrisse Cullors is on record as saying she and co-founder Alicia Garza are "trained Marxists."[1, 2] By all appearances, her "problem" is to turn the U.S. toward communism. The "issue" used to address the problem by creating class conflict is alleged "systemic racism."

Equally, do you think election "reform" bills offered by the left actually have anything to with claimed "voter suppression?" Nonsense. The phony issue they exploit is intended solely to perpetuate voter fraud in order to elect more leftists.

What differentiates my tactics from the left is that each issue I cited was a *legitimate* issue which would in fact be addressed by the campaign I created, even if the issue was only tangentially related to the underlying problem I intended to solve. Fundamental honesty is critical. Lying creates two problems: First, it allows your opposition to depict you as the liar you are. Second, if you get caught lying to your followers, they will never believe you again, damaging not only your fundraising, but also your political effectiveness. As detailed in Chapter 11, "predatory fundraising"– raising money on false threats or threats you either cannot or will not address – destroys organizations.

Issue plans

And what do each of the campaigns cited above share? An "issue plan" laying out clearly the objectives and methods for solving each problem. Rather than doing it in your head, lay it out on paper and consult it frequently to ensure you are staying the course. (See Appendix II for example.)

Issue plans should contain the following:

❏ **Objectives:** These lay out in detail the problem to be addressed, including goals and subgoals for each of what might be a multi-stage project. Have measurable metrics of success for each. In the Judicial Fairness Project mailing above, for example, my primary goal was to take out Christy Clark, who had come into office as a gun control zealot, sponsoring several bills even as a freshman. Subgoals included taking out other leftists, of course, but the principal subgoal was to force the other gun control zealots to do a cost-benefit analysis. "If I sponsor this gun control bill, I will have to spend $50,000 defending myself against these people in the next election. Is it really worth it?" In the next legislative session after we defeated Clark, the legislative agenda for gun control advocates was considerably more modest, suggesting we achieved the subgoal.

❏ **Target demographic:** When I hear activists spout hair-brained messaging, my first question is, "Who exactly are you appealing to?" When pressed, the answer is usually themselves. I've heard activists plan to address county commissions with talking points which, rather than enlisting help from sympathetic commissioners, would terrify them. Step out of your own head, ask exactly whose help you are enlisting, and ask what would appeal to *them*. Be very specific about your target demographic.

❏ **Message:** Your message must be carefully tailored to the target demographic. You might be motivated by things like "freedom" and "liberty." In fact, I hope you are. But the cold reality is that such abstractions will rarely inspire people to follow you. As depicted in Fig. 10B, the five-tier Maslow's Hierarchy of

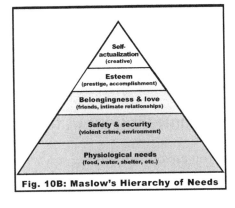

Fig. 10B: Maslow's Hierarchy of Needs

needs hypothesizes that basic needs must be met before moving to the next level of the pyramid. Accordingly, I tailor issue campaigns to *the lowest plausible level of needs*. As a gun rights advocate, I probably can't impact their physiological needs like food and shelter, so normally I pick the next highest: safety. With politicians, the target "need" is generally esteem and prestige. Whatever level you appeal to, your message must indicate clearly and simply what you want the target to do.

❏ **Delivery method:** Possibilities include email, website, social media, snail mail, Robocall/Robotext, radio, or TV. Again, this should be appropriate to the target demographic. I routinely reject suggestions from my leadership to save money on snail mail by issuing our newsletter only by email. The reality is that gun rights supporters are not always technically sophisticated. Some don't even have computers. Being a bit of a Luddite, I generally appeal to the lowest common denominator, which is snail mail. Whatever you use should require the absolute minimum of effort on the part of the target. Whenever somebody says, "Don't print a return vehicle for contributions; just give them the website," I point out that many recipients won't take time to go to the website. Never underestimate the laziness and short attention span of your constituency. If they can't respond *right now*, preferably in three minutes or less, there is an excellent chance they won't do it at all.

❏ **Budget:** Obviously, available funds will impact your delivery method. Hopefully, as outlined in Chapter 15, you've incorporated your organization as a not-for-profit and gotten a non-profit bulk mail permit, which dramatically reduces mailing costs, and hopefully you have a robust fundraising operation. Yes, electronic communications reduce costs. But beyond the fact that part of your constituency might not reliably use them, email providers such as Constant Contact and Mailchimp get picky about how you build lists and your rate of spam reports. For viable alternatives capable of reaching thousands, email is far from free.

Channeling input for change

You are but a lightning rod whose task is to collect energy and channel it to a target, be it a politician, committee, or corporation. The key to successful grassroots mobilization lies in channeling massive constituent input to particular legislators and particular committees. To paraphrase a quote from the late Senator Everett Dirksen, "When they feel the heat, they see the light."

"When they feel the heat…"

Activists seem to want to preach to each other, as though that will somehow change things. Whenever a supporter asks, "Do you guys have meetings?" I respond, "We can either spend time and energy speechifying to each other, or we can recruit new people to the cause. Why don't you help us distribute legislative alerts at gun shows?"

I want to channel input to politicians, committees, and corporations from as many supporters as possible. To that end, I don't require people to join my organization in order to receive alerts. We will cover list-building elsewhere, but suffice to say that your goal should be to reach 100,000 people, and your alerts should encourage a significant number to respond.

Channeled input for political action should be:

❏ **Appropriately targeted:** When possible, avoid targeting political staffers. To preserve their jobs, they tend to insulate their employer from unpleasantness, which includes you. Similarly, targeting unelected bureaucrats is generally a waste of time and resources because they don't answer to you, but to the elected officials who hired them. Ignore them and target the elected official to whom they report. If, for example, you have a problem of crime in city parks, don't bother with the chief of police; target the mayor. As one activist manual says, "Many local groups work to pressure unelected government, administrators, or regulators to do what is needed. Their success depends, in large part, on how such people perceive the group's ability to bypass them and take the case directly to the elected officials who appoint them."[3]

❏ **Civil but direct:** Although you don't want supporters to be rude (which gives pols an excuse to disregard you), the fact is that angry voters scare politicians. Rather than being deferential, the message delivered should be clear, direct, and commanding.

❏ **Massive and overwhelming:** There is rarely an advantage to "limited" constituent input. Any time you direct input to a legislator or committee, it must overwhelm input generated by your opposition. Bury them in phone calls, emails, and/or postcards. I refer to this as the "contact ratio" and I generally look for a 5:1 contact ratio, or five times as many contacts from my people as from my opposition.

❏ **Appropriately timed:** I've seen gun control idiots do a superb job of whipping up righteous indignation from their core constituency … just after we killed their bill. Why bother? Similarly, if you are targeting a bill that must be dealt with in committee before being reported to the floor for a vote, targeting legislators not on the committee represents a waste of resources. They will forget about you long before they deal with the bill.

❏ **Directed to "swing voters":** Although an occasional reminder to "friendly" legislators can be useful in reminding them who "brung 'em to the dance," regularly burying reliable supporters with constituent input creates unnecessary ill will. (Note: having constituents deliver the occasional "attaboy" can be useful.) Equally, targeting legislators who will never support you, and who are safe from retribution in their districts, is a waste of resources. In line with "Five Column Analysis" (Chapter 9), the focus of your efforts should be the fence-sitters—centrist voters who could swing against you … even if they claim they won't. Assess the vulnerability of each: How close was his last election? How heavily Republican or Democrat is the district? In previous elections, was the seat contested? Do you have supporters or sympathetic organizations in the district? Does the pol have other problems brewing?

❏ **Instantly available:** Things happen very quickly in a legislature. A bill not scheduled for a committee hearing might be added to the calendar just hours beforehand. If you are not "in" with the committee chair, you might not find out when it will come up for a hearing until you see it on the calendar, typically published on the day prior. For a timely response, your alert channels should be fully operational and virtually instant. Legislative team members should monitor legislative calendars (typically available via email subscription). Alert personnel should be ready to deliver email, website, or phone alerts within a couple of hours. Then you will discover how satisfying it is to have a bill show up on the calendar at 9:00 PM, then attend the committee meeting the following morning and have committee members, who've already gotten 250 emails and calls, plead, "How do you guys *do* this?"

"…they see the light"

A bill we opposed was scheduled for a Judiciary Committee hearing on Wednesday. On Monday, one of our volunteers delivered boxes of Godiva chocolates to legislative assistants for the committee chair and two swing voters.

On Monday night, our alerts went out advising supporters to *phone* (not email) the targeted legislators, plus other committee members, on Tuesday morning. Beginning Monday afternoon and stretching through Tuesday evening, radio spots aired in swing voters' districts across conservative programming favored by gun rights supporters. It gave phone numbers for the targeted legislators, and delivered a simple (if slightly "spun") message: "Immediately call Representative Nelson and tell him to *stop registering guns!*"

On Tuesday, phone lines for Rep. Nelson and his cohorts were so overwhelmed that they were unable to make outgoing calls. Better still, the complaints were coming largely from within their own districts. One legislative assistant told me she had to disconnect the phone. Another collared me in a hallway and said, "Now I know why you gave me those chocolates!"

When I got word that Rep. Nelson was screaming to see me ASAP, I sent a winsome volunteer who smiled sweetly as she apologized, "Yes, Rep. Nelson, I agree that Paul is being entirely unreasonable in shutting down your office and stirring up your district. But unless we have your vote on this bill, I'm afraid I can't persuade him to stop. We need your vote on this bill, Rep. Nelson."

"I'd rather get one well-written letter…"

Politicians and inept activists alike pontificate that politicians don't pay attention to postcards or copy-and-paste email. "I'd rather get one well-written letter than a thousand emails," says Sen. Blowhard.

Sen. Blowhard is telling the truth. He *would* rather get one letter. (In fact, he would rather get no letter at all, in order to screw you with impunity.) The reason he would rather get one letter is that a lone voter can't hurt him. By contrast, when he gets 1,000 of the same email, that implies **organization**, and it is organization he fears. Why? Because in the next election, the same somebody who can organize 1,000 people to send an email can organize 1,000 votes against him.

Incidentally, politicians will complain when they get contacts from voters outside their district. When they do, I gave the same response every time. "Oh, gee. Sorry. I'll have to talk to my alert crew about that." I never do. If they want to figure out which emails come from within their district and which from outside, that is their problem.

Similarly, congressional representatives who use web contact forms rather than email generally have the forms set up to reject input from out-of-district addresses. To bypass that, I give supporters the address of the politician's main district office and instruct them to use it on the form.

Channels for directing input

In *increasing order of effectiveness*, here are the ways you can channel input from angry voters to politicians:

❑ **Letters:** As described above, letters are ineffective, first, because nobody takes the time to write them, and second, because small numbers imply the absence of organization. Moreover, given screening protocols created in response to anthrax threats, letters to Congress might take months to arrive.

❑ **Petitions:** Although petitions are poor vehicles for channeled input because they are easily ignored or round-filed, they are excellent tools for list building, so make sure to gather all contact information, particularly emails. When doing petitions (e.g. online, at gun shows, etc.), make sure each petition signatory occupies a full page. Once you get a few thousand, you can wheel in the stack of boxed petitions to the politician's office, preferably with someone taking photos as you do.

❑ **Email:** "I don't read those form emails," say politicians and staffers. Maybe they don't, but they don't have to. All they have to do is *count* them, which they do. At the end of one legislative session, I found my email inbox filled with thousands of emails, as a somewhat vitriolic legislator took time to forward back to me each and every one we had directed to her. (Incidentally, she voted our way.)

❑ **Postcard campaigns:** When huge stacks of pre-printed postcards arrive by mail, all in a uniform shocking color (say, neon pink), politicians notice. Whenever possible, kick off postcard campaigns by distributing cards at gun shows, conferences, or other events. Always have people fill them out at your table and tell them *you* will mail the cards, then ask them to kick into the kitty for postage. Assure them you will mail the postcard regardless of whether they donate. That way, you accomplish two things: first, you compensate for the fact that, left to their own devices, most people will forget to mail the postcard; and second, you increase fundraising because they generally throw more than the cost of postage into the donation jar (often much more).

❑ **Phone calls:** I like to tell followers to call AND email. Concentrate phone calls for one period of time – preferably a morning, when they are doing office business – in order to shut down the office. I call this a "feedback day" and shoot for the first business day following a gun show at which we hand out thousands of alerts instructing people to call.

❑ **Talk radio:** This one works best when targeting squishy Republicans (R.I.N.O.s or "Republicans in Name Only"), since conservative talk radio dominates the forum. I once had the Senate President Pro Tem doing a rug dance on a prominent station when he refused to move our restaurant carry bill. To the talk show host, he said, "It's not a matter of *if* we move the bill; it's a matter of *when*." To his credit, he did so in the next legislative session.

❑ **Social media:** Yakking to each other on social media is useless. But when you go after a politician, shaming him on his Facebook page, or via Twitter or other social media platform, it becomes far more productive. As an example, the Wake County (NC) Board of Commissioners tried to shut down gun shops as "non-essential" during the COVID pandemic. They ignored our F.O.G. letter (see below) promising litigation until supporters roasted them on Facebook, creating enough public embarrassment to get them moving.

❏ **Leafleting:** The left has become quite adept at this. Going after politicians in their own districts with leaflets or demonstrations scares the crap out of them. In fact, the mere *threat* of leafletting is often sufficient to extract compliance. I have put a demonstration in front of a county commissioner's hotel and threatened to put demonstrations in front of a house representative's car dealership and even in front of a speaker's home in a posh neighborhood. I've benefitted every time.

❏ **Hijacking events:** As the crème de la crème of channeled input, putting a few dozen angry activists at a politician's fundraising event genuinely terrifies them because it erodes their support not just from the party faithful, but also from that most precious entity: donors. Best of all, it takes only a limited number of people. Because ridicule is your most effective weapon (Alinksy's Rule 5), a variation of this is to have a costumed character show up at a politician's fundraising events to lampoon the pol. Say, for ex-

Fig. 10C: "Squish the Magic R.I.N.O." visits the General Assembly.

ample, "Squish the Magic R.I.N.O." showed up at all of a Republican's events, bringing along a couple of friends holding a banner that says: "Sen. Bombast: Giving Conservatives 'the Horn' since 2010". Equally effective venues include party conventions, barbeques, or other political gatherings. We have leafletted Virginia's venerable "Shad Planking" and the North Carolina Republican Convention (twice).

Tactics & Treachery

What follows are basic tactics that all activists should use, and then some commonly used dirty tricks. (For additional "Dirty deeds, done dirt cheap," see also Chapter 13.) Personally, I'm comfortable using any tactic the opposition would use against me. But that is your call. Even if you aren't comfortable using them, however, read the section in order to recognize what can be used *against* you.

Basic tactics

Presuming you have absorbed rudimentary legislative process, what follows are techniques used by activists and politicians to advance friendly legislation and stymie the opposition. For some of them, you will have to recruit legislative advocates (i.e. politicians who act on your behalf in committee or on the floor).

General pointers:

❑ **Develop a persona:** This depends on your personality, of course. I find it is best to stay somewhat aloof when delivering pain to politicians. (In fact, I'm told that within the Republican caucus, I have a reputation for beating the crap out of anybody who doesn't comply.) When a pol is screaming at my people to have me come to his office, I generally don't. Instead, I find a winsome young female to play "good cop" by apologizing for my unreasonableness, saying: "I'm sorry Paul gets like this. He can be very unreasonable, but I'm afraid I won't be able to dissuade him unless we have your vote on this bill."

❑ **Get a poster child:** "Caylee's Law," "Jennifer's Law," "Leandra's Law," the list is endless. Every bill needs a poster child, a sympathetic figure (preferably a child) who personifies the need for the law. For our bill to expand concealed carry into restaurants, it was Danielle Watson, the pregnant woman stabbed to death while working at the Flying Biscuit Café and left behind a dumpster. Accompanied by her photo, our fliers implored legislators to "Stop Restaurant Homicide!"

149

Rules for Anti-RADICALS

❏ **Make one or more people responsible:** The idea is to personalize the target (Alinksy's Rule 13). Whatever problem you want solved, find an appropriate elected official and make him responsible. Generally, the higher the rung on the food chain he occupies, the better off you are. When I want a hearing for a bill in the state house, I channel input to the speaker, the committee chair, and the Rules Committee chair (who usually assigns bills to committees). *They* are responsible, and every alert we send instructs our supporters to contact not only their own representatives, but also party leaders.

❏ **Avoid debating the bill with hostile legislators:** When you address hostile legislators, they will tell you all the reasons your bill is wrong (or all the reasons the opposition's bill is right). Don't bite. For example, when doing literature drops, tell lower level volunteers not to debate politicians. Instead:

- Soften up the office for a few days with massive numbers of phone calls and emails from angry voters.
- Have volunteers walk into the office and say, "Hi, we're from Organization X. I think you know what we want."
- *Every* time the pol begins to whine, make placating noises and then say, "Senator Bombast, we need your vote on this bill."

❏ **Build your organization:** Every legislative project should be undertaken with an eye toward strengthening your organization, including both list-building and fundraising. Chapter 15 covers this in greater detail.

❏ **Use force multipliers:** You don't want just your own paid members responding to alerts. Get as many people as possible to direct angry calls and emails at targets by distributing legislative alerts at gatherings of sympathetic people (e.g. gun shows, conservative conferences or seminars, town festivals). We often schedule a "feedback day," shutting down the target's office with phone calls on the Monday morning immediately following a gun show at which we distribute thousands of fliers.

On one occasion, we held a "'Million' Mom Countermarch" by using vans to take people back and forth from a nearby gun show in order to outnumber the opposition. We also got a Concerned Bikers

Association motorcycle rally to divert and circle the block around the "Million" Mom March event, revving engines and drowning out speakers. Amusingly enough, they were escorted by motorcycle cops who gave *us* the thumbs up. It was quite a spectacle, and thoroughly demoralizing to the gun control group.

❑ **Form coalitions (or not):** As you draft your bill, or when killing opposing bills, assess which other groups and organizations might share your interest. Ask people in your group who are familiar with them to make contact. Evaluate both the extent of their interest and their capability to mobilize members. Encourage them to support the effort by funding it, providing volunteers, and either channeling input themselves or giving you direct access to their members. That said, be careful who you forge coalitions with and make sure they are suitable, since anything they do will reflect on you.

❑ **"Stalk" legislators:** No, don't do anything that will get you arrested. Appointments with politicians (particularly leadership) can be hard to come by and may require more lead time than you have. You can simply stop by Senator Bombast's office, but odds are you'll miss him. Why? Because whatever their shortcomings, politicians are busy devils. When not in session, they are likely in committee meetings.

Sometimes you can post a watch on an office, tagging the politician when he passes through. Better yet, research his committee schedule, including rooms and times, then skulk nearby with a legislative directory containing the politician's photo in hand, if necessary, intercepting him when he appears. Have your spiel ready; you're going to have to talk fast, especially if he doesn't want to see you. A caveat: stalking legislators might be more difficult in state legislatures that restrict access to the legislative building, and is utterly impossible in Congress.

❑ **Probe insiders:** As a grassroots activist, you are outside the inner sphere of decision-makers regarding when (and if) legislation moves. Constantly probe lobbyists, staffers, and politicians for information, including asking the same question of multiple sources and comparing the answers, which may differ dramatically.

Rules for Anti-RADICALS

❑ **Watch who's plotting with whom:** Learn who the players are. I can tell a lot about the political landscape by noting which lobbyists have decided to darken legislative doors on any given day (particularly if a national lobbyist comes from out of town). Depending on how the legislative building is laid out, you can learn much by observing who is speaking with whom.

❑ **Prepare talking points:** Ready a *literate* sheet of bullet points on your issue. Distribute it to your legislative advocates, leadership, and eventually politicians who will next deal with your bill. "But," you ask, "didn't you say the merits of the argument rarely win the day?" Yes, but talking points accomplish several objectives:

- **They put your position on record:** Nobody can claim they "didn't know" what you want.
- **They give your committee advocate a fig leaf:** They give cover to friendly legislators arguing your position, quite often for reasons unrelated to the nobility of your cause.
- **They frame the landscape for debate:** Gun control advocates, for example, have a harder time whining about "children killed by guns" when you've proven that the "children" they cite are drug-dealing gang members up to age twenty-four. Talking points my organizations distribute often shape committee and floor debates.

❑ **Count votes:** Whether in committee or on the floor, you should develop a close approximation of "who's fer ya and who's agin' ya." One shrewd legislator kept wall charts of relevant committees. Here is where your candidate evaluation system comes in handy. (You did do candidate evaluations, right?) But barring that, you might be able to use previous votes, party affiliation, or evaluations by other organizations as proxies. (Be aware that due to the NRA's propensity to make "deals" for candidate ratings, NRA ratings are unreliable predictors of politicians' voting behavior.)

❑ **Don't preemptively concede:** Some grassroots activists practice "preemptive concession" by trying to push "lite" versions of opposing proposals. For example, when the Obama administration pushed S. 649 for "universal background checks" (aka universal gun registration), a few players tried preemptive concession with the "Toomey-Manchin compromise" for a milder version. Having anticipated the effort, we forged a coalition of 39 "no compromise" organizations which prevailed, killing S. 649 altogether.

Preemptive concession has two problems: First, it never satiates the leftist appetite for more. They just take whatever you give them and come back later (often not much later) for what they didn't get the first time. Second, watering down hostile legislation makes it more likely to pass. (See "bad bills are better" below.)

❏ **Bad bills are better:** In general, don't water down opposing legislation to make it "better," since doing so de-motivates your core constituency, who will decide "Hell, it isn't that bad anymore" and go back to watching football, making it more likely to pass. For example, when we expanded concealed carry into state and municipal parks, a R.I.N.O. ("Republican in Name Only") weakened our bill by amending it to allow local governments to continue banning guns in ill-defined park "recreational facilities." Rather than watering it down, we refused to concede. The bill passed with the bad language, after which the city of Winston-Salem immediately started posting entire parks against concealed carry by claiming they were "recreational facilities," exactly as we predicted. First, we sued the city. Then, with a fresh example of how bad the measure was, we went back to the legislature and got it rolled back. Now, any time a city posts a park, I just send a F.O.G. ("Fear of God") letter telling them we will sue and they will have to pay attorney fees, court costs, and damages. The signs come down pronto.

❏ **Use preemptive accusation:** At the first inkling a politician will cross you, accuse him of it. Doing so forces him to defend himself by saying that what you accuse him of doing is not true and that he is not doing it, thereby shutting down that particular avenue. That said, be very careful not to say anything about a politician that is false. Examples of preemptive accusation include branding "universal background checks" as "universal gun registration," or predicting an anti-gun governor will veto pro-gun legislation and nailing him with the accusation before he does.

In committee:

❏ **Do "vote roundup":** So you've softened up swing voters on the committee with hundreds of emails and calls. You've earned a hearing for your bill. Now you have to make sure your votes show up. (You've already added up who will likely support you, who opposes you, and who's sitting the fence, right?) Just because a legislator supports your position doesn't mean he will attend the meeting. Especially toward the end of legislative sessions, overloaded schedules and conflicts might mean your votes don't show. Stop by supporting politicians' offices on the day of the hearing and ask them to attend. If you can't find the legislator in question, drop a business card on which you've written "Senator Bombast: Please attend Judiciary Committee today and support H. 666."

❏ **Pack the committee room:** Your supporters should civilly but visibly dominate the room, delivering to committee members a clear message that they are being watched. Signs might be prohibited by chamber rules, but matching T-shirts with coordinated messages or stickers worn on clothing help get your point across.

❏ **Sit front and center:** I send volunteers into the committee room early to reserve at least four seats at the front of the gallery so committee members can see I am watching them (and occasionally glare at me, to which I generally respond with a smile and a little wave).

❏ **Hold legislators accountable:** It is no accident that committee votes in state legislatures are often not recorded. Again, the politician's goal is to claim support for *you* while actually doing whatever benefits *him*. By contrast, your goal is not only to hold him accountable for his actions, but also to convey the message beforehand that you will do so. Start by putting a contingent of your supporters dead center in the front of the committee room gallery. If possible, videotape the meeting and *do* use politicians' words against them. When a vote is taken – be it an amendment or the main motion – votes are generally taken by voice. Depending on the rules of the chamber, however, your "committee advocate" (a sympatico committee member you previously recruited) may be able to call for "division" – a brief show of hands revealing who's for you and who's against. Plan and be ready.

❏ **Anticipate opposing arguments:** If your opposition issues membership alerts, talking points, or position papers, study them. Make sure your sponsor and/or your committee advocate are equipped for rebuttal. Consider what tactical compromises you are willing to accept, and under what circumstances. (Once again, do not compromise principles.)

❏ **Target swing voters:** Using input channels and advertising, make the swing voters "feel the heat" from constituents. Keep the input polite, but pour it on, with all input delivering a coordinated message.

❏ **Use "floaters":** If the vote is tight and your sponsor is from the majority party, ask him to work with party leadership to bring in supporting "ex officio" committee members—party leaders who may vote on any standing committee—to vote your position.

❏ **Talk ... or not:** The chair will likely solicit public input on the bill. If it's your opponent's bill, *always* testify against it. If it's yours, whether you should speak depends on whether the bill will go to a quick motion for favorable report and be sent to the floor. If your committee advocate has the votes lined up, sit down and shut up. If you do testify, plan on three minutes or less, so have your sound bites in order. Talking points previously given to the Sergeant at Arms for distribution to committee members will support your case.

❏ **Don't lose:** If your votes didn't show up for committee and success is in doubt, avoid having a vote if possible. In a friendly committee, that might mean having the chair displace it from the calendar or bring up the bill for discussion only. In marginal committees, consider running a "Proposed Committee Substitute" (P.C.S.) to pick up more votes. If all appears lost, have your committee advocate try to get the bill referred to a subcommittee where you might be able to make it more palatable to the full committee. In fighting hostile bills, anticipate these tactics from your opposition. Just remember: Whether yours or the opposition's, if a bill receives a recommendation for unfavorable report, it is D.O.A. unless you can resurrect the language in another bill.

Rules for Anti-RADICALS

Floor Fights:

❏ **Soften them up:** Just as military battles start by softening up the opposition with artillery fire, so too you should precede floor votes by pummeling swing voters (as identified in Chapter 9 under "Five Column Analysis") with overwhelming channeled input from your supporters.

❏ **Watch the calendar:** You should subscribe to legislative calendars and monitor them daily. That said, legislative agendas can be highly fluid, particularly as deadlines approach. Cultivate relationships with staffers for friendly legislators and ask them to notify you of relevant changes in schedules.

❏ **Make sure your sponsor gets his caucus on board:** Each party will likely hold a caucus meeting to plan tactics before a floor session. Make sure your sponsor coordinates with the caucus on your bill, including your position, whether you will be tracking votes, and which amendments you consider friendly or hostile.

❏ **Make your position known:** Politicians love to screw you by claiming they "didn't know" your position. Before a vote, send an email to all *except* 0-star or (--) legislators (i.e. those you *know* are ideologically opposed to you) letting them know your position and that you will track votes.

❏ **Get recorded votes:** As mentioned elsewhere, recorded votes not only tell you who your friends are, but also motivate mediocre politicians to vote with you because they know you are watching. Track votes not only for Second Readings, but also for hostile or friendly amendments. I generally don't score recorded votes for Third Readings because politicians, having seen a bill pass on Second Reading, often change to vote with the victors in order to give the appearance of support. The exception is for the odd case in which the bill gets amended on Third Reading.

❏ **Recruit advocates:** For friendly legislation, your sponsor will argue your position on the floor. For hostile legislation, recruit several legislators to argue against it and give them appropriate talking points. You might also have to recruit multiple legislators to sling amendments at a bill.

❏ **Track procedural votes:** Politicians use procedural votes (e.g. motions to "lay on the table") to avoid putting themselves on record, particularly in hostile chambers. Accordingly, use procedural votes as appropriate to evaluate legislators' positions. Similarly, you and your advocates can use procedural votes to kill hostile legislation or amendments, but make sure you let friendly legislators know you will be doing so. As recounted in Chapter 9, I had a solid conservative vote against no fewer than twelve motions to table hostile amendments to our bill, all because his sense of fair play led him to believe that all legislators, regardless of position, had the right to be heard.

❏ **Use flexible defense:** Like the old NATO doctrine in defending Europe against numerically superior Warsaw Pact forces, this utilizes controlled retreat. In a hostile chamber, winning might not be an option. You can, however, extract a price for the opposition's victory – a price paid in recorded votes you use against politicians in the next election.

Extracting a price even in defeat has two advantages. First, you can punish opposing politicians in the next election. Maybe you can defeat them, maybe not. Regardless, you deliver a message to any legislators who might contemplate crossing you, forcing them to ask, "Do I really need the aggravation if I sponsor this bill? These guys will come after me. What will it cost me in mailings in the next election?" Only by attacking turncoat politicians – each time, every time, regardless of chances of victory – can you force them to do that cost-benefit analysis.

Tricks & Treachery

If you have a solid advocate in the chamber, you might be able avail yourself of tricks like the ones which follow. Other times, be ready for hostile politicians or lobbyists to use them against you. Because pols are clever devils whose main talent is scheming and who come up with new tricks every day, the list is by no means exhaustive. These are just a few you can expect to see on a more or less regular basis.

Rules for Anti-RADICALS

In general:

❏ **Opposition research:** As an example, thanks to opposition research, we have filed complaints against Michael Bloomberg's various astroturf entities when they failed to get the required Charitable Solicitation License in my state. We have also filed complaints for potentially impermissible legislative lobbying by IRS 501(c)(3) organizations. In conducting opposition research, check at least the following items:

- **Regulatory compliance:** Check PAC reporting, required licenses, corporate filings, IRS Form 990s, etc. If violations are found, file a report with the applicable regulatory agency.
- **Publicly stated lies:** If you catch the opposition in a lie, continue stating it over and over, on multiple forums and media outlets, each time asking whether, having been caught in a lie once, they can ever be trusted again.
- **Backgrounds of opposition leaders:** Lots of things are public information. Has a leader had a DUI? A criminal conviction? A domestic violence charge? A nasty divorce with unpleasant details?
- **Unsavory connections:** One of my people – a journalist with strong research skills – once discovered that a supposedly non-partisan entity calling itself "Americans for Gun Safety" was actually an unincorporated "donor advised fund" of the Tsunami Fund, which was itself a PAC associated with the leftist Tides Center, which itself gave money to various left-wing extremists such as the Ruckus Society, responsible for destruction in the Seattle World Trade Organization riots in 1999.[4] We had great fun with that one.

❏ **Tactical intelligence:** This involves researching general strengths and weaknesses of your opponent. Does your opposition have any weaknesses in organizational finances, relationships between leaders, or history of hypocritical actions (e.g. a radical Democrat claiming to be an advocate for the poor who is also a slumlord). Incidentally, *the corollary of all of this is to make sure you don't have anything your opposition can exploit.*

In committees:

❏ **Running the clock:** Typically used in committees as a defensive measure to kill legislation by literally "talking it to death," the technique is most useful when facing an approaching legislative deadline (e.g. crossover deadline or adjournment). Conversely, if you know you have the votes to pass your bill, shut up. The committee meeting at which nobody debates the bill is the meeting where "the fix is in."

❏ **Preemptive concession:** A diehard gun rights activist – who was highly valuable to my organization – once made the mistake of educating the lobbyist for the state gun control group, telling him how errors in definitions in their gun show bill made it vastly over-reaching. At the next meeting, the lobbyist showed up with a P.C.S. that softened the language, denying us an angle of attack and making his side look eminently "reasonable." (That said, I generally don't believe in using preemptive concession, as outlined above.)

❏ **Shell game (also bill stripping, or "gut and go"):** This is a process by which legislators take unrelated bills, strip out the contents, and replace them with whatever they want, often in ad hoc committee meetings with little public notice. Following a spate of murders by domestic violence offenders defying restraining orders, we had already passed a bill which notified domestic violence victims of their ability to get emergency concealed handgun permits. At the end of the session, when things were hot and heavy, Democrats tried to repeal it before it even become effective by playing "gut and go" in a series of bills, even convening a Rules committee hearing on the house floor during a short recess. Fortunately, our sponsor kept us apprised and we blasted them each time they tried. Failing that, they tried (and failed) to add the repeal to a "technical corrections" bill intended to fix errors in previously passed legislation, as though our entire bill was a typo. You might be able to get legislators to use bill stripping to bypass crossover or other deadlines.

❏ **Ad hoc meetings:** See "gut and go" above. Quite often, leadership will call for committee meetings during a floor session, with the meetings taking place after the session adjourns.

- ❑ **Amendment or PCS:** In Congress, committees may do a "mark-up" on a bill, meaning they don't actually change the text of the bill, instead recommending amendments to be made on the floor. In state legislatures, the preferred vehicle is a "Proposed Committee Substitute" (P.C.S.), which is new language offered in lieu of a bill's language as it was originally referred to the committee for consideration. Technically, the committee substitute is an amendment to the original bill.

- ❑ **Layered defense:** When killing your opposition's bill, don't attack all points at once. Save attacks for later use in case the bill passes and goes to another committee or to the floor, attacking only one point at each stage. Layered defense allows you to create new and unanticipated hassles for legislators and your opposition at each stage of the process. As they address one of your objections, a new one arises.

The "Rapist Protection Act"

When leftist freshman Rep. Jennifer Weiss offered a mandatory gun storage bill in a Democrat chamber, we dug up research indicating states adopting such laws experienced increases in rape, murder, and aggravated assault. Before its committee hearing, my leadership urged me to release the bill brand I had developed. I replied, "Wait." When it passed committee, they again wanted to release it. I said, "Not yet."

We waited until it was scheduled for a floor vote before unleashing upon every legislator hundreds of irate emails and phone calls, demanding they "Oppose, HB 320: the 'Rapist Protection Act.'" This so unnerved the radical feminist sponsor that she actually stood before the North Carolina House to defend her bill by whining, "I would *never* introduce a 'Rapist Protection Act!'" Gotcha. The bill went down in flames in a recorded vote, allowing us to later unseat Democrats in marginal districts.

(continued on next page)

(continued from previous page)

Consider her remarks to a gun control fundraiser: "*Sometimes ... you are discouraged from rocking the boat when it needs to be rocked. The safe storage bill I introduced ... was such a bill. All we wanted to do was clarify and strengthen the safe storage law and require all homeowners to be careful with their guns when children were in their homes. You would have thought that I had threatened to take people's children. In retrospect, the whole process was wrought with fear and intimidation. The bill's contents were distorted and it was renamed 'The Rapist Protection Act' by a gun rights group. Legislators received hundreds of emails from gun rights groups warning them that they were causing people to be unsafe in their homes and that they would be remembered at the ballot box in November. I was told by other legislators who had sponsored the bill that they could no longer support it because, I quote: 'Do you know how many [gun owners] live in my district???' ... The undercurrent of fear at the legislature was that we would be voted out of office if we supported the bill. And many legislators took that threat very seriously and would not vote for the bill...*"

As you will see in "Scorched earth" below, we weren't done with Rep. Weiss.

Floor fights:

❏ **Poison pill amendments:** These may pose as "friendly" amendments in order to camouflage a legislator's opposition to a bill. I once had a senator offer a poison pill amendment to a hostile bill by telling the entire chamber that, "This makes a good bill better." When the amendment passed, the sponsor sent it back to committee to die rather than pass his bill with our language.

❏ **Bill branding:** This is a personal favorite I've used many times. As noted in Chapter 4, you should never accept your oppositions' verbiage, since terminology defines the debate. The same is true of bill names. For example, the great 2021 election power grab by Democrats was deceptively titled the "For the People Act." In response, Sen. Ted Cruz and Republicans promptly dubbed it the "Corrupt Politicians Act." As depicted below, branding a bill is a fine way to kill it, particularly when combined with a floor ambush. Bill brands should be:

- Powerful and evocative
- Concise
- Memorable

❏ **Floor ambush:** This involves holding your objections to hostile legislation until it hits the floor before unleashing. Pols often do it by lining up members to offer a long series of hostile amendments, a tactic that produces mixed results. When combined with bill branding, however, the results can be dramatic, as outlined in the accompanying sidebar.

❏ **Motion to "lay on the table":** This postpones debate on a motion (a bill or amendment) until some later time, but is actually used to delay voting indefinitely in order to kill it. It is commonly used to avoid recorded votes on the substance of an issue.

❏ **Discharge petition:** This a hard core tactic to force a bill out of committee if the chair won't give it a hearing. Requiring signatures from a simple majority of the chamber, the tactic is rarely used and, if successful, embarrasses leadership, meaning members of the majority party will be under considerable pressure from their leaders not to sign. Because it is divisive within the majority party, a credible threat of a discharge petition might induce leadership to dislodge a bill from committee.

❏ **Objecting to third reading:** *If* your legislature has a rule prohibiting second and third readings on the same day except upon unanimous consent of all members, and *if* a legislative deadline is looming (e.g. crossover deadline), you *might* be able to kill a hostile bill by having your advocate in the chamber object to third reading if all else has failed. If this Hail Mary tactic is used, it should probably be in conjunction with running the clock, above.

❏ **Walkouts (denying a quorum):** Under chamber rules of any legislative body, a minimum number of legislators, called a "quorum," is required to conduct business. If the minority party walks out to deny the chamber a quorum, hostile legislation cannot be debated or passed. Ballotpedia lists eight significant walkouts in the past one hundred years5, and it has been an increasingly popular tactic by Republicans in leftist-dominated Oregon (2019, 2020, and 2021).

Quorums may also vary depending on the type of legislation debated (e.g. taxes or state budgets). It is of limited use, since legislative rules must require more than fifty-one percent (e.g. 2/3) for a quorum, and the minority party must hold enough seats to deny the applicable number. Incidentally, denying a quorum is also valuable for running political organizations. I once used it to defeat rogue members of my organization who tried to call a special meeting to take it over.

❏ **Scorched earth tactics:** Because conservatives are civilized beings, we are entirely too merciful to the left. Once we win a legislative battle, we tend to go back to mowing the lawn and watching football. Instead, I suggest you emulate the left by pressing the advantage to weaken your opponent. Defending the future of our republic is not the time for sportsmanship. In the "Scorched earth applied" sidebar below, we weakened bureaucratic leftists and both defunded and demoralized the state's primary gun control organization, rendering them ineffective for roughly ten years.

"Scorched earth' applied

Rep. Jennifer Weiss was a slow learner. After we killed her mandatory gun storage bill (see "Rapist Protection Act" above), she sponsored legislation requiring release of mental health data for gun purchases.

The NC Child Fatality Task Force (CFTF) comprised leftist bureaucrats to whom gun ban advocates routinely "sunshined" gun control bills, including Weiss' latest nightmare. At a meeting, I requested but was denied a handout presented by the lobbyist for North Carolinians Against Gun Violence (NCGV), so I got it from a legislator who owed me a favor and discovered the group had received a $60,000 grant for the effort from billionaire Andrew McKelvey's "Americans for Gun Safety" thanks to an endorsement by Democrat Governor Mike Easley.

Since the bill might pass if it moved, we decided to deny it a hearing by branding it the "Medical Records Disclosure Act." Knowing Easley already had problems stemming from misuse of the gubernatorial helicopter (he eventually pled to a felony) and didn't need additional aggravation, we ran radio spots implying it would forever harm children with Attention Deficit Disorder, giving the governor's phone number, and telling people to call and register opposition to "*Governor Easley's* Medical Records Disclosure Act."

(continued on next page)

> **(continued from previous page)**
>
> On day two of the campaign, I called Easley's office to register my opposition. When an exasperated voice sighed, "Thank you." I asked, "Don't you want my name and address?" Another sigh. "No. At this point, we're just keeping a number."
>
> Gotcha.
>
> To let Easley know the source of his pain, our website featured his letter endorsing the grant proposal and identifying both the Democrat lobbying firm disseminating it and the Child Fatality Task Force ounching it. I can only imagine the call from the Democrat governor to the Democrat Speaker saying, "What the Hell are you doing to me? Bury this thing!" as well as the lobbyist's and CFTF director's rug dance for the governor.
>
> Next day, the NCGV lobbyist collared me at the legislature, exclaiming, "This is the lowest thing you've ever done!" I replied, "Bruce, from you I'll take that as a compliment." Not only did the bill die, the gun control grant dried up (AGS apparently decided its money was better spent elsewhere), the CFTF got its funding cut, and we didn't hear much from the gun ban group for about ten years. (Check "Astroturfing applied" in Chapter 13 to find out how we further demoralized our opposition.)

References:

1. Yaron Steinbuch, "Black Lives Matter co-founder describes herself as 'trained Marxist'," *New York Post,* June 25, 2020, https://nypost.com/2020/06/25/blm-co-founder-describes-herself-as-trained-marxist/

2. Jared Ball, "A Short History of Black Lives Matter, The Real News Network, 7/23/2015, https://therealnews.com/pcullors0722blacklives

3. Kim Bobo, Jackie Kendall, Steve Max, *Organizing for Social Change: Midwest Academy Manual for Activists,* Seven Locks Press, 2001, p.14.

4. Gretchen Randall and Tom Randall, "The Tides Foundation: Liberal Crossroads of Money and Ideas," Capital Research Center, Foundation Watch, December, 2003, https://mirror.explodie.org/x3797262231.pdf

5. As I write this, Texas Democrats staged a ninth major walkout to avoid voting on election integrity legislation, branding it (entirely without validity) "Jim Crow 2.0."

Chapter 11
Election Operations

"When buying and selling are controlled by legislation, the first things to be bought and sold are legislators." – P. J. O'Rourke[1]

This is the part where you demonstrate to politicians what a bad-ass you are ... or not. To repeat Machiavelli's quote, "...it is much safer to be feared than loved because ... love is preserved by the link of obligation which, owing to the baseness of men, is broken at every opportunity for their advantage; but fear preserves you by a dread of punishment which never fails."

Mike Rothfeld of the Foundation for Applied Conservative Leadership (FACL) puts it more succinctly: "Unless you are politically feared, you will never be politically respected."

As noted previously, a politician's goal is to make you believe that legislative and election seasons are unrelated. Yours is to ensure they are inexorably intertwined. Before we talk about what makes an effective political organization, however, let's talk about some that aren't.

Ineffective political organizations

Fangless wolves

Think of election action as hunting by wolf pack. Hunting as a lone wolf, you can pick off stragglers and weaker members of the herd (politicians in marginal districts or who have alienated voters). But because the alpha of the herd (party leadership) circles the herd to protect its members through things like reallocating soft money donations, your best chances of taking down the bigger, stronger members of the herd lie in hunting in concert with others (i.e. piling on with other groups).

Unfortunately, a certain number of fangless activists seem to think they can gum their prey to death. When I meet a grassroots leader, the first thing I ask is whether they have a political action committee (PAC). Without a PAC, they lack the teeth to enforce compliance with demands made during the legislative season.

Some grassroots leaders without PACs are just inexperienced and naïve. Others, unfortunately, are either too lazy or obtuse to be politically effective. Avoid the latter.

A few regard their PAC as just a way to throw money at friendly politicians, hoping to buy their allegiance. (Remember what Machiavelli said about love?) Many times, I've advised one prominent state-level leader to expand beyond political donations by doing independent expenditures. Skating along for years as his state gradually turned from "red" to "purple," his refusal to do so eventually resulted in an election disaster with all of the expected consequences.

Phony gun groups (and other charlatans)

Worse than fangless wolves, however, are those who prey on their own. These groups exist less to defend conservative values than to monetize fear. The gun rights movement seems to have more than its share, perhaps owing to its abundance of very real threats. What makes these charlatans particularly reprehensible is that they siphon off time, money, and effort from legitimate players.

Such organizations thrive on what I call "predatory fundraising" – raising money by generating fear over issues the group either cannot or will not effectively address. During the Obama administration, for example, one group relentlessly raised money on international gun control allegedly promulgated by the Wicked Witch herself, then-Secretary of State Hillary Clinton. Supporting the campaign were slick graphics featuring Evil Hillary and demanding people sign petitions to prevent Americans being saddled with United Nations (U.N.) gun control.

While I don't dispute the dangers of the U.N. Arms Trade Treaty, there wasn't a damned thing this organization could do to prevent the U.S. signing it (which it did under Clinton's successor as Secretary of State, John Kerry). Nor did the group have N.G.O. ("Non-Governmental Organization") status with the U.N. Translated, it built lists and raised money using petitions for things over which it had little or no influence.

Nor are phony activist organizations limited to the national stage. When gun rights supporters figured out what the group above was all about, the resulting flight of donors forced it to downsize. Are you old enough to remember the "Halloween Massacre," when Jimmy Carter decimated the CIA, forcing spooks to earn a living by fomenting revolution in South America? Yeah, well the downsizing of this organization was a lot like that. Political operatives trained in predatory fundraising, finding themselves out of jobs, returned to bilk their own states.

As a result, I constantly entertain questions from potential donors that go something like this: "I just got an email from this group calling itself 'Blood Suckers for Gun Rights.' Should I contribute?" Here are some attributes to help you decide. They aren't hard and fast, since fledgling organizations may also exhibit some of the same attributes.

Five questions to ask before donating:

1. **What has the group actually done?** Laws it passed or killed? (And evidence that it actually did so rather than the ever-popular parasite tactic of taking credit for other people's work.)

2. **Is it just a PAC?** Political Action Committees (PACs) are a cheap and easy way to tax shelter donations, but are far better vehicles for election operations than for long-term legislative operations. Serious legislative operators take the time, trouble, and money to incorporate IRS 501(c)(4) not-for-profit organizations, allowing them to raise money without paying taxes, to advocate for passage or defeat of legislation, and generally *not* to disclose donors. The best among them have not only c4s and PACs, but also incorporate non-profit 501(c)(3) education and legal action arms.

3. **Do politicians they claim to be cozy with confirm it?** I'm not saying the group should be tight with politicians in general. (Hell, most of the ones I know hate me.) But if the group claims to be working with one legislator, is it true? For example, the guy behind one phony gun group publicly denounced a permitless concealed carry bill we helped a stalwart legislator draft, claiming he helped a different legislator draft a better bill. But not only was the "better" bill virtually identical to ours, when I asked the other legislator about the guy in question, his response was, "Who?"

4. **Is there a human you can actually talk to?** Money-grubbers often create elaborate websites, but when you try to actually talk to the leader of the supposed organization, he is nowhere to be found. In many cases, the organization's "office" is a UPS Store.

5. **Does the organization have concrete objectives?** It is a favorite activity of certain gun rights organizations to raise money by beating on pro-gun politicians for supposedly not being pro-gun enough. Beating on politicians, while great fun, should not be the sole objective of the organization. It should have tangible goals, with beating on politicians as a *means* rather than an *end*.

Effective election operations

Now let's talk about how it *should* be done. The reason you conduct election operations is to put teeth into your legislative operations. If politicians know they can screw you with impunity, they will. Having the ability to punish errant politicians – and elect good candidates – will not only reshape the political battlefield in your favor for the long term, but also offers the short-term benefit of motivating marginal candidates to vote your way because they fear you. If you still doubt that, re-read "The Rapist Protection Act" sidebar in Chapter 10.

Is our political system "broken?"

Activists routinely complain that our political system is "broken" because it is often corrupt. I reply that it has been dirty and corrupt since the inception of the republic. That said, it remains the best model on earth because, unlike socialism, the rulers and the ruled are not fixed, immutable classes.

Moreover, the Framers understood what Machiavelli calls the "base" nature of man, and designed a balance of power between competing interests to compensate for it. It is precisely that balance which leftists are working to erode for that most base and eternal of human motives: absolute power.

Steps to effective election operations

Conservative activists tend to approach elections with methodology that can best be described as "scattershot." They might help a few candidates or target one or two, but they don't think in terms of shaping the entire legislative battlefield. To do so, we need to break down election operations into three steps, identifying the objective of each. After a short synopsis, the following sections will cover them in detail.

The three critical steps to impacting elections:

1. **Evaluate candidates:** As the old baseball line goes, "You can't tell the players without a program." In this case, you can't elect good candidates without a metric to judge their performance. You might think you know where some politicians stand on your issue, but can you identify all of the players in your legislature? New Hampshire, for example, has 400 members in its House. To know which to support and which to target, you need an organized and effective candidate evaluation system. In doing evaluations, you are not advocating the election or defeat of candidates, instead merely making a systematic analysis of where they stand. You might disseminate the information to voters in order to allow them to make up their minds, but you are not saying, "Throw the bum out" … yet.

2. **Identify voters to influence and mobilize:** Most activists make the mistake of appealing only to the small universe of their paid members. To win elections, you need to swing many more votes. But which voters and how many? Fortunately, the commonly held notion that you must influence 50%+1 of voters is wrong. As depicted in Fig. 11D, FACL says you need influence only "3%+1." That's closer, but still oversimplifies who you need to mobilize. To swing elections, you must mobilize potentially sympathetic voters. To develop messaging that *resonates* with those potentially sympathetic voters, you must correctly identify who they are. Because you probably don't have the money to do extensive polling, we will look at cheap shortcuts to identify and mobilize target demographics.

3. **Advocate election or defeat of candidates to appropriate voters:** Referred to as "express advocacy," this is the fun part of election operations. There is little more satisfying than unseating a hostile politician, then holding his scalp high for other politicians to see. It is generally done with one or more political action committees (PACs) which, as described below, means you have to do additional

fundraising beyond that required for your organization. In order to get more bang for the buck (and to make sure your money isn't used against you), your PAC should do "independent expenditures" for or against candidates rather than throwing money at them.

Evaluating candidates

If you are creating a new organization, or if your organization has not previously evaluated candidates, this might mean using information from other organizations. Your long-term goal, however, should be creating your own metrics to gauge candidates as my organization did, beginning in the mid-1990s, with our "Remember in November" objective candidate evaluation program.

One advantage of *objectively* evaluating candidates is that because you are not engaging in "express advocacy" (advocating the election or defeat of specific candidates), you don't have to use precious PAC money. As you will see below, there must be a firewall between organizational money and political action committee funds, making it difficult to raise PAC money from people who have already donated to support your group.

Apart from Remember in November, our organization does use PACs (at least two, sometimes more) which most definitely *do* advocate election or defeat of specific candidates, but they use different funds to achieve different goals.

Methodology

To objectively evaluate candidates, we compile voting records on gun-related legislation, survey scores, bill sponsorship, and a measure we call "bill support," which are entered into a spreadsheet to calculate a percentage of the time a given candidate agrees with a control group

Name	Party / District	Survey	Voting	Other	Star Evaluation
US President (sorted by name)					
BIDEN J	D-US President	0	0	0	
BLANKENSHIP D	C-US President				0
HAWKINS H	G-US President				0
JORGENSEN J	L-US President	100			★★★★
TRUMP D	R-US President			83	★★★
US Senate (sorted by name)					
BRAY S	L-US Senate				0
CUNNINGHAM C	D-US Senate				0
HAYES K	C-US Senate	94			★★★★
TILLIS T	R-US Senate		100	59	★★★
NC State offices (sorted by name)					
CAUSEY M	R-Insurance				0
CHATTERJI R	D-Treasurer				0
COOPER R	D-Governor		58	0	0
DIFIORE S	L-Governor	96			★★★★
DOBSON J	R-Labor		86		★★★
FOLWELL D	R-Treasurer	91	100	98	★★★★
FOREST D	R-Governor	96			★★★★
GOODWIN W	D-Insurance				0
HOLLEY Y	D-Lt Gov	7	0	0	
HOLMES J	D-Labor				0

Fig. 11A: Objective candidate evaluation criteria

of conservative gun owners to whom we have also administered the survey. A candidate who concurs with the control group at least ninety percent of the time gets a four-star evaluation (****), eighty percent gets three stars (***), seventy percent gets two stars (**), etc. These are not "ratings" and are not meant to imply how "good" a candidate is, just how closely he agrees with the control group. The result is a guide to political candidates which carefully and deliberately does not advocate election or defeat of any candidate. For simplified candidate evaluations, see Fig. 11A. For the candidate evaluation spreadsheet criteria, see Appendix V.

Three criteria for candidate evaluation:

1. **Voting record:** Going back for a reasonable number of years of your choosing, research your state legislature or Congress to find relevant votes for which the candidate went on record, potentially including amendments and procedural motions. Set up your spreadsheet to weigh votes more heavily than other variables (we use a factor of two), since voting record represents the best indicator

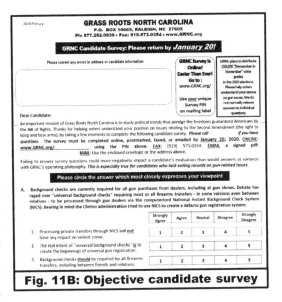

Fig. 11B: Objective candidate survey

of a candidate's proclivities. Going forward, make a spreadsheet for each legislative session and enter relevant votes. Continue to update records even for candidates who don't run again or are defeated, since they might surface again in the future, often in entirely different districts or races.

2. **Candidate surveys:** Unlike most organizations, which issue candidate surveys demanding to know if a candidate would support specific policies (on which candidates often lie and which cannot be objectively scored), we issue a statement on a given policy together

with a five-point "strongly agree" to "strongly disagree" scale that allows us to correlate responses with our control group. (See Fig. 11B.)

Prior to primary elections, we mail surveys to the candidates' address of record with the state board of elections, giving them a firm "return-by" date, and allowing them to submit it by mailing the original copy (we include a stamped, addressed return envelope), emailing a scanned and signed copy, completing online with a PIN we provide or faxing it to our office. To avoid being construed as express advocacy, we mail *all registered candidates* in races we choose to cover. Incidentally, for candidates lacking voting records on relevant issues, we regard failure to return the survey as evidence the politician is hiding his position, and we automatically and unwaveringly award a zero-star evaluation. Note: If you put a neon-colored sticker on the outer envelope exclaiming: "IMPORTANT CANDIDATE SURVEY: RETURN BY JAN 20!", you will get slightly fewer gripes from politicians claiming they "didn't receive" the survey.

3. **Bill support:** The metric contains two measures of support: First, it includes bills for which the legislator is a primary sponsor (not co-sponsor). To align numerically with other metrics, we award a "100" for each bill supported by the control group for which the candidate has been a primary sponsor, and "0" for each bill he sponsored in opposition to control group preferences. Second, it is applied to chamber leadership (speaker or president pro tem), the rules committee chair (since he generally participates in deciding which bills get hearings), and the chair of the committee to which a relevant bill has been assigned, each of whom are assigned "100" or "0" for each relevant bill given or denied a hearing.

Calculating candidate evaluations

Our system uses a simple mean (average) of each of the metrics above, with votes over-weighted to count twice because votes are the most reliable metric. The resulting rate of concurrence with the control group (e.g. 80% concurrence) is converted to the star evaluation listed above.

Distributing candidate evaluations

Here you will have to wade through the swamp of IRS regulations. I would argue that using the methods above, you are not "rating" candidates, which constitutes "electioneering" by non-profit organizations, because you are applying objective criteria usable by anyone, from any political perspective.

If your organization uses 501(c)(3) (non-profit) money, however, you will likely run afoul of IRS regulations. Using 501(c)(4) (not-for-profit) money for distributing candidate evaluations is safer because "campaign activity" is permissible by c4s provided it is not the organization's "primary activity." (And no, the IRS is not particularly clear on what constitutes "primary activity.") In any case, you probably do not have to use precious PAC money. Chapter 15 discusses regulatory compliance in greater detail. To the extent your finances permit, you should distribute objective candidate data far beyond the core constituency of your paid members, as we have done in election years by distributing up to 150,000 voter guides across the state. (See Fig. 11C.)

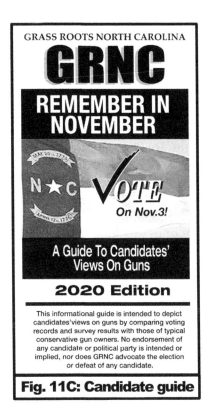

Fig. 11C: Candidate guide

Identifying and reaching appropriate voters

FACL uses a "How politics works" diagram which is useful for illustrating the point that you don't have to swing fifty percent of the vote plus one in order to win an election. (See Fig. 11D for my version of FACL's presentation.)

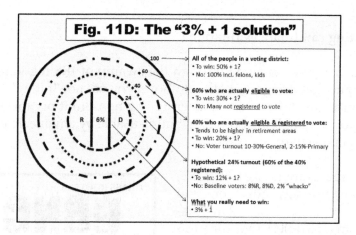

Fig. 11D: The "3% + 1 solution"

All of the people in a voting district:
• To win: 50% + 1?
• No: 100% incl. felons, kids

60% who are actually **eligible** to vote:
• To win: 30% + 1?
• No: Many not registered to vote

40% who are actually **eligible & registered** to vote:
• Tends to be higher in retirement areas
• To win: 20% + 1?
• No: Voter turnout 10-30%-General, 2-15%-Primary

Hypothetical 24% turnout (60% of the 40% registered):
• To win: 12% + 1?
• No: Baseline voters: 8%R, 8%D, 2% "whacko"

What you really need to win:
• 3% + 1

Their point is that the entire population of voters (100%) includes felons, children, non-citizens, and others who are ineligible to vote (at least until Democrats bus them to the polls). Although perhaps 60% of the total population are eligible to vote, only perhaps 40% of the total population are actually registered. Of the 40% who are registered, only about 60% of those (24% of the total population) actually turn out to vote. And finally, of the 24% who actually vote, roughly 8% vote straight Democrat, 8% vote straight Republican, and 2% vote "other" (Libertarian, Constitution, Green, etc.) leaving only 6% in play. Hence, says FACL, you only need to swing 3%+1.

Problems with the FACL model

Obviously, in a political district hypothetically containing 100,000 people, FACL is correct in saying you don't have to swing 50,001. But if the FACL model was always accurate, we would be able to win in any district, which we clearly cannot. The generic model fails to account for variation of party affiliation between districts.

Some districts (or entire states) lean "blue" (Democrat) and some lean "red" (Republican). Trying to apply the FACL model to a blue state would be a waste of money. (We will save for later the discussion of "purple" states suffering influx of left-leaning voters from other states.)

Even in a "friendly" state, when a majority party draws political districts every ten years, it concentrates voters from the minority party into as few districts as possible in order to maximize the number of seats it (the majority party) controls. This is called "gerrymandering" and, despite what leftists claim, has been a legitimate and constitutional practice since the founding of the republic.

But there is a consequence: when Republicans draw the districts, those few in which they concentrate Democrats cannot be won by Republicans, and vice versa. In a district where not 8%, but instead 12% of those who turn out to vote are Democrat and only 4% are Republican, swinging 3%+1 won't win the day for Republicans. In that race, you would have to win a probably impossible 8%+1. (Beyond the 4% who are Republican, which you can presumably count on, you would need all 6% of unaffiliated voters plus another unobtainable 2% from Democrats or third party voters.)

Political triage

Although all this might seem obvious, I say it because I am routinely pitched by ideologically sound but overly optimistic candidates making Quixotic runs in unwinnable districts by predicating their planned victory on winning *all* of the unaffiliated voters which, in truth, will never happen.

You need to understand the dynamics of redistricting in order to avoid wasting precious PAC money on unwinnable races, even when the greatest candidate in the world is running against the likes of Chuck Schumer or Nancy Pelosi. Investing in a race like that flushes money down the toilet – money that would be better spent on races you *can* win.

Such realities motivate leftists like former Attorney General Eric Holder and his National Democratic Redistricting Committee to "sue 'til they're blue" – to litigate against Republican drawn districts on inflated claims of "racism" in order to increase the number of left-leaning seats in a given election. It is also why leftists routinely decry gerrymandering, instead pushing for "non-partisan" redistricting commissions which, in practice, would be anything but "non-partisan."

Identifying target demographics

The other problem with the FACL model is that it doesn't address which demographic to target. Books are written on this; campaigns spend millions of dollars on it. Presuming you don't have millions to pay consultants, how then can you identify who you will appeal to beyond your immediate supporters?

Start with your board of elections. Included among data kept on voters are: name, address, gender (sorry lefties, only two allowed), age, race, party affiliation, and voting history (including elections voted in by year and whether primary and general election, but not how they voted).

If I wanted to activate voters against a pro-abortion candidate in an off-year election, for example, I might use a target demographic of Republican women over age fifty who vote only presidential elections. They are likely to agree with the message, but less likely to vote unless I motivate them to do so. If the number is too large to afford the mailing, however, you will have to find ways to whittle it down.

In some cases, targeting is relatively straightforward. For example, in a Republican primary election, you would target only Republicans (usually Republicans with a history of voting in primaries, but under the right circumstances you might try to mobilize less motivated voters) and, if your state has "open primaries," perhaps unaffiliated voters. (This is slightly over-simplified. For a detailed examination of types of primary elections, see "State Primary Election Types," published by the National Conference of State Legislatures.[2])

Another way to hone the target demographic is to data mine your list against other special interest lists, either provided by the state or from commercial sources (which are admittedly more expensive). Gun rights organizations might have an easier time of that if concealed handgun permit lists or hunting license lists are public record. In our case, we matched the state voter database with the concealed handgun permit-holder list to produce roughly 400,000 matches, for which we have district information allowing us to target specific legislative districts. For how to do such mailings, see Chapter 16.

Express advocacy

Disclaimer: I am not a lawyer and nothing herein constitutes legal advice. What follows are only general principles which do not necessarily reflect recent changes in the law. For specifics, check with the Internal Revenue Service (IRS)[3], Federal Elections Commission (FEC)[4], and your state board of elections. Although registering a PAC is relatively simple, it will require some research of arcane regulations and rigorous adherence to reporting schedules to ensure you stay within the law.

Express advocacy refers to advocating the election or defeat of specific candidates. You are now entering the "Twilight Zone" of your state board of elections if you are using a state PAC, and the FEC if you have a federal PAC. If you register as a federal PAC with the FEC, which I advocate, you will be able to cover not only state races, but also congressional and presidential races.

Although you can do some express advocacy using an IRS 501(c)(4) "social welfare" not-for-profit organization (see Chapter 15), it may not be the "primary activity" of that c4 organization.[5] "Primary activity" is not clearly defined by the IRS, which alleges a vague "facts and circumstances" determination. While some have construed it to mean 51% of expenditures, that is by no means a hard-and-fast rule. If you use your c4 for express advocacy, understand that you might be responsible for taxes and reporting requirements may apply. The good news is that for a c4, as opposed to a PAC, you need not disclose donors.

"Dark money" groups

"Dark money" is a derogatory term for advocating election or defeat of candidates by nonprofit groups – typically 501(c)(4) social welfare organizations, 501(c)(5) labor unions, and 501(c)(6) trade associations – that do not report the names and addresses of their individual donors to the government.

Foremost among leftist dark money is Arabella Advisors, a $1.7 billion-a-year dark money group and its "pop up" front group, called the 1630 Fund. *The Atlantic*, a left-leaning magazine, has called the Sixteen Thirty Fund "the indisputable heavyweight of Democratic dark money" which funneled "roughly $61 million of effectively untraceable money to progressive causes," making it the "second-largest super-PAC donor in 2020."[6]

What is a PAC?

Think of a political action committee as a separate checking account whose funds are strictly segregated from organizational funds. Unlike raising non-profit funds, however, PACs have limits on donations and expenditures, and are subject to reporting requirements, violation of which may result in significant penalties. The reason you should undergo the inconvenience of forming a PAC is to do unlimited express advocacy that you may not do with a c4 or c3 organization.

Contributions to candidates are limited to relatively low amounts. The big advantage of a PAC is the ability to do unlimited "independent expenditures" – mailings, email, social media advertising, radio and TV ads, etc. – for or against candidates *provided you do not in any way "coordinate" those independent expenditures with the candidate who benefits*.

Basic PAC limits and requirements:

❏ **Registration:** A federal PAC must register with the FEC within ten days of its formation, providing name and address for the PAC, its treasurer, and any connected organizations.

❏ **Tax ID number:** Although PACs do not have to pay taxes, the IRS says:

"...a tax-exempt political organization may be required to obtain an Employer Identification Number (EIN), also known as a Federal Tax Identification Number, even if it does not have employees. A political organization can apply for an EIN by completing an online Form SS-4, Application for Employer Identification Number, or by calling the toll-free Business & Specialty Tax Line (800-829-4933). You can also submit a paper Form SS-4 PDF via fax or mail to the address listed on Where to File Your Taxes - Form SS-4. TIP: An organization must file Form 8871 within 24 hours of its creation, and is not tax-exempt until it does so. An organization must have an employer identification number in order to file Form 8871. You can receive an Internet EIN on-line that can be used immediately to file Form 8871."[7]

❏ **Donations:** For your purposes, the FEC donation limit per person is presently $5,000 per calendar year. Your state will likely have different limits (in my state it is currently $5,600). You will have to solicit donor information, including the donor's profession and employer. Since privacy-minded conservatives tend to avoid disclosing private information, we inform them it is permissible to respond to those items with "decline to state."

- **Prohibited donors:** Donations by corporations (including non-profits), labor organizations, federal government contractors, foreign nationals, or those contributing in the name of another person are all expressly prohibited by the FEC. For state PACs, limits on corporate contributions vary between states. For a general idea, the League of Women Voters of Maine has a chart of state-by-state limits[8], but I wouldn't depend on it for regulatory compliance. For that, check with your state election board.

❏ **Campaign contribution limits:** Federal PACs can give $5,000 to a candidate committee per election (primary, general or special). They can also give up to $15,000 annually to any national party committee, and $5,000 annually to any other PAC. Again, I do not recommend donating to candidate committees. (Contributing $15,000 to the RNC for unspecified purposes would be truly stupid.) If you have it together, your money is far better spent doing "independent expenditures." Contribution limits for state and local elections vary by state.

❏ **Disclosure:** In the reports described below, PACs must report names and addresses of donors, as well as donation amounts. (Note: If you are interested in secrecy, at least temporarily, it might be possible to manipulate donation timing to avoid reporting until after applicable deadlines, including the election itself. If the Super PACs described below elect to make monthly reports, for example, they might not have to disclose donors until after the election.[9])

❏ **Reporting:** Generally speaking, a non-connected PAC is required by the FEC to make quarterly reports, as well as pre- and post-election reports. Again, check the FEC for specifics and your state board of election for state PAC reporting requirements.

Other relevant political entities:

❏ **527 organizations:** The number "527" refers to the section of the tax code governing such entities, which are typically parties, candidates, committees, or associations organized for the purpose of influencing an issue, policy, appointment or election, whether federal, state or local. They can raise unlimited funds from individuals, corporations or labor unions, but they must register with the IRS and disclose their contributions, donors, and expenditures. To be exempt from federal income tax, they must electronically file notice of section 527 status (Form 8871) with the IRS with the exception of:

- Committees required to file with the FEC;
- State or local candidate or party committees; and
- Organizations anticipating annual gross receipts of less than $25,000.

❏ **Super PACs:** Also called "independent expenditure-only committees," the advantage of super PACs is that they may raise unlimited sums of money from corporations, unions, associations and individuals, then spend unlimited sums to overtly advocate for or against political candidates. Unlike traditional PACs, however, super PACs are prohibited from donating money directly to political candidates. Their activities may not be coordinated in any way with those of the candidates they benefit.

Like conventional PACs, super PACs must identify donors. However, if one or more 501(c)(4) (c)(5) or (c)(6) organizations – which don't have to report donors – were to fund a super PAC, the only donors reported would be the non-profit organizations, not the individuals who funded those organizations.

Coordination or not?

Regardless of the type of PAC involved, independent expenditures may not be "coordinated" with the candidate who benefits. If the expenditure is construed to be coordinated, it will be treated as an "in-kind contribution" even if it is not a monetary contribution, and thereby subject to FEC reporting, contribution limits, and prohibitions. Your state regulations may vary, but the FEC claims to apply a three-pronged test[10], and the communication must meet all three prongs to be considered coordinated.

FEC three-pronged test of coordination (communication must meet all three):

1. The source of payment (payment prong)

2. The subject matter of the communication (content prong)

3. The interaction between the person paying for the communication and the candidate or political party committee (conduct prong)

In the FEC's "Coordinated Communications" synopsis, you will almost certainly meet the payment and subject matter prongs, meaning you must remain clear of the conduct prong in order not to be construed as coordinating with the candidate. This becomes particularly important if you are using a super PAC.

Whether or not to "endorse"

As a c4, the IRS allows you to "endorse" a candidate to your own members. To distribute the endorsement more widely without your c4 being construed as electioneering, you can use your PAC to endorse candidates. Although political organizations routinely endorse candidates, however, I would argue that endorsements can come back to bite you.

For example, you typically get about two terms out of a good legislator before being called "the honorable" starts going to his head and he starts getting pulled toward ideological compromise by party leadership. But your endorsement stays out there, often regurgitated by the politician even if he later becomes a R.I.N.O.

If you endorse a candidate, you also become responsible for any whacky or stupid thing he might do in the future. That is why my PAC "recommends" voting for a candidate rather than endorsing him, meaning only that he is the strongest candidate *in a given race* and *on our issue*. It is a blanket endorsement of neither him nor his character.

Some argue that is a distinction without a difference, but I have been able to use it to advantage. When a state house candidate we recommended later said something the media construed as racist, they tried to discredit *us* by claiming we had "endorsed" him. But when I responded that we didn't endorse anybody, including him, they were forced to walk back the accusation.

We've used the system of "evaluations" and "recommendations" successfully since 1994. If it has a problem, it is that I constantly have to explain the difference between evaluations and recommendations, as well as how recommendations differ from endorsements.

Reaching voters and donors

Having identified which candidates to help or pummel, which voters to reach, and what types of organizations need to do the reaching, now let's talk about *how* to reach them and what to say.

The classic vehicle is snail mail. While effective, it is expensive. At current rates for a PAC (which is prohibited by USPS from using non-profit bulk rates), sending even a postcard using USPS First-Class Mail, presorted on a bulk permit, costs about $.44 per card (including printing, postage, and mailing house costs), making a 20,000 piece mailing an $8,800 proposition. If you can't afford that – and even if you can – look to other distribution channels to supplement U.S. Mail.

Top ten channels for reaching voters:

1. **Snail mail:** Even if your organization has a non-profit bulk permit (see Chapter 16), postal regulations prohibit using it to mail PAC express advocacy materials. To reduce time and workload, I use mailing houses that have their own commercial bulk permits, the rates for which are still significantly below regular (unsorted) First-Class Mail. In terms of designing mail pieces, you can reduce costs by doing it yourself. If possible, recruit volunteers with graphic design skills. If not, you can either pay for graphic design software or simply use PowerPoint, which will allow you to do far more graphic design than you might expect.

2. **Email:** While far cheaper than snail mail, email on the scale you will

need to be truly effective is not free. You will build lists by a variety of methods described in Chapter 17, not all of which are acceptable to email providers like Constant Contact and Mailchimp. During elections, our organization routinely sends a million or more emails per month, costing $2000 per month or more. The key lies in finding a provider that won't be too picky about how you compile lists, but also won't be tagged as spam by Internet Service Providers. My mentors recommended Paramount Communication Group (www.paramountcommunication.com), which we have used reliably for many years. Incidentally, anti-spam laws don't apply to political speech, which is protected by the First Amendment.

3. **Robocalls/Robotext/Ringless Voicemail:** You say you hate them? So do I, but they work. Moreover, I defy you to find another way to reach voters at the typical $.04/call rate for Robocalls. And if you say people don't listen to them, I will respond that the many high-dollar campaigns using them suggest otherwise.

   Although you can't legally make automated calls to the ever-growing population of cell phones, current rates for Ringless Voicemail to cell phones run about $.12 each. Basic SMS (Short Message Service) text messages are only $.08, but are limited to 160 characters. MMS (Multimedia Message Service) are more flexible but pricier, running between $.10 and $.12, depending on volume.

   Other options are phone banking (very workload intensive and volunteers avoid cold calling like the plague) and Peer to Peer Testing platforms which, in my experience, require large volumes to be economical. I use Robocalls, Robotext, and Ringless Voicemail extensively ... and then don't pick up phone calls forwarded from our office for a day or so afterward in order to avoid obscenities from the few people who become truly unhinged at receiving them. Incidentally, like email, the National Do Not Call Registry does not apply to political speech, which is protected by the First Amendment. Unfortunately, irate callers will not know that.

4. **Social media:** Facebook and Google provide fairly cheap advertising, allowing you to target audiences by a variety of criteria, including age, interest, and geographic location. The problem is that if you are conservative, there is an excellent chance they will terminate

your account. In the 2020 election, we ran Facebook ads with excellent effect in nearly forty races. (See Fig. 11E.) But when we tried to do advertising in the infamous Georgia Senate runoff elections, they cut us off because, after all, censorship lives large within the leftist "voice of tolerance."

Fig. 11E: Social media advertising

5. **Simpatico gatherings:** Gun rights activists have a relatively easy time of this because gun shows abound. Buy a table if you can't get one donated, then distribute as many candidate fliers as you can. (Incidentally, gun rights organizations who maintain they cannot legally do this are idiots. See above.) Other possibilities include conservative (or other) conferences or forums, town festivals (if the town's political leanings allow), even trade shows.

6. **Clubs and civic organizations:** These include wildlife or shooting clubs, Kiwanas Clubs, Fraternal Order of Masons, Rotary Clubs, Veterans of Foreign Wars, etc. Because civic organizations tend to promote mainstream American values, they tend to be friendly to conservative causes.

7. **Distribution via commercial shops:** Again, this is easier for gun rights supporters, since they can distribute literature at gun shops and ranges, but you might find applicability for other issues.

8. **Radio/TV spots:** In talk radio, conservative shows have a numerical advantage, allowing you to mobilize core constituencies by advertising on even local talk shows. Advertising rates for "issue ads" go for a premium at election time, but reasonable rates can be had at smaller stations. Make sure the broadcast area overlaps the

political district you are working, and use a professional-sounding radio spot, lest you alienate the people you are trying to influence. Unless you have deep pockets, TV spots are likely out of your price range, the exception being local cable networks which, frankly, few people watch.

9. **Door-to-door canvassing:** Politicians love this one. It is highly effective at increasing voter turnout, but very workload intensive and most effective for smaller races. You will need lots of dedicated, extroverted volunteers. Software like i360 Walk can optimize routing and even provide scripts for volunteers, reportedly starting at around $265/month.

10. **Website:** Obviously, you should have your candidate recommendations on your site. That said, nobody will go there except your members, and only some of them unless, of course, you link it from the millions of emails you send.

One method I didn't include in the "Top 10" but which should be considered is using poll workers. Beyond the fact that most voters have made up their minds before going to the polls (although perhaps not for all races on the ballot), early voting has diminished the impact of working polls because voting is spread out over days or even weeks. That said, if you can summon the manpower, sending out poll workers isn't a bad idea. One advantage of early voting is that it usually takes place in a selected, smaller number of locations than on election day.

If you do it, however, be prepared for some irate voters. Once as I worked a poll with hit literature on a state senator, a woman berated all of the poll workers, saying, "Shame on you for preying on weak minds." My answer? "Madam, has it dawned on you that if their minds are that weak, perhaps they shouldn't be here?"

Election planning and execution

Whether by incapacity or laziness, election operations tend to be plagued by lack of planning. To produce an effective election effort, you should draw up an election plan several months before early voting starts for primary elections. You should include critical election dates, and task allocation to your volunteers.

Critical election dates:

❏ **Candidate filing deadline:** This is the deadline by which candidates must file for a particular race. It is important for two reasons:

- First, you should produce a spreadsheet of all registered candidates in the races you intend to cover as soon as your board of elections produces a candidate list.
- Second, this is the deadline for recruiting people to run against wayward politicians, either in the primaries or general election.

❏ **Voter registration deadline:** Each election cycle (primary, general, runoff, special) has a deadline for registering voters, with the exception that some states use same-day voting and registration, typically *only* if one uses early voting. Ballotpedia lists twenty states plus D.C. that allow same-day voting and registration.[11] Although FACL claims voter registration drives are useless because people who aren't registered aren't interested, in truth lots of people change addresses and don't remember to change their registrations. You don't need supporters showing up to vote and discovering they can cast only provisional ballots that probably won't get counted. In email alerts leading up to elections, remind supporters to check their voter registrations and give them a link to do so.

❏ **Early voting dates:** Once upon a time, I could crank out voter guides and PAC recommendations a month before the first Tuesday after the first Monday in November, secure in the knowledge that I could reach relevant voters. Not anymore. The National Conference of State Legislatures (NCSL) lists twenty-two states (plus D.C.) that use unrestricted early voting[12]. States now begin early voting as early as fifty-five days before elections, and that doesn't include attempts by Democrats to expand absentee voting. Check your state board of elections for the dates early voting begins and ends, and have materials ready for distribution at least a month beforehand.

❏ **Absentee/mail ballot deadlines:** These include deadlines for requesting and returning absentee ballots. Although I don't especially trust what are too often Democrat-controlled local election boards to honestly tally absentee ballots and therefore don't recommend absentee voting, you will likely have supporters who are disabled or otherwise unable to vote in person.

❏ **Election day:** Federal elections (and usually state elections) are set by statute for the first Tuesday following the first Monday in November of even-numbered years. That said, some states can be oddball, like Virginia, that runs elections for governor and other state legislative offices in odd years.

Overall plan

Your PAC should primarily target politicians who have crossed you *and* are in vulnerable districts. To be sure, I try to deliver the message that we will pay back all attempts to introduce hostile legislation (which might mean opposing a politician in a Democrat primary, even if his opponent isn't friendly to our issue), but I only invest significant money into races I can win.

Race	Dist r	POL supported	Comments/Opponents	Target	Mail#	Email	Phonex2	Cell	JFP Mail#	Facebook
NC HOUSE										
NCH001	D+1	EDWARD GOODWIN	OPPOSE Emily Bunch Nicholson	REP & Ul	1233	119	748	466		
NCH007	R+4	MATTHEW WINSLOW	OPPOSE PHIL STOVER	REP & Ul	2244	265	1298	913		
NCH009	D+1	PERRIN JONES	Oppose Brian Farkas -- signed ple	REP & Ul	1615	110	662	937	4232	
NCH012	R+1	CHRIS HUMPHREY	Oppose Virginia Cox-Daugherty	REP & Ul	1709	139	971	705		
NCH014	R+10	GEORGE CLEVELAND	Oppose Marcy Wofford	UNA	587	111	228	328		
NCH037	R+3	ERIN PARE	Oppose Sydney Batch -- signed pl	REP & Ul	2729	356	1360	1288	9525	
NCH043	D+1	DIANE WHEATLEY	Oppose Kim Hardy -- signed pledg	REP & Ul	1745	255	922	804		
NCH045	D+1	JOHN SZOKA	Oppose Frances Jackson -- signed	REP & Ul	1772	306	880	798	3799	
NCH046	D+1	BRENDEN JONES	Oppose Tim Heath	REP & Ul	833	96	473	344		
NCH051	R+3	JOHN SAULS	Oppose Jason Cain	REP & Ul	1767	154	980	773		
NCH059	R+3	JON HARDISTER	Priority 4: Oppose Nicole Quick --	REP & Ul	2541	286	1516	959	5955	
NCH063	D+1	STEPHEN ROSS	Oppose Ricky Hurtado -- signed pl	REP & Ul	1411	178	706	569		
NCH066	R+2	BEN MOSS	Oppose Scott T. Brewer	REP & Ul	1810	301	1131	647		
NCH079	R+10	KEITH KIDWELL	Oppose Nick Blount	UNA	716	165	442	299		
NCH083	R+7	LARRY PITTMAN	Oppose Gail Young -- signed pledg	REP & Ul	2683	466	1512	1069		
NCH084	R+16	JEFFREY MCNEELY	Oppose Gayle Wesley Harris	UNA	963	242	558	366		
NCH093	R+3	RAY PICKETT	Priority 3: Oppose Ray Russell -- s	REP & Ul	1960	192	1370	515	7057	
NCH096	R+13	JAY ADAMS	Oppose Kim Bost -- signed pledge	UNA	710	210	371	366		
NCH098	R+7	JOHN BRADFORD	Priority 1: Oppose Christy Clark --	REP & Ul	2078	198	1061	932	8305	
NCH103	R+0	BILL BRAWLEY	Oppose Rachel Hunt -- signed ple	REP & Ul	1461	144	872	547		
NCH104	R+1	DON POMEROY	Priority 2: Oppose Brandon Lofto	REP & Ul	1453	116	843	575	6852	
NCH105	D+1	AMY BYNUM	Oppose Wesley Harris -- signed pl	REP & Ul	1171	95	623	529		
NCH119	R+2	MIKE CLAMPITT	Oppose Joe Sam Queen -- signed	REP & Ul	1750	124	1004	707		
HOUSE COUNT					36941	4628	20531	15436	45725	
HOUSE COST					$ 16,777.13	$55.54	$ 1,642.48	$1,852.32	$ 22,688.85	

Fig. 11F: PAC expenditure planning

Fig. 11F depicts an election plan for some of what we call "focus districts" – districts in which there are clear differences between candidates on our issue, and where I think we can make the margin of victory. To help determine which districts to focus on, we use a state legislative variation of The Cook Partisan Index[13], which rates national, statewide, and congressional districts on how Republican or Democrat they voted in the last election compared to the nation as a whole (e.g. R+3 or D+10). In my state, the Civitas Partisan Index[14] applies similar metrics to state house and senate races. Some other states have similar tools, some do not. If you don't have an equivalent, you might have to look at raw percentages for party affiliation (e.g. Republican, Democrat, Libertarian, etc.) for the district.

You will note the plan in Fig. 11F has priorities, mail counts, phone counts, and budgets for each district. (Although the figure here is black and white, the spreadsheet is actually color-coded.) For important races, we might use not only postcard election alert mailings, email, and social media, which are the basics, but also Robocall/Robotext, radio spots, and possibly mailings from *other* political action committees we control. Incidentally, I get out voter guides early (at least 45 days) before the general election (not primaries), but save express advocacy via election alert postcards until just before the start of early voting for both primary and general elections.

Five key questions in prioritizing PAC expenditures:

Our PAC does candidate "recommendations" (or "endorsements," if you prefer) in all races in which we have a truly simpatico candidate, but we only spend money where we can make a difference. This is where "political science" intersects with "political art" because only so many things can be quantified, meaning that at some point, you will have to go with your gut. When deciding how to triage limited PAC resources, ask these questions:

1. **Is there a clear distinction between candidates?** For example, if both the Democrat and the Republican in a given race received only a Remember in November 0-star evaluation (see above), there is no point in spending precious PAC money in the race. To get involved, my personal criteria are that: (a) one candidate must be at least 3-star; and (b) one candidate must be demonstrably "better" than the other.

2. **Is the race winnable?** If a district is not D+2 or better (i.e. D+2, D+1, D+0, R+1, R+2, R+3, etc.), then it's likely that doing independent expenditures in the form of mailings, Robocalls/Robotexts or radio

spots would waste limited PAC money. Consequently, I do recommendations but not independent expenditures. The rationale, of course, is that a district of D+3 or worse (i.e. D+3, D+4, D+5, etc.) is too heavily left-leaning for us to achieve the margin of victory.

3. **What other factors are at play?** Partisan indices are not necessarily predictive for a given race because they don't factor in other variables. For example, incumbency is a strong force. Against a long-time and powerful Democrat incumbent, I might be reluctant to invest even in a D+1 district. But for an open seat, I might get involved in a D+2 district. Other variables include (but are not limited to) redistricting, national sentiment (which might mobilize voters in a red or blue "wave"), or local controversies (e.g. a road or development issue) which might make an incumbent vulnerable.

4. **Can I accomplish my goal in a primary election?** Primaries are relatively cheap. If I can install a simpatico candidate via a primary in a heavily red district (e.g. R+10) where the winner of the primary is unlikely to lose the general election, I am more likely to get involved.

5. **Will the "good" candidate win regardless?** In many cases, long-time conservative incumbents occupy heavily red seats (e.g. R+15). If they crossed us in the legislative season, I might plan to bump them off with a primary, but there is little point in spending heavily in general election races they will almost certainly win. Here, there are two possible exceptions: For a legislator who helped us significantly, I might do a limited "attaboy" mailing. For a normally friendly legislator who crossed us, I might do limited mail against him (e.g. to his donors or to dedicated Republicans who will tell him they received it) as a slap on the wrist. But in both cases they are limited expenditures made more for commentary than impact.

The joys of low voter turnout

Maybe I lack civic-mindedness, but *I love low voter turnout*. Forget the crap about how "everyone should vote." Nonsense. *Your* people should vote; the rest are welcome to stay home.

In elections with low turnout (e.g. primaries, runoffs, or special elections), smaller numbers of voters allow you to increase your impact by effectively turning out *your* supporters. That is one reason primary elections are my preferred weapon against wayward Republicans. (That and the fact that you can no longer find Democrats who aren't leftist.) In fact, we have become notorious for primarying Republicans who cross us.

The upside to primarying Republicans is that it does not, by itself, reduce their numbers in the targeted chamber. The downside is that Republican leadership knows that, and leadership experiences less fear when they know that although some of their caucus members might get ousted, *they* will stay in power.

Even better than primaries are runoffs and special elections, both of which are typically characterized by low turnout. In one runoff, we installed the dark horse candidate, Patrick McHenry, in the U.S. House by 85 votes. In another, we ousted incumbent Congressman Robert Pittenger, who seemed to have forgotten who brung him to the dance, by 134 votes.

Yes, 134 votes removed a sitting congressman. Rest assured that in both cases *we claimed the victory*, since we more than made the margin. This brings us to an important rule: If you pile on to a candidate who is already having problems, and he loses, *claim his scalp*. Rothfeld expresses it to the effect that if you find a hostile politician stabbed to death in the street with the murder weapon lying next to him, raise the bloody knife high and claim the killing as your own (metaphorically speaking, of course).

Multi-seat races

Occasionally, you will find races with three or more candidates from the major parties vying for two or more seats. Examples include city councils or county commissions with multiple "at large" seats, and sometimes multi-seat state house or senate districts.

In multi-seat races, advise your supporters to vote *only* for your candidate, even if others may be acceptable. The reason is that the other "acceptable" candidate might bump yours out of the seat. Take, for example, a two-seat, at-large county commission race for which four candidates have registered. The two with the highest vote tallies will win the seats. Assume your candidate is vying for the second highest vote count. If your supporters vote for another candidate in addition to yours, however, it could relegate yours to third place, denying him the seat.

Third party candidates

I am routinely denounced for not adequately supporting Libertarian and Constitution Party candidates because, after all, they are stalwarts for freedom, are they not? In truth, however, I make a point of not supporting *any* candidate who doesn't run a serious campaign. The problem with such campaigns is threefold. First, they often act as "spoilers" for good candidates in marginal districts by siphoning off just enough votes to elect leftists. Second, they siphon off your precious PAC money, if you make the mistake of supporting them. Third, in rare cases like the one below, they can even hand control of entire chambers to leftists.

I couldn't possibly recount the number of third party candidates I have seen run Quixotic campaigns not only with no chance of winning, but also with no serious *intention* of winning. Among those who seem to think it is enough to just appear on the ballot, I've seen Libertarians *celebrate* getting 4% of the vote.

On our Facebook page, after making our 2020 GRNC-PVF candidate recommendations, I had Libertarians screaming that we should support a state house candidate who had by then raised a grand $507.41 in donations, with an additional $3,259.28 of in-kind contributions from the Libertarian Party. At that point, his candidate committee report showed he had spent only $410.41 on his race.

When I pointed that out, Libertarians cried: "Oh, so it's all about the money!" My reply? "Without money, how exactly do you expect to reach voters?"

At around the same time, a Constitution Party candidate hounded us because we recommended re-election of Thom Tillis for Senate. Was Tillis a great candidate? No. He falls into the large category I call "votes right when squeezed." But as you may recall, at issue in 2020 was control of the entire U.S. Senate, for which ours was one of the critical races. Tillis won the race by only 1.7% of votes cast. The Constitution Party candidate in question neatly siphoned off 1.25% of the vote, nearly costing Tillis the race and Republicans control of the Senate. If we had recommended the Constitution Party candidate, Tillis might have lost to a truly vile leftist.

Did the Republicans ultimately lose control of the Senate anyway? Yes, thanks to probable election fraud in Georgia. But if Tillis had lost his race, we would now be facing a 51-49 Democrat-led Senate rather than 50-50 that currently needs Vice President Kamala Harris to break tie votes. If the split was 51-49, resistance to the leftist agenda by "The Last Blue Dog Democrat," West Virginia Senator Joe Manchin, wouldn't make a damned bit of difference. By now, Democrats would have ended the filibuster in a 51-49 vote and then, needing only a simple majority, would have "packed" the Supreme Court, rammed through an "assault weapon" ban, and passed the horrifically misnamed "For the People Act" to federalize a permanent leftist lock on power.

That is the impact of third party candidates. If a candidate doesn't run a decent campaign, with a reasonable chance of success, I have absolutely no use for them and neither should you.

References:

1. P.J. O'Rourke, *A Parliament of Whores: A Lone Humorist Attempts to Explain the Entire US Government*, Atlantic Monthly Press, 1991.

2. "State Primary Election Types," National Conference of State Legislatures, January 5, 2021, https://www.ncsl.org/research/elections-and-campaigns/primary-types.aspx

3. "Tax Information for Political Organizations," Internal Revenue Service, https://www.irs.gov/charities-non-profits/political-organizations

4. "Registering as a PAC," Federal Election Commission, https://www.fec.gov/help-candidates-and-committees/registering-pac/

5. "Social Welfare Organizations, Internal Revenue Service, https://www.irs.gov/charities-non-profits/other-non-profits/social-welfare-organizations

6. Emma Green, "The Massive Progressive Dark-Money Group You've Never Heard Of," *The Atlantic*, November 2, 2021, https://www.theatlantic.com/politics/archive/2021/11/arabella-advisors-money-democrats/620553/

7. "Employer Identification Number - Political Organizations," Internal Revenue Service, https://www.irs.gov/charities-non-profits/political-organizations/employer-identification-number-political-organizations

8. "State Limits on Contributions to PACs," League of Women Voters of Maine, https://www.lwvme.org/sites/default/files/pdfs/State_Limits_on_Contributions_to_PACs.pdf

9. Maggie Severns, "'Oh that's cool — do that!: Super PACs use new trick to hide donors," *Politico*, 8/17/2018, https://www.politico.com/story/2018/08/17/super-pacs-hidden-donors-disclosures-741795

10. "Coordinated Communications," Federal Election Commission, https://www.fec.gov/help-candidates-and-committees/candidate-taking-receipts/coordinated-communications/

11. "Same-day voter registration," Ballotpedia, https://ballotpedia.org/Same-day_voter_registration

12. "State Laws Governing Early Voting," National Conference of State Legislatures, 6/1/2021, https://www.ncsl.org/research/elections-and-campaigns/early-voting-in-state-elections.aspx

13. David Wasserman and Ally Flinn, The Cook Political Report with Amy Walter, April 15, 2021, https://cookpolitical.com/analysis/national/pvi/introducing-2021-cook-political-report-partisan-voter-index

14. "Civitas Partisan Index Measures the Partisan Leanings of New Legislative Districts," John Locke Foundation, November 8, 2021, https://www.johnlocke.org/civitas-partisan-index-measures-the-partisan-leanings-of-new-legislative-districts/

Chapter 12
Legal Action

"Litigation: A machine which you go into as a pig
and come out of as a sausage."
– Ambrose Bierce

Litigation in activism is typically used for one or more of three objectives: to change public policy, to enforce compliance with a law (or your reasonable interpretation of a law) from a governmental body or corporation, or to damage an opposing political player. Because I am not a lawyer and in all likelihood neither are you, what follows will be oriented toward managing legal projects for which you will almost inevitably recruit lawyers, either as volunteers or by retaining them. As mentioned previously, by virtue of cost and uncertain outcome, it should be an activist's last recourse.

Types of legal action

Top three objectives of legal action:

❏ **To change public policy:** The most common course is to litigate against perceived violations of the Constitution with the intent to induce the U.S. Supreme Court (SCOTUS) to make a precedent-setting decision. For example, attorney Alan Gura argued and won *D.C. v. Heller* and *McDonald v. Chicago* to establish precedent on the individual right to keep arms within the home. Our case, *Bateman v. Perdue* (see below) was Gura's attempt to establish a precedent on the right to bear arms *outside* the home. Unfortunately, we won. I say "unfortunately" because the state, reading the tea leaves, chose not to appeal and our case never went to SCOTUS. At long last, however, the Court has granted a "writ of certiorari" (agreed to hear) a similar case, *New York State Rifle & Pistol Association Inc. v. Bruen*. As of this writing, our organization has signed on to an "amicus curiae" (friend of the court) brief on the case.

❏ **To enforce compliance:** The left is fond of using this tactic to perpetuate voter fraud by litigating against voter ID laws and election reform. North Carolina, for example, has passed voter ID laws twice – the second time by voters via ballot initiative – only to have activist judges strike them down as "racist." To force redistricting more favorable to leftists, former attorney general Eric Holder created the National Democratic Redistricting Committee and its "sue 'til they're blue" campaign to strike down Republican-drawn districts, and was largely responsible for leftist victories in Virginia.

Compliance-oriented litigation can also be used on smaller targets. My organization has litigated against a sitting agriculture commissioner, a city, and two sheriffs over non-compliance with state statutes on carrying concealed handguns. That said, because it often requires "novel" interpretations of the law, the tactic works best for leftists, particularly if they can get the case before an activist judge who will legislative from the bench.

❏ **To damage the opposition:** As the nastiest use of legal action, litigation is often used to damage hostile players usually, but not always, on the other end of the political spectrum. For example, a group I helped organize in another state was forced to dissolve by court order after a hostile politician sued over alleged non-compliance with state law governing not-for-profit organizations. More than once, I've had opposing players make spurious (and unsuccessful) complaints to our state board of elections over supposed election law violations. I even had a large national organization which is ostensibly on our side try to sue us out of business, also unsuccessfully. Whether or not you choose to use this tactic against others, the lesson is to "keep your sh-t wired tight" by ensuring you are always in compliance with the law, thereby denying your opposition a weapon to use against you. (See "Defending against legal attacks" below.)

When to employ legal action

For the reasons below, I regard using litigation for activism as the course of last resort, to be used when economic and political action have either failed or are not applicable. In fact, I refer you once again to the Flow Chart for Activism in Fig. 12A.

Why legal action should be your last resort

Every neophyte activist I encounter thinks we should immediately sue governmental entities, public officials, and corporations for their various malfeasances, all blithely ignorant of what is actually required. After all, "Anybody can sue anybody over anything," right?

Wrong. Lawyers who file frivolous litigation are subject to disciplinary action by their state bar associations, and any lawyer worth a damn won't file such litigation. As detailed below, the three largest problems with legal action are the expertise required, cost, and outcomes that may bear little relation to the merits of your suit.

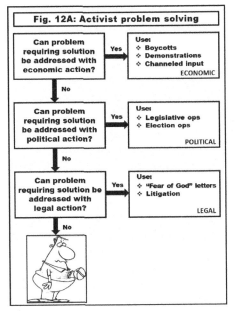

Fig. 12A: Activist problem solving

Can problem requiring solution be addressed with economic action? — Yes → Use: ❖ Boycotts ❖ Demonstrations ❖ Channeled input — ECONOMIC

No ↓

Can problem requiring solution be addressed with political action? — Yes → Use: ❖ Legislative ops ❖ Election ops — POLITICAL

No ↓

Can problem requiring solution be addressed with legal action? — Yes → Use: ❖ "Fear of God" letters ❖ Litigation — LEGAL

No ↓

Incidentally, if volunteers start talking about "common law courts," "sovereign citizens," "illegitimate governments," and filing lawsuits themselves, cut them loose. Immediately. They probably subscribe to some version of the very out-there "sovereign citizen" ideology, and nothing good will come of it.

Top three problems with legal action:

❏ **Arcane and highly specific expertise required:** Everyone I encounter seems to think they know the law. They rarely do. My father, a lawyer, used to call such people "jailhouse lawyers." Unless you have a J.D. and have passed the bar, you probably don't know enough about the law to give an informed opinion. Hell, I've *written* laws and don't consider myself knowledgeable. (Fear not; the laws I write are always vetted by lawyers.) Because you don't know the law, you will have to find someone who does, which brings us to the second problem of legal action.

❏ **Exorbitant expense:** Lawyers start at about $300 per hour and up. Yes, you can mitigate costs by doing some of the footwork yourself, as we discuss below. And yes, recruit all the simpatico lawyers you can find in the hope they will do at least some pro bono work. But in litigating to change public policy or force compliance, which I have done a number of times, I don't recall a suit that cost less than about $15,000, usually far more. Economic and political action, if they are viable options, offer far more "bang for the buck."

❏ **Uncertain outcome:** Judicial activism, in which leftist judges impose the law *as they want it to be* instead of the law as it is written, is an increasing problem. The left even has a doctrine for this: "living document theory," which effectively says, "We don't have to amend the Constitution or law. We will just reinterpret it to mean whatever we want it to mean."

Even if you are dead right, you may lose. The classic example was our lawsuit against a sitting agriculture commissioner over allowing concealed carry at the state fair. We had repealed the law prohibiting concealed carry at events that charge admission, leaving the state absolutely no legal grounds to prohibit carry at the fair.

But the result was best described in the following headline: "Gun-rights group is probably right about the law but loses anyway." Understand that the headline came from a *hostile* newspaper editor, who went on to say:

> "I'm not sympathetic to the firearms-everywhere gun-rights group Grass Roots North Carolina, but this time I think it has a point.

> "Superior Court Judge Donald Stephens pretty much ignored the intent of the law when he ruled yesterday that Agriculture Commissioner Steve Troxler can ban concealed handguns from the State Fair.

> "GRNC President Paul Valone issued a statement this morning saying:

> "'Judge Donald Stephens' decision in the GRNC lawsuit against posting the state fair against concealed carry can best be summa-

rized in his own words: "…I do believe it would be unwise and imprudent for firearms to be carried into the State Fair, and if there is some way I can interpret these statutes to prohibit that, I will.""[1]

Stephens' ruling pretty much defined judicial activism or "legislating from the bench," and is what you may well encounter if you choose legal action to solve a policy problem.

Avoiding litigation

Over the years, I've learned that the threat of litigation is infinitely more efficient in solving problems than litigation itself. Accordingly, I've made art of what I call a "F.O.G." (as in "Fear of God") letter.

The rationale for F.O.G. letters is to convince the target that you are a serious person on serious business, and that you have both the will and the means to inflict significant legal, political, or economic damage if he fails to comply. The objective, by so doing, is to avoid having to expend precious time, manpower, and money to actually inflict that damage. Incidentally, letters from lawyers and/or delivered by certified mail tend to be taken more seriously. For pointers on writing effective F.O.G. letters, see chapter 16.

Assessing the viability of legal action

So you've gone through the activist problem-solving flow chart in Fig. 12A and you've decided that, alas, your problem can't be solved by either economic or political action. That means it's off to court, right? Not so fast, bucko. There are some very big hurdles to clear before filing litigation.

Four questions to ask before deciding to litigate:

❏ **Is there cause for action?** A cause of action, in law, is a set of facts sufficient to justify suing to obtain money, property, or the enforcement of a legal right against another party.

So you say, "That's unconstitutional!" Well, I have bad news for you: a law is constitutional until you prove it isn't. The burden of proof is on you. That's not to say you can't sue on constitutional grounds. As described above, together with the Second Amendment Foundation and the lawyer who won the precedent-setting cases of *D.C. v. Heller* and *McDonald v. Chicago*, we took down our state's blanket ban on carrying firearms outside the home during declared states of emergency in the case *Bateman v. Perdue*. That said, however, your life will be far easier if you can find a specific state or federal statute that your target is violating.

☐ **Do I have plaintiffs with "standing?"** Standing ("locus standi") means the party seeking legal remedy must demonstrate to the court sufficient connection to, and harm from, the law or action challenged to support that party's participation in the case. A large part of public policy litigation involves recruiting plaintiffs with standing.

According to the Cornell Law School, "… at an irreducible minimum, the constitutional requisites under Article III for the existence of standing are that the plaintiff must personally have: 1) suffered some actual or threatened injury; 2) that injury can fairly be traced to the challenged action of the defendant; and 3) that the injury is likely to be redressed by a favorable decision."[2]

☐ **What relief can I seek?** Consider this a ridiculously brief overview of a topic on which lawyers write volumes. Again, your life will be far easier if you are litigating violation of a statute which allows specific damages. For example, cities and counties in our state often ignored our objections to violation of our "statewide firearms preemption" law which, generally speaking, prohibited them from enacting gun laws more stringent than state law … that is, until we passed a measure allowing us to recoup court costs, attorney fees, and damages. Now we almost always get compliance when we send a F.O.G. ("Fear of God") letter explaining the realities of the situation.

Understand, too, that you might have to navigate around "sovereign immunity," the legal doctrine protecting governmental entities from civil suit or criminal prosecution. That said, relief from violation of constitutional rights may include[3]:

- Injunctive relief to restrain a party from doing certain acts or to require a party to act in a certain way;
- Compensatory damages for injuries or costs directly resulting from the constitutional violation;
- Punitive damages assessed to punish a defendant for conduct, and to reform or deter the defendant and others from engaging in similar conduct; and
- Attorneys' fees and costs. The federal civil rights enforcement statute, 42 U.S.C. § 1983, recognizes that often only "nominal damages" (e.g., $1) are available, as the violation of a plaintiff's rights may not have caused provable economic damage, and expressly provide for the award of attorneys' fees, expert fees, and other costs to a prevailing plaintiff.

❏ **Can I afford it?** The first question to ask is what your lawyer will be doing for his $300+ per hour, and what you can do to minimize costs (e.g. recruiting and vetting plaintiffs). If possible, recruit a volunteer lawyer to oversee the project, even if the area of litigation is not his specialty. Another possibility is recruiting one or more interns to do research. If you can get a ballpark figure for basic litigation (not appeals), you will at least know how much money you have to raise to fund the case.

Whatever you do, be honest with yourself about your fundraising capabilities. Bake sales and flea markets won't do it. You will need solid fundraising lists (either developed or rented) to which you send competent fundraising mail. You might also be able to raise at least some money via "crowdfunding" sites such as GiveSend-Go (*not* GoFundMe which, as described in the "Freedom Convoy" sidebar to Chapter 13, tried to confiscate funds from the demonstration). Another option is to recruit other non-profits to join you as plaintiffs and split litigation costs. Be very careful who you add to your suit, however, since the wrong co-litigant can turn your project into a nightmare. (Ask me how I know.)

Legal project management

To manage legal action projects, do not under any circumstances just task it to lawyers or others and forget about it, however tempting that may be. Doing so may run up inefficient and unsustainable legal costs, as well as potentially lose the direction you want the litigation to take.

If you have co-litigants, be prepared to act as "cat-herder-in-chief." In forming a coalition with two other organizations to sue a sheriff who refused to issue handgun permits as required by law, for example, it gradually became apparent that one of the organizations was far more interested in recouping damages and declaring "victory" than in fully accomplishing the goal. To do that, my organization had to separately file yet another suit, at additional cost.

Considerations for legal project management:

❑ **Funding:** Whenever possible, fund litigation from a 501(c)(3) non-profit organization rather than a 501(c)(4) not-for-profit organization, since the IRS allows c3's to do unlimited legal action and because, as you will see in Chapter 15, it is easiest to raise money for a c3 since donations are tax deductible, offering advantages to donors who itemize deductions. In general, political non-profits with multiple entities (a PAC, a c4, and a c3) should prioritize *fundraising* for the entity which is most restricted in fundraising but least restricted in spending (the PAC). Conversely, prioritize *spending* from the entity least restricted in fundraising but most restricted in spending (the c3). This is because you can't use the more restricted c3 money for express advocacy and are limited in using it for advocating legislation.

  • **Using a c4 as a litigant:** If you don't have a c3, it is perfectly acceptable to use c4 money for litigation provided it is consistent with activities in the bylaws filed to get your IRS letter of exemption. In fact, having your c4 out front shows donors what they are getting for their money. Never forget that organization building should be part of every plan; you should come out of the battle stronger than you went in. Accordingly, do fundraising using the techniques listed in Chapter 17 to highlight the suit. If your group has been invited by a national organization to join an amicus brief on a large case with costs underwritten by the national organization, using your primary c4 as the litigant is a no-brainer.

- **Using a c3 to underwrite costs:** If you are underwriting litigation but want the name of your c4 out front, you have two options: First, you can list both organizations as plaintiffs but fund the suit from the c3. Alternatively, your c3 can donate to your c4 if the donation is restricted to a charitable purpose that aligns with the c4's mission, as stated in its organizational documents, and if the activity the money is used for does not violate the c3's eligibility. To that end, I suggest segregating funds by setting up a separate checking account specifically for the permissible activity.

❏ **Retaining counsel:** Obviously, the lawyer you retain should be proficient in the requisite area of law. Although you might get recommendations for lawyers from "insiders" such as political party leadership, understand that those insiders, likely having more money to work with than you do, aren't necessarily sensitive to billing rates and billable hours. In interviewing for counsel, I prefer young, "hungry" lawyers over established firms not only because they work cheaper, but because they tend to be more motivated. To estimate their effectiveness, check references, the state bar, Yelp, and third-party rating services.

Presuming you are forced to retain counsel rather than recruiting volunteers, items to consider include billing rate, required retainer, and whether or not the retainer is refundable if not fully used. In particular, avoid the sort of lawyers who seem to work for what I call the "billable second." For example, I dumped the lawyer who incorporated our c3 when it became evident that he thrived on writing memos for five-minute phone calls and then billing me for time spent writing each memo in addition to time spent on the call.

❏ **Recruiting plaintiffs:** The plaintiffs are those for whom you seek legal remedy. Make sure to let the plaintiff know that costs will be underwritten by your organization. In recruiting plaintiffs, first and foremost they must have standing as defined above. Second, you must vet them to ensure nothing in their background might preclude eligibility (e.g., if I sue for a sheriff's failure to issue handgun permits, my plaintiff must have nothing in his background that makes him ineligible for a permit). Third, the more sympathetic a plaintiff is, the better off you will be. For example, in looking for a plaintiff to sue the sheriff for failure to issue pistol purchase permits, we found a single mother who didn't own any firearms and wanted, but was unable, to buy a handgun for protection during the civil unrest of 2020. Fourth, your plaintiffs should not have a problem with their name being associated with the case, particularly in a "cancel culture" environment that could get them fired from their jobs. I've had several back out when I raised that possibility.

❏ **Managing media.** Your goal is to cause your target pain. Negative media increases pain. Use the press contact list you have developed (see Chapter 18) to issue press releases at appropriate times, typically at the time of filing and after significant decisions. Consider having a press conference at the time of filing. I once even had press follow us in for photos when the suit was filed. Another possibility is to time the filing to coincide with related significant events in order to increase coverage.

❏ **Monitoring performance:** Keep a close eye on legal counsel to ensure correct procedures are followed, critical deadlines are met, and appropriate arguments supporting your cause are made. For example, one of our lawyers screwed up serving the complaint on a sheriff we sued, requiring us to refile the case. (In fairness, he more than made up for it when the sheriff tried to dodge service – yes, you heard that right – by claiming he no longer lived at his address of record, only to have our lawyer produce photos proving otherwise.) Again, if you can have a volunteer lawyer bird-dog the lawyers you retained, so much the better.

Resolution

Don't count on getting rich from public policy litigation. In most cases, you will be lucky to recoup costs. We've had some cases go to trial, some were settled, and one was dismissed after the city we sued quietly complied with our demands without acknowledging it had done so and then moved for dismissal. (The latter was less than satisfactory because we were unable to recoup legal costs.)

If settling, I urge you not to be "that group" – the one that's in it more for money and the ability to claim a "win" than having a serious impact on public policy. And if you receive a settlement or win an award, I also encourage you to reinvest whatever you win into achieving additional objectives.

Defending against legal attacks

Having been on the receiving end of legal attacks designed to damage not only my organization, but also my personal life, I have learned to be very careful with every political operation I conduct. Do not give leftists the ammunition to degrade your operational effectiveness.

Nowhere does this appear to be more true than at the NRA, which *appears* to have given leftist New York Attorney General Letitia James the ammunition to seriously damage the organization and, with it, the gun rights movement in general. Rumors of financial malfeasance by NRA Executive Vice President Wayne LaPierre and his cronies had *reportedly* by circulating for years. But when Michael Bloomberg's propaganda "news" organization, "The Trace," did an exposé on the NRA leadership's spending habits, the result was potentially unrecoverable. (For why I used the words "appears" and "reportedly," see below.)

SLAPP suits

If you are too effective against a target, you could face a "strategic lawsuit against public participation" (SLAPP) suit intended to censor, intimidate, and silence you by burdening you with the cost of a legal defense until you give up and go away. In SLAPP suits, the plaintiff may not expect to win, but merely to subject you to fear, intimidation and exorbitant legal costs.

Defensive tactics

The most important thing in defending against malicious litigation designed to silence you is to anticipate it, even expect it, and to take the following steps *ahead of time*.

Avoiding or blunting legal attacks:

❏ **Comply with the law:** The more effective you are, particularly in attacking candidates with your political action committee (PAC), the more vultures you will draw. Strict adherence to regulations governing non-profit organizations and PACs, including reporting requirements and deadlines, will deny them the carrion they seek. In response to a leftist lawyer who complained to the board of elections that we were conducting independent expenditures without required reporting, it was my greatest pleasure to respond, "Sorry, dude. Wrong PAC. The PAC you are complaining about ceased to exist five years ago when we federalized it. Go nip at somebody else's ankles."

❑ **Use weasel words (sort of):** Don't you hate it when a corporation uses weasel words? Yeah, well, having been on the receiving end of a defamation suit, I now understand why they use them. Rather than saying that "Senator Bombast is a lying sack of sh-t!", say "Senator Bombast *appears to be* a lying sack of sh-t!" No, I'm not saying you should adopt the politician's habit of stringing together pleasant-sounding words that mean nothing; I'm just saying that when attacking other players, think carefully about how you do it.

❑ **Get umbrella insurance:** What will happen to you if you organize a rally, a whacked out "supporter" assaults a member of the opposition, and the aggrieved party sues *you*? My advice to anyone in the leadership of a volunteer political organization is to carry at least a $1 million comprehensive liability policy, and preferably $2 million. It is a cheap add-on to your home or auto insurance. (Note: If you are being paid for your political participation, a comprehensive insurance policy won't protect you. Instead, have the non-profit indemnify its directors.)

❑ **Shut up and lawyer up:** If a hostile organization or individual starts threatening litigation, *do not reply*. (Ask me how I know this...) Instead, immediately seek legal advice. That way, not only will you avoid "pre-counsel remarks" (i.e. stupid statements, something which I am apparently quite good at), the fact that a lawyer responds to them projects strength, and strength deters bullies.

❑ **Use it against them:** Depict you and your organization as poor little concerned citizens being attacked by the big corporate (or governmental) interest. Do so in press releases, interviews and, if possible, channeled input directly to members of the plaintiff's board of directors. If it is a membership organization, bleed them for members.

References:

1. Doug Clark, "Gun-rights group is probably right about the law but loses anyway," *News & Record*, October 14, 2014, https://greensboro.com/townnews/legislation/gun-rights-group-is-probably-right-about-the-law-but-loses-anyway/article_3961e6dc-53a4-11e4-b874-0017a43b2370.html

2. "Constitutional Standards: Injury in Fact, Causation, and Redressability," Cornell Law School Legal Information Institute, https://www.law.cornell.edu/constitution-conan/article-3/section-2/clause-1/constitutional-standards-injury-in-fact-causation-and-redressability

3. "Measuring Damages for Violations of Individuals' Constitutional Rights, 8 Val. U. L. Rev. 357 (1974), https://scholar.valpo.edu/vulr/vol8/iss2/7

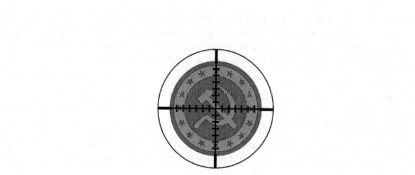

Chapter 13
Non-Legislative Operations

"The majority of people were always sitting in the stands.
When I find people who are willing to go against the grain,
who are willing to make tremendous sacrifices to change an
unjust situation – that's what blows my mind out."
– Abby Hoffman

The left has been kicking our ass more or less continuously since about 1968. Would you like to know how? It isn't by employing effective legislative operations. They generally don't. It isn't by mobilizing to win elections. With the exception of a relatively small number of power-hungry manipulators of *true* liberals, leftists are generally too absorbed with their own perceived intellectual "superiority" to actually do anything effective.

Nope. We lose because, paradoxically, leftists have convinced a large number of mainstream Americans that *they* hold the moral high ground. Whether the issue is open borders, free college or global warming, those who redistribute *your* money to others have convinced the ignorant and inattentive that *they* "care" more; those who suppress *your* voice have convinced them that *they* are the "voice of tolerance"; and those who ride around in private jets have convinced them that *you* should "minimize your carbon footprint."

And as much as my mentors might argue otherwise, you don't win that fight in the legislature. You win it in the streets, and you win it in a media which, unfortunately, the left has already infiltrated to use against you.

Public demonstrations

Given that radicals started perfecting demonstrations in the 1960s, they have almost a sixty-year head start on you. They also have an advantage in that many (if not most) of the Antifites and BLMers, lacking real jobs, have far less to lose in demonstrating than do mainstream Americans. If *they* get arrested at a demonstration, it's a badge of honor. For *you*, it could be the end of your career and an impediment to relationships with family and friends. Despite this position of disadvantage, however, you are going to have to learn to deliver our message on highly public forums.

Fig. 13A: Richmond gun rights rally
(Samira Bouaou/The Epoch Times)

Why demonstrate?

"We need to hold a rally," my supporters tell me with depressing regularity, usually without a clear idea what they intend to accomplish with said rally. I've come to regard the desire to rally as a necessary first step into activism. Hell, *I* started my political advocacy by holding a rally. With experience, however, I have decided that while rallies have certain uses, they are generally ineffective instruments for impacting public policy.

If you need an example, consider the huge Second Amendment rally in Virginia after their off-year 2019 elections gave Democrats a political trifecta in state legislature and gubernatorial races. Although tens of thousands attended, Democrats rammed through nearly all of their gun control agenda regardless.

In the days leading up to the Virginia rally, scores of gun rights supporters implored me to organize a similar rally in North Carolina. Here was my response:

> "If I were in Virginia, I'd organize a rally too. Do you know why? Because they already lost the election. They don't have any recourse. We, on the other hand, have elections coming up in a few months, and we are suffering all of the court-ordered redistricting and out-of-state money here that caused them to lose. So I can either spend all of our time, money and sweat holding a rally, after

which nothing will have changed, or I can expend it winning the 2020 elections. I plan to do the latter."

We won the 2020 elections in "purple" North Carolina, by the way. We won not only the presidential election, but also three heavily contested U.S. House races and a U.S. Senate race targeted nationally by Democrats. We increased both the Republican majority in the General Assembly and the number of conservative seats on the North Carolina Supreme Court. My organization won nearly every race we targeted. In fact, the only failures we experienced were to unseat a sitting governor and a sitting attorney general. And why did we win these victories? Because we *didn't* split our resources by holding a rally.

Changing landscape

In 2020, however, leftist demonstrations following the death of George Floyd shifted the battle decidedly in favor of such events. In response, I have changed my position on public demonstrations and now say, "It depends." Specifically, it depends on your goals.

Sometimes referred to as "direct action," public demonstrations are intended to take the target out of its comfort zone by intimidating or embarrassing its leadership, or by alienating its traditional base of support. What demonstrations do *not* do is to change legislative outcomes, with the exception of those which are so "in the face" of politicians that they produce fear of being unseated.

Location, location, location

As the cliché goes, the three most important factors in determining the desirability of real estate are "location, location, location." The same holds true for public demonstrations. Few things are funnier than watching leftists spend time, money, and effort organizing a demonstration in a place few people notice.

Locations for public demonstrations should be:

❑ **Visible from roads, streets, or walking malls:** Put people with signs out on the street getting passersby to honk in support.

❏ **Accessible for your supporters:** Make sure you have parking, water, toilets, and other facilities as well as suitable road access. Equally, it should be positioned such that passersby can join.

❏ **Photogenic for the media:** Make sure your location will look good on TV and in printed media.

❏ **Seen by decision-makers:** We once held a rally in a legislative walking mall directly under legislators' offices. Because the mall was an echo chamber, our chants of "We will not compromise!" literally rattled politicians' office windows.

Objectives of public demonstrations:

❏ **Raise public awareness of (or create) an issue:** Exploiting the death of George Floyd with what were undoubtedly pre-planned nationwide demonstrations, the left created a new issue they called "systemic racism." As previously noted, "systemic racism" may have been the *issue* raised, but the *problem* the left intended to solve was to foist socialism on the U.S.

❏ **Intimidate a political or commercial target:** Using a variety of tactics up to and including throwing paint at fur-wearing celebrities, PETA ("People for the Ethical Treatment of Animals") has been highly effective at getting high end department stores to stop selling fur and getting restaurant chains such as Kentucky Fried Chicken to change meat processing practices.

❏ **Financially damage a target:** When targeting merchants or corporations, demonstrations often fail to change the target's behavior unless they directly impact its "bottom line." For this objective, public demonstrations are inefficient unless combined with other tactics, since corporations have become adept at hunkering down and waiting out the storm. Boycotts are more effective at changing corporate behavior.

❏ **Build organizations:** Demonstrations can be highly effective in organizing or activating a specific group of potential supporters. At our first Second Amendment rally in 1994, we circulated petitions we later used to create the mailing list from which we built our organization. Given good media management, they also provide an opportunity to build your organization because, sadly, perception is more important than reality. Holding a demonstration—even one which accomplishes little in concrete terms—creates the impression among supporters that you are "doing something."

Types of demonstrations:

❑ **Rallies:** This is the basic venue for people who want to "do something." The formula goes like this: Put the word out and gather a bunch of angry demonstrators holding signs, chanting, etc. The upside is that rallies can be photogenic. The downside is that rallies require considerable resources and skill to organize.

The worst of possible (and highly likely) outcomes is to organize a rally for which nobody shows up. In 1994, with the "assault weapon" ban moving in Congress, a group calling itself the "Committee of 1776" organized state rallies leading up to a well-attended rally on Washington's National Mall. With nationally renowned speakers, including G. Gordon Liddy, it went so well the organizer decided to do it again the following year, *after* we won the 1994 elections. At the Gun Rights Policy Conference later that year, he gave the following speech: "My topic is 'If You Rally, Will They Come?' The answer is no." With that, he sat down.

Learning from him (and understanding that people are basically lazy and apathetic), I plan either "limited" rallies that require only a few people or use the following methods to increase turnout:

- Plan it at times when working people can attend;
- Plan at times when people are angry;
- Pile on to other events that draw people; or
- Use a variation of "astroturfing" (see later in this chapter).

❑ **Protests/picketing:** In this case, you are generally reacting to an opposition event (e.g. a widely acclaimed leftist speaking at an event). The upside is that your people are likely to be pissed off. The downside is that not only don't you get to pick the location, you probably don't have much lead time to plan it, especially if your opposition hides the venue to avoid your protest. To convey a coordinated message, either print signs for protestors yourself or instruct protestors to use your themes. (See Fig. 13B.) When we had a lot of these going on during the Obama years, we actually created a text-based "flash mob" to respond with minimum notice.

Fig. 13B: Messaging for marches

When Gabby Giffords and Mark Kelly of "Americans for Responsible Solutions" announced a Raleigh stop on their national "conversation with gun owners" (to which gun owners were not invited), we made statewide news with a play on "Where's Waldo?" We called it "Where's Gabby?" and offered 1,000 rounds of ammo to anybody who could tell us where the event would be. As a result (and much to their chagrin), a sizable group of those gun owners she claimed to want a "conversation" with actually showed up at her luncheon. I've used these types of limited protests to very good effect over the years, including the "Truth Vigil for Sarah Brady," the "'Million' Mom Countermarch," and a couple of Michael Bloomberg protests. We often draw more people than the event we are protesting.

❏ **Marches:** Logistically more challenging than static demonstrations, marches may require permits to close streets. At a minimum, you will need event marshals to coordinate street crossings. We held a "Solidarity March" during the Charlotte NRA convention in 2000, which was the year after anti-gun activists responded to the Columbine killings by all but shutting down the NRA annual meeting in Denver. Determined not to give them a toehold in North Carolina, we dominated the national news with thousands of marchers bearing identical lime green "Guns Save Lives" signs. (Fig. 13B.) What the media didn't know was that after marchers walked from Charlotte's Fourth Ward park to the NRA event at the convention center, they boarded vans taking them back to the park to start over again, greatly increasing their apparent number.

❏ **Street theater:** Requiring fewer organizational resources, street theater can help you drum up media coverage. The key to street theater is imagination: Your themes must compel and your delivery must be graphic. For example, animal rights activists once crashed a Repub-

Fig. 13C: Effective street theater

lican National Convention by streaking through, dressed in cow suits, chanting: "Cut pork! Tax beef!" Bear in mind that although we call it "theater," skits—particularly those that require people to stop for long periods of time—aren't likely to hold attention long enough to deliver your message. One glance should tell people all they need to know. That means delivering it visually and/or via a repeated chant. Don't be subtle. Although you might think symbolism for something is unmistakable, a newspaper camera will not. Put your message into words via a short, memorable sign.

At the 2000 NRA convention mentioned above, we got a permit for the busiest corner in Charlotte to do a piece we called "The Rape of Justice." (Fig. 13C.) As a cross between the infamous picture of the child Elian Gonzalez being dragged from his Miami home at submachine gunpoint, and the cover of the gun rights novel *Unintended Consequences*, it featured the blindfolded, semi-naked and supine figure of Lady Justice, draped in the American flag, hands held up in a plea for mercy and the scales of justice lying discarded on her body, as four storm-troopers in full SWAT regalia pointed submachine guns down at her. Above it all was the banner, "Your future under gun control." So realistic was the display that we needed an FBI escort to set up on the street. Instead of gun control protestors, national media coverage was dominated by our "Guns Save Lives" signs and "The Rape of Justice."

❏ **Vigils and sit-ins:** This is primarily a leftist tactic, and not one I recommend. Unless you have a sympathetic media (which conservatives rarely do), a few people sitting silently with signs, or empty shoes of "victims" (or whatever) generally don't make news. At the same time as our "Rape of Justice" street theater, gun control activists held a pathetic vigil of black-clad protestors and a beating drum that was utterly ignored.

Necessary elements of public demonstrations

As the organizer, you are responsible for the safety of your demonstrators. You are also responsible for ensuring that messaging to the media and public is consistent with your objectives, as well as ensuring the opposition doesn't derail your effort. Unlike twenty years ago, when leftists were cute, stupid,

Fig. 13D: Coordinated messaging

and ineffective, your opposition today is organized and dangerous. They are also committed to disrupting conservative events. Don't give them that opportunity.

Four elements to effective demonstrations:

1. **Command and control**: The organizers of the January 6, 2021 demonstration in Washington lost control of their event, resulting in the debacle witnessed by the world. By contrast, your command structure should be highly visible, tightly coordinated, and consistent in applying rules. Your leadership should have a copy of the demonstration permit, if required, and copies of any applicable regulations. Command and control should include the following:

    a. **Command center:** For the Solidarity March and "Rape of Justice" street theater, we got a suite at the Hilton overlooking the city convention center which served not only for staging the various components of the operation, but also for press conferences and meetings with law enforcement contacts. For smaller demonstrations, you might work from a van, a pop-up shelter or even a street corner, but have a place where your leadership can meet.

b. **Event team:** Designate who will serve as leadership, event marshals, and media contacts.

c. **Event marshals:** These are your points of contact with demonstrators. They should have armbands, T-shirts or other garb identifying them as such. At the Solidarity March, one marcher dropped over with a heart attack. Our people were on him with medical attention immediately. (He and his family thanked us profusely from the hospital.)

d. **Communications:** At a minimum, publish a list of cell numbers for leadership, event marshals, and media contacts. Radios have the advantage of instantaneous contact, as well as allowing all members of your event team to listen to and be aware of developments.

2. **Security:** If possible, have large, imposing people as your event marshals. At our first Second Amendment rally, many of ours were prison guards. I've also used off-duty police. However you handle it, you should deliver a clear message to the opposition that you are not people to mess with.

a. **Video:** Either designate specific people or have everyone prepared to video interactions with law enforcement and the opposition. Because the left loves doing this and then misrepresenting conservatives, you should be ready to provide your own narrative.

b. **Weapons:** Adhere to the law. Depending on state law, deadly weapons are often prohibited at public demonstrations, right down to potential restrictions on the staffs used to hold signs. Pepper spray or Tasers, however, might be permissible and, if so, should be carried by event marshals.

c. **Law enforcement:** Be proactive in working with law enforcement, delivering the message that you are the "good guys." At the Solidarity March, we worked closely with a liaison from the FBI who, after the event, repeatedly thanked us for our cooperation.

3. **Regulatory compliance:** Make sure to have all necessary permits

in place and adhere to regulations on signage and any sticks used to hold signs (which local regulations may restrict to avoid being used as weapons), not blocking sidewalks or public thoroughfares (if applicable), and sanitation, including trash receptacles, portable toilets, and event cleanup.

4. **Messaging:** *You*, not the media and not your opposition, must control the messaging for your event. Incidentally, that means you must *have* a message. That message must be simple, direct, and evocative. If it isn't, the media will ignore it and substitute their own, which will almost certainly not be complimentary.

   a. **Appearance:** Tell demonstrators to "dress for the press," since the leftist media will invariably gravitate to the one guy in the crowd wearing camo and a racist T-shirt.

   b. **Interviews:** Designate well-dressed press liaisons, give them talking points, and ensure they rehearse your message. Because media will try to interview the least articulate person in the crowd, have demonstrators refer media to your press team, and instruct your press team to actively intervene if necessary.

   c. **Signage:** Your signs display the message the world will see. They should be professional, coordinated to your demonstration theme, contain your website, and be large enough to read on television. I leave it to you whether to permit signage brought by demonstrators but if you do, edit the content. For the Solidarity March, we printed two hundred lime green signs saying: "GUNS SAVE LIVES" and "GRNC.org" along with hundreds of matching T-shirts. As a consequence, national media on the NRA convention, rather than showing anti-gun protestors, showed a sea of lime green.

How to lose control of messaging: The January 6, 2021 "March to Save America" in Washington was an exercise in how *not* to do a demonstration. I saw little in terms of event marshals, instructions to demonstrators, or infrastructure such as portable toilets, medical stations, or press contacts. Consequently, during Donald Trump's speech, people lacking instructions just began to wander off from the Ellipse toward the Capitol Building. That militants in the crowd, spurred by "agents provocateurs," would get out of control was not only likely, it was inevitable. Even Women for America First, the 501(c)(4) organization holding the event, was later depicted negatively as a "dark money" group.

Demonstration timing

As the organizer behind the Committee of 1776 described above would tell you, timing is everything. In early 1994, when the "assault weapon" ban was moving through Congress and gun owners felt threatened, tens of thousands showed up. The following year, after we won the election with the Republican Revolution, nobody bothered. If the political environment isn't getting your people seriously riled up, your event will fail.

Always hold demonstrations *before* legislation passes, never after. Hold events on weekends unless circumstances dictate otherwise (e.g. you want to confront legislators). If possible, plan events for synergy with other events (speakers, conventions, etc). Finally, let your people know you expect them to show rain or shine (and prepare accordingly).

Required equipment

Obviously, the type of equipment required depends on the type of event. If you can't find donors to lend it free, most of it can be rented. The most demanding in terms of equipment are fixed rallies, which may require:

- ❏ Raised dais and chairs for speakers
- ❏ Podium, with signage in front and banners behind which deliver your message in photos and video
- ❏ Portable public address system and power cables or portable generator
- ❏ Pop up shelter and chairs for event leaders and VIPs
- ❏ Seating for speakers
- ❏ Water coolers and paper or plastic cups
- ❏ Trash receptacles
- ❏ Portable toilets
- ❏ Medical kit with qualified personnel
- ❏ Radios and/or a cell phone contact list containing all event organizers
- ❏ Petitions, pens, and clipboards
- ❏ Table, chairs, and signage for petition signups and administration
- ❏ Donation jar and/or membership forms (if applicable)

Organization building

If you hold an event which ends when everyone goes home, you will have wasted an opportunity for organization building. Your goal is to come out of the event stronger than you went into it. Have petitions or other sign-up sheets for use in list-building. Hold a free drawing, requiring that people give you their email addresses in order to win.

Demonstrations in non-permissive environments

Everything above assumes you have permission to be where you are demonstrating. If on private property (e.g. a corporate campus) where you don't have a right to be, however, deliver your message quickly and leave when instructed.

In fighting the sewage treatment plant slated for my cove on Lake Norman, I called media contacts and told them to meet me at "high noon" in front of the Ramada Inn owned by a county commissioner. A dozen protestors lined the road (a major thoroughfare) with pink "Stink Zone" signs we had printed up to line roads around the proposed plant site.

When reporters arrived, I led them into the hotel lobby. I greeted the receptionist with, "Correct me if I'm wrong, but isn't Commissioner Ikerd a principle in this hotel?" She allowed that he was. "And isn't his office right over there?" I gestured at the building roughly two hundred yards away. "Yes, it is," she replied.

"Then would you please tell Commissioner Ikerd that Concerned Citizens of Lake Norman has a demonstration set up in his front yard?" Then I walked to the demonstration area and waited. Five minutes later, the red-faced commissioner barged onto the scene trailing a lawyer to restrain him from assaulting me (alas). As he started his finger-pointing tirade, newspaper cameras began snapping pictures. For good measure, we brought our own video camera. Given the potential impact of the sewage plant on residents' home values, the media found a certain irony in the commissioner's vehement protest that this was, after all, just a political matter having nothing to do with his private interests.

The next day, the perception that the sewage plant was a "done deal" was replaced by newspaper headlines saying, "Concerned Citizens of Lake Norman Fight Sewage Plant." We followed up with a mailing for money and volunteers to area residents and raised nearly $60,000 in a month from homeowners who reasoned that $500 to us was cheaper than a $50,000 hit in their property values. Incidentally, the property purchased by the county for the sewage plant remains vacant to this day.

Hostile action

This constitutes what the left calls "direct action." Because I define direct action more broadly to encompass any action directed to change the behavior of a target, however, I will call this category of activism what it really is: hostile action.

Hostile action is intended to economically, emotionally, or physically intimidate the target. It is undeniably the ugliest form of activism, which makes it a favorite of the nasty losers of Antifa, BLM, and various other radical elements (e.g. the Weather Underground, Students for a Democratic Society or SDS, etc.).

Occasionally, hostile action works. More often, it hardens the target against you. I won't say I have never dabbled in it (particularly doxxing), but I use it only as a last resort and even then only with extreme caution. Suffice to say that if you do, it should be for very specific purposes and you should understand the risks, not only to your cause but to your humanity.

❏ **Doxxing:** This refers to revealing private information about the target on the Internet, and has become a popular tactic of the left. To steal a line from former Senator Phil Graham, however, "I was doxxing before doxxing was cool."

After the Sandy Hook shootings in 2012, the *Journal News* of New York thought it would be cute to publish names and addresses of handgun permit-holders, pretty much inviting theft and violence upon them. I swore that if anybody did it in North Carolina, it would only happen once. Sure enough, a leftist television station in Raleigh published an address-searchable database of concealed handgun permit-holders. So, after unsuccessfully warning the station to remove it, we published the reporter's name, cell number, partial address, voter affiliation, home value, names and photos of his family, where he vacationed, and much more. When the station refused to relent, we did the same for his editor (who, as I recall, had a nasty divorce in Maryland). To avoid charges of criminal harassment, we told our people to call him only once and to be civil. When newspapers across the state wailed about how "unfair" we were, I replied, "In the era of the Internet, we all live in glass houses. So y'all better play nice." As I predicted, it only happened once.

The second, slightly more limited occasion on which we used doxxing was against gun control lobbyists who opposed our "constitutional (permitless) carry" bill. The problem was that we had indications that the ostensibly "Republican" lobbying firm (which routinely contracted leftist causes) was hiring out to a high-dollar national gun control organization. To deliver the message that risks were involved in so doing, we distributed limited personal information on the lobbyists. Although I took some heat even from friendly legislators, the fact that the national organization has had a much more low-key and limited presence since then suggests that our message got across.

- ❏ **Non-contact harassment**: The preferred tactic of Antifa and various other radicals, it involves getting in the faces not only of police, but often opposing organizations and even neutral parties such as patrons at outdoor restaurants. Typically, "black block" –clad radicals get within the personal space of the target, sometimes using bullhorns, screaming insults and obscenities, and trying to evoke a physical response from the target while themselves staying just shy of chargeable offenses. Rest assured that somebody nearby will be making a cell phone video. I describe the tactic not because you should use it, but because any conservative activist holding a public demonstration should be ready for it.

- ❏ **Civil disobedience**: Given that the tactic usually involves getting arrested, it is far less popular among responsible conservatives who have something to lose than among jobless leftists living in their parents' basements. The funniest example that comes to mind was the "unilateral nuclear disarmament" protest, circa 1980, when lefties decided to "clog the justice system" in New York City by lying down in the street, getting arrested, and refusing to give their names to police. But the cops were ready: They promptly dragged off protestors to Rikers Island and locked them up with what Arlo Guthrie's "Alice's Restaurant" describes as "the mother rapers" and "father stabbers." It didn't take long for the lefties to do whatever it took to get out.

❏ **Violent protest:** If burning and looting is your "bag," put down this book and steal a copy of *The Anarchist Cookbook*. The only thing we will cover below is *security* against this particular species of miscreant.

'Dirty deeds, done dirt cheap'

With apologies to AC/DC, what follows are tactics that range from benign to nasty. They are not solely for public demonstrations, although some of them can be applied there. Decide for yourself what you are comfortable doing, but understand that whether or not you are willing to use them, your opposition is.

❏ **Agents provocateurs:** On January 6, 2021, John Sullivan allegedly egged on protestors at the Capitol Building, exclaiming *"Let's go. This sh-t is ours! F-ck yeah. ... We accomplished this sh-t. We did this together. F-ck yeah! We are all a part of this history ... Let's burn this sh-t down."* [1]

He was eventually arrested for his participation in the protest. By his own admission, however, he was not a Donald Trump supporter, but instead a leftist acting as an "agent provocateur," a troublemaker who entices others to commit illegal or rash acts or falsely implicates them in illegal acts in order to ruin the reputation or induce legal action against the group they appear to belong to. People like Sullivan have been causing trouble in public demonstrations for as long as there have been public demonstrations. Given the dangers of doing so yourself, I don't recommend it, but you should be alert to the possibility of leftists infiltrating your demonstrations.

❏ **Astroturfing:** This political term of art describes creating the impression of a grassroots movement where none actually exists. It is a favorite of gun control activists up to and including Michael Bloomberg because on the gun issue, pro-gun grassroots activists invariably outnumber anti-gun activists. One example was Bloomberg's "No More Names" tour in which he rolled a bus into a city, after which (probably paid) gun control advocates rolled out of the bus to hold a gun control rally by reading out the names of victims of "gun violence" which included, among other upright citizens, the Boston bomber and cop-killer Christopher Dorner, both killed by police. I called this tour "demonstration in a can."

That said, milder versions of astroturfing have their uses. As noted above, at our Solidarity March, we shuttled marchers who arrived at the convention center back to the end of the line to increase perceived numbers. On another occasion, we held a "'Million' Mom Countermarch" by shuttling demonstrators from an adjacent gun show. (At the same show, one of our leaders made a deal with the Concerned Bikers, who were holding a rally, to ride motorcycles around the gun control demonstrators, drowning out their speakers.)

❏ **Preemptive accusation:** Another leftist favorite, one variation of this involves accusing your opposition of what you are either doing or intending to do such that when they make the accusation, it is dismissed as a child's "Well you did it too!" A milder variation involves accusing your opposition of something you anticipate they will do, or which you have unfounded assertions they might do. At the Solidarity March, we got word from the FBI that some leftists had discussed disrupting our march, so to deter them I immediately convened a press conference and accused them of plotting to do so. It never happened.

❏ **Social media "cyberbullying":** If you have ever had the misfortune to "debate" a leftist on social media, you know that, lacking cogent arguments, they immediately resort to name-calling and general nastiness, often attacking like packs of jackals. We encountered lots of this when we ran Facebook ads against Joe Biden, Cal Cunningham, and other leftists in the 2020 elections. Despite the vitriol, it is perfectly valid to hold elected officials responsible for their actions on Facebook and other platforms. We used the tactic to good effect in pressuring the Wake County Board of Commissioners not to shut down gun stores during the pandemic.

❏ **Spoofing:** Another leftist favorite, this one involves targeting conservative activists with ridicule or embarrassment. In what became known as the "Puppy Pistol Incident," the most infamous recent example occurred when Sasha Baron Cohen of "Borat" fame posed as an Israeli anti-terror expert to convince elected officials and gun rights supporters to support a fake "Kinderguardians" scheme for children as young as three. More recently, gun control activists convinced two national figures to do "dress rehearsal" commencement speeches on the Second Amendment to empty auditoriums, later claiming the empty seats represented victims of "gun violence." Again, I present this not as something of use, but instead something to guard against.

❏ **Computer hacking:** This is an increasingly popular way for the left's self-professed "voice of tolerance" to shut down any who dare disagree. In the "Freedom Convoy" sidebar below, for example, GoFundMe shut off the convoy organizers, instead plotting to send the money to its favorite leftwing causes until various state attorneys general promised investigations. Convoy organizers switched to GiveSendGo which, when ordered to freeze funds by the Canadian government, politely told them to bugger off. So what happened next? You guessed it: hackers took down GiveSendGo. Obviously, I don't advocate you use this technique, since it can land you in jail. I do, however, encourage you to recruit web designers with strong security skills.

❏ **Street warfare:** This sounds like fun, doesn't it? Again, I have included street warfare not because you should use it, but because you should be prepared for the left to use it against you. To learn more, I refer you to a charming online document entitled, "Street Warfare in Portland: A manual of military strategy"[2], which purports to adopt military tactics to go after "fascists" (that would be you) with tactics such as "neutralization of enemy personnel," "area denial," and "resource denial." Among its recommendations are those for things like helmets, gas masks, and body armor. Nor is this manual alone in its recommendations. Other favorites are "40 Ways to Fight Fascists", "Antifa: The Anti-Fascist Handbook", and "The Antifa Manual (Do not distribute to any cis white males non-PoC non-LGBTQ peoples a.k.a. fascists)". Incidentally, in the language we can call "Leftese," "PoC" means "person of color."

The Freedom Convoy: Effective or not?

The most fascinating exercise of direct action in recent memory came in January and February of 2022 by truck drivers protesting mandatory COVID-19 vaccination for truckers crossing between the U.S. and Canada.

The protest picked up steam as somewhere between 36,000 and 50,000 heavy trucks in several convoys converged on Ottawa, blasting air horns and clogging streets. The demonstration moved to a phase of civil disobedience when organizers announced they would stay in Ottawa until vaccine mandates were lifted. Meanwhile, sympathetic demonstrations broke out in Toronto, Quebec City, Vancouver, and Winnipeg, as well as in other countries.

First, Canadian Prime Minister Justin Trudeau implored them to go home. When that failed, however, a 78-year-old grandfather who stood all of four feet, ten inches, was dragged from his car and wrestled to the ground for the grand crime of honking his horn in support of the truckers.[5]

Citing "disruptive" behavior by demonstrators which later turned out to be little more than traffic citations, police began arresting people for bringing fuel needed by truckers for heat in the Canadian winter, charging them with the "Aiding and Abetting of Mischief."[6] In response, demonstration supporters hampered enforcement with a shell game in which some carried fuel cans filled with water.[7]

Far from quitting, the truckers began a devastating series of selective shutdowns, starting with two major ports of entry — the Ambassador Bridge connecting Detroit to Windsor, Ontario, and the Coutts crossing linking Montana to Alberta. When they clogged traffic at the Ottawa International Airport, police threatened arrest without warrant.8 Eventually, Canadian provinces began to capitulate by rescinding vaccine mandates.

Ultimately, the ordinarily "Tea-and-Crumpets" Canadian government bared its autocratic fangs when Trudeau invoked the "Emergencies Act," suspending civil liberties and freezing bank accounts of protestors without benefit of court orders. Although Trudeau eventually sent in baton-wielding police to break up the protest, I would argue that protestors won the fight by forcing Trudeau to show the world the autocrat he is. As I write this, it has spurred another trucker convoy, this time in the U.S.

The Freedom Convoy was effective for two reasons. First, superior issue management in making the demonstration about freedom rather than just vaccine mandates. Second, its prolonged, roving, and targeted disruption of commerce. Had the organizers protested and gone home, they would have been promptly forgotten. Instead, they brought two countries to their knees. Their one major mistake was using GoFundMe to fund the protest. The platform not only cut them off, but claimed it would redistribute contributions to its pet leftwing causes until promises of fraud investigations by various attorneys general convinced them otherwise.

References:

1. Jordan Davidson, "Far-Left Agitator John Sullivan Posed As A Cameraman At Capitol Riot To Stir Up Violence: 'Let's Burn This Sh-t Down'," *The Federalist*, January 15, 2021, https://thefederalist.com/2021/01/15/far-left-agitator-john-sullivan-posed-as-a-cameraman-at-capitol-riot-to-stir-up-violence-lets-burn-this-sh-t-down/

2. "Street Warfare in Portland: A manual of military strategy", https://rosecitycounterinfo.noblogs.org/files/2021/10/Street-Warfare-in-Portland-PRINT-1.pdf

3. Spencer Sunshine, ""40 Ways to Fight Fascists: Street-Legal Tactics for Community Activists", https://spencersunshine.com/2020/08/27/fortyways/

4. "The Antifa Manual (Do not distribute to any cis white males non-PoC non-LGBTQ peoples a.k.a. fascists) - Found on the campus of The Evergreen State College", https://fromthetrenchesworldreport.com/wp-content/uploads/2020/07/ANTIFA-MANUAL.pdf

5. Lee Brown, "Video shows Canadian great-grandad, 78, arrested for honking horn in support of 'Freedom Convoy' truckers," *New York Post*, February 9, 2022, https://nypost.com/2022/02/09/man-78-arrested-for-honking-horn-in-support-of-freedom-convoy/

6. Josh Pringle, "Several people arrested for bringing gas to 'Freedom Convoy' demonstrators in Ottawa, police say," *CTV News*, February 6, 2022, https://ottawa.ctvnews.ca/several-people-arrested-for-bringing-gas-to-freedom-convoy-demonstrators-in-ottawa-police-say-1.5770413

7. Ryan Tumilty, "Ottawa protesters employ gas can subterfuge to frustrate police," *National Post*, February 8, 2022, https://nationalpost.com/news/canada/ottawa-protesters-employ-gas-can-subterfuge-to-frustrate-police

8. Amy Cheng, Jennifer Hassan and Miriam Berger, "'Freedom Convoy' protesters shut down third border crossing as Ottawa police warn of arrests 'without a warrant'," *The Washington Post*, February 11, 2022, https://www.washingtonpost.com/world/2022/02/10/canada-freedom-convoy-alberta-ottawa-protests/?utm_campaign=wp_post_most&utm_medium=email&utm_source=newsletter&wpisrc=nl_most&carta-url=https%3A%2F%2Fs2.washingtonpost.com%2Fcar-ln-tr%2F3600b16%2F620545689d2fda34e78790ff%2F598a8514ae7e8a68161fad5f%2F11%2F72%2F620545689d2fda34e78790ff

PART THREE
Grassroots
Organization

Chapter 14
Grassroots Leadership

"All that is necessary for the triumph of evil is that good men do nothing." — Edmund Burke

"Leadership is the ability to have other people follow where you go, or go where you direct." – Mike Rothfeld

Quick. Look behind you. Are you being followed? If you aren't, then you aren't a leader ... at least not yet.

If nearly three decades of grassroots mobilization have taught me anything, it is that activism is a constant talent search. I have had the good fortune to work with many competent, dedicated volunteers, but relatively few leaders. Of those, many were ineffective not because they didn't display leadership characteristics, but because they lacked one or more critical skills – skills like organizing and communicating.

But leadership skills can be taught, meaning even if nobody is following you right now, you, too, might have grassroots leadership potential. (God help you.) Even if you have no interest in leadership, preferring instead to follow others, I suggest you read this chapter anyway, since it will describe how to effectively execute activist projects.

Becoming an effective leader

Describing leadership problems among conservative activists, Senator H.L. "Bill" Richardson, founder of Gun Owners of America and author of *Confrontational Politics*, put it thus:

> *"For Conservatives, the cause is all-important. However, the organizational advantages presented to them for recruitment, education and long-range political planning rarely cross their minds. They react, do battle, and then disband, perceiving each struggle as an entity within itself. Not the Left, they build on every engage-*

ment, knowing full well the present effort is but one engagement in a protracted conflict, a fight that will take them decades to win completely."[1]

I became a grassroots leader not because I intended to, but because nobody else would. When I called my state's NRA affiliate and asked to get involved, I was told to "write a one-minute letter." When I asked whether they were tracking votes on a gun control bill that just passed, they said: "Well, it's not that easy and we really can't do that because Yada, Yada, Yada."

The last straw was when I discovered that although the "Committee of 1776" was organizing rallies in state capitols across the country, nobody was organizing one in my state. So three guys with just telephones (this was before common use of the Internet) put a thousand people on the capitol steps in less than thirty days. We took names at the rally, built an organization, and have been kicking tail ever since.

In the early years I relied solely on instinct. Only three years later did Dennis Fusaro, then-Director of State and Local Affairs for Gun Owners of America, together with Huck Walther and Mike Rothfeld, the self-described political "thugs" from the National Right to Work Committee contracted by GOA, set about teaching us the hard core tactics which, with modifications and additions, I continue to apply to this day.

As Rothfeld preaches, failures in conservative activism usually result from failure of leadership. The goal of this chapter is to ensure you don't have to learn by trial-and-error as I did. With apologies to Mike, below is my take on the leadership tenets taught by his organization, the Foundation for Applied Conservative Leadership.[2]

What makes effective leaders?

Effective grassroots mobilization relies on four things: planning, preparation, action, and evaluation. To their own detriment, most grassroots leaders jump into the action phase with little or no planning or preparation. They then fail to objectively evaluate their successes and failures, virtually assuring that mistakes will be repeated.

The four pillars of effective grassroots leadership:

1. **Planning:** Thanks to inherent laziness, even after nearly three decades of political action I have to push myself to draw up an "action plan" for each project. But draw them up I do, particularly for our elaborate, multi-pronged Remember in November election effort. (For an example of a legislative action plan, see Appendix III.) An action plan should have the following elements:

   Objectives: Whether control of a legislative chamber or just media attention, each operation should have specific goals.

   - **Resources needed:** What do you need to implement the action plan? (See "preparation" below.)
   - **Methods:** Detail the methods used, be they for channeling input, mobilizing voters, or hijacking media limelight.
   - **Critical deadlines:** Include specific dates by which tasks must be completed, particularly in election operations where early voting has changed the landscape. It is both ineffective and a waste of resources to distribute electioneering communications after half the voters have already gone to the polls.
   - **Assigned roles:** Make specific volunteers responsible for specific tasks. Include what is expected of them and when.
   - **Contingencies:** Because, as the cliché goes, no plan survives first contact with the enemy, work out an "if-then" flow chart for when the plan goes sideways.
   - **Metrics for success:** Does success mean passing a bill? Unseating a politician? Sometimes success lies even in failure – in just proving something can be done, such as primarying a strong incumbent or introducing a bill you know has little chance of passing. (See the "Overton Window" in Chapter 5.)

2. **Preparation:** Lack of adequate preparation is the Achilles' heel of conservative activism, which requires compiling necessary implements such as money, lists, and people. In particular, recruit people with relevant skills such as database management, web design, graphic arts, printing, legal, etc.

3. **Action:** A certain type of person gets hung up on infinite planning, perpetually honing and perfecting a plan that gets implemented

too late, if at all. Once you draw up the plan and put resources into place, don't dither. Pull the trigger and act, particularly if time-compressed decision making is called for. Action should be swift, decisive and unapologetic, including when even your own side is whining, "That's not how we do things here."

4. **Evaluation:** Nobody likes to take a hard look at what they did wrong, yours truly included. But when the dust settles, write (yes, I said "write") an evaluation of what went right, what went wrong, and what to change next time. If you failed to meet the objective, don't be unduly harsh on yourself. If you stretch to make change, you can expect to occasionally fail. More importantly, understand that losing is often winning. (Again, see the "Overton Window" in Chapter 5.)

"Jim Crow-era" permit repeal

Incidentally, the planning phase may encompass decades. For example, in our effort to repeal North Carolina's pistol purchase permit system, I spent twenty years instilling into public consciousness the phrase "our Jim Crow-era pistol purchase permit law." I used it in alerts, position statements to politicians, and op-eds. Eventually, even our opposition started using it. Not long after, the powerful North Carolina Sheriffs' Association, which had opposed us for decades, reversed its position and issued a statement supporting repeal.

Ten things effective grassroots leaders do:

1. **Communicate:** To be taken seriously in politics, you must be a serious person on serious business. That requires clear communications, which themselves require the ability to write and speak clearly. If writing or public speaking isn't your forte, find someone for whom it is.

   - **Public speaking and media:** The good news is that in Chapter 17 ("Media Management"), you can find techniques for effective public speaking. As someone for whom it didn't come naturally, trust me when I say that, to a degree, it can be learned.
   - **Written communications:** In issuing alerts to supporters, position statements to legislators, and press releases to the media, few things will undermine your credibility more thorough-

ly than pervasive errors in grammar, spelling, and syntax. In growing organizations, it's easy for them to slip through (as a big-picture type of person, I'm a lousy proofreader). So, if possible, create an alert team to check each other's work for typos.

2. **Recruit talent:** Rothfeld is fond of saying that leaders create other leaders. True, but they also find people with specific skills such as database management, web design, printing, graphic arts, writing, office management, social media, etc. Create a spreadsheet of names, contact information, and skill sets for potential volunteers, and call them when needed. To find sympatico volunteers, search politicians' offices, social media, newspaper comments sections or letters to the editor, and like-minded gatherings. Steal them from other groups, if necessary, particularly if the other group isn't effective. The best communications director I ever recruited originally come to me for advice on how he could start an effort. In recruiting a potential volunteer, you must appeal to their "enlightened self-interest," which could be:

- **Personal** (how your issue impacts them)
- **Professional** (to develop new skills)
- **Moral** (to further their values or vision)
- **Power** (to be part of your organization's influence)

3. **Delegate:** Leaders tend to be perfectionists, and perfectionists tend not to delegate tasks to others they deem less capable. Get over it. Even worse than "logjam management" resulting from failure to delegate is the resulting burnout you will experience. Yes, you will need to monitor volunteers' performance, but tell your people what you expect and let them do it without micromanaging them.

Our organization uses an online leadership network that not only allows people to volunteer for tasks they prefer, but also conveys a sense of "belonging," of being one of the team. As I discovered the hard way, effective delegation also means *not* assigning a task to someone who either lacks the requisite skills or doesn't want to do the task. If you do, they will drop the ball, often at critical moments. Volunteers help because they want to, not because they need to. I tell them we fully understand the demands of families and jobs, and ask only that if they can't do something, they let us know

ASAP. Incidentally, saying "Can someone do this task?" will get nobody. When you need something covered, decide who is best to cover it and call them. Note that I didn't say email them, text them, or message them via Facebook. I said *call* them.

The corollary to delegating is that there are also things to *avoid* delegating, including control of finances (that doesn't mean you have to sign all checks), marketing and framing issues, raising money, and making contacts with powerful politicians or leaders.

4. **Lead by example:** Don't ask your people to do anything you wouldn't, and *do* assist with dirty work nobody wants to do (at least some of the time). For example, volunteers hate pitching people for memberships and money. When our people work gun shows, I constantly have to ask them to get out in front of the table, actively draw people in, and then *ask* for the membership. Because they hate to do it, anytime I visit a gun show, *I* do it to set an example.

5. **Pace themselves and others:** It's been said that 95% of the work is done by 5% of the people. Since you can't change that, embrace it by "rewarding" your most productive volunteers with more responsibility. That said, however, do not over-involve your organization. In a target-rich political environment, you might have a tendency to simultaneously launch against a dozen threats. Don't, since doing so will not only dilute your effectiveness against any single threat, but will also contribute to burnout, either for you or for your volunteers. Instead, prioritize and tackle only threats against which you can make an impact. Similarly, discourage your more enthusiastic volunteers from tackling too many projects at once. By encouraging volunteers to pace themselves, I keep most of my leadership for at least ten years, and several have been with me since the beginning, twenty-eight years ago.

6. **Prioritize:** Did I say "prioritize" in the bullet point above? Let me say it again: prioritize. In the months leading up to the 2020 elections, everybody wanted us to pass worthless "Second Amendment sanctuary" resolutions and hold rallies for the sole reason that it was what Virginia was doing. After all, we needed to "do something," right? As noted in Chapter 13, I told them we could either hold rallies or we could win elections, not both. I chose to win

elections rather than expending precious resources on rallies that felt good but accomplished nothing. The result? In stark contrast to other states during the dark days of the 2020 elections, we won, including several races with national significance.

7. **Manage burnout:** Have you noticed that this is the third time I've mentioned burnout? It is a big problem for activists. When it afflicts you (and it will), work through it by staying politically active and focusing on tasks you enjoy. Eventually, it will pass.

8. **Fire unsuitable people:** In volunteer organizations I direct, we joke that incompetence is punishable by promotion (explaining how I got to be president). In volunteerism, screw-ups are something you will have to accept. Bad attitude, however, is corrosive and must be eliminated. I've had two volunteers who bitched constantly. Nothing was ever good enough, other organizations did it better (they didn't), or we should be doing whatever *they* decided should be a priority. Those people I terminated from our leadership network summarily and without notice, saying, "Thanks for your help. Goodbye."

9. **Praise performance:** As a demanding taskmaster and perfectionist who expects people to perform superbly as a matter of course, this is my weak point (and I have lost volunteers because of it). Offer perks and "attaboys" for volunteers' achievements.

10. **Persevere:** You will sometimes lose. At points, the political environment in your state and your country will turn to sh-t. You will be demoralized. It will seem that our republic is lost. But suck it up, snowflake, and press on. Maybe the republic is dead, maybe not. But I can tell you one thing for sure: I'm not going down without a fight.

Managing legislative/election projects

In conducting issue campaigns, the extent to which a problem is controversial is *inversely* proportional to the ability of access-based lobbyists to solve it. The more controversial it is, the less likely it is that conventional lobbying can effectively address it.

Unfortunately, that's where you – the grassroots mobilization specialist – come into the picture. I say "unfortunately" because the big, ideologically compromised national groups will pass the easy stuff, leaving you to slug it out over what politicians will insist can't be done.

Worse, big national organizations ostensibly on your side may *oppose* you on controversial bills. Back in the 1990s, when some of us first began offering what eventually became known as "constitutional carry" legislation – which has so far become law in twenty-one states – NRA lobbyists reportedly actively worked to undermine the measure.

Problems to anticipate:

❑ Politicians selling you out
❑ People failing to follow through
❑ Hard work being the order of the day
❑ Hardship and adversity dogging you
❑ Fighting "conventional wisdom" from both politicians and people on your side

Picking fights

FACL teaches that political battles divide into three categories: survival, obligatory, and opportunity. The type of battle determines what proportion of your available resources you should devote to fighting it. All three types of battles share one thing in common. In each, your goal should be that your organization emerges from the fight stronger than before – if not in money, then in supporters, lists, and gravitas.

As eloquently expressed by "Dirty Harry" Callahan, "A man's got to know his limitations." Pick battles you can win. Additionally, in political action, like economic action, you should achieve maximum effect by concentrating your fire on a single target (or at least a limited number of targets) whenever possible.

The three types of political battles:

❑ **Survival battles:** This is a battle which, if lost, will debilitate either your organization or your cause. In the past, Rothfeld has said that very few battles are truly for survival. Given the existential threats to the right to keep and bear arms we have faced over the past three decades, however, I respectfully disagree. In fact, given the dramatic rise of "Wokeism" (Marxism) in the U.S. in recent years, I would argue that we face many such existential threats. As such, I err toward "balls to the wall," particularly in elections. Presuming an election is realistically winnable, having PAC money in the bank after losing it is like holding unexpended ammunition after losing a war (unless, of course, there are additional battles looming).

❏ **Obligatory battles:** These are battles to which you are committed, by virtue of affiliation or supporters' expectations, but don't present either an immediate threat or benefit to your organization or cause. As such, you should devote fewer of your precious resources to the fight. Over the years, various groups have asked for help in promoting Second Amendment rallies in Washington and elsewhere. Did we issue alerts telling people to attend? Yes. Did we organize transportation pools? Yes. Did I personally attend? Yes. But did we devote significant amounts of precious money and resources? Hell, no.

❏ **Opportunity battles:** These are battles in which either your organization or cause stands to gain. Most legislative battles fall into this category, and could be either offensive or defensive. The resources you devote should be directly proportional to its benefit if won or damage if lost. To determine that, FACL teaches an evaluative method known as the "Red Fox Four."

"Red Fox Four"

Although the name of this evaluative method sounds like a military acronym, the story goes that "Red Fox Four" (RF4) originated from the name of the drinking establishment in which conservative activists developed it. RF4 involves scoring potential projects on the criteria below. While useful, however, you should understand that because it relies on subjectively assigning values to the various measures (what psychologists call "free assessment"), it can be unintentionally biased to arrive at whatever conclusion you consciously *or unconsciously* want. One way to minimize unconscious bias is to solicit RF4 analysis *separately* from each member of your leadership – denying them a chance to compare notes with others – and average their answers.

Red Fox Four evaluation criteria:

❏ **Win _or_ lose:**

1. Just by fighting the fight, will it attract more money or people to my cause? (Rate +10 to -10)

2. Will it help friends or allies? (Rate +10 to -10)

3. Will it hurt enemies or their allies? (Rate +10 to -10)

   - Will it defund them?
   - Will it help beat them in the next election?

❏ **Win _and_ Lose:**

4. What is:

   - The value to policy if we win? (Rate 0 to +10)
   - The cost to liberty if we lose? (Rate 0 to -10)

Once you've scored each metric, add them up to determine a score. Although there is no hard-and-fast "good" score, the process forces you to think about whether a given project is worthwhile. Understand, too, that once started, a project's score can change with time or other variables, and should be re-evaluated as necessary. Start a spreadsheet and save the score for each evaluation. For an RF4 analysis of the "Medical Records Disclosure Act," see Appendix IV.

A coalition ... or not?

Coalitions with other organizations have the potential to create force-multipliers, as greater numbers of supporters deluge target politicians or corporations with channeled input.

In 2013, for example, we forged a highly effective coalition of thirty-nine state and national organizations to kill S. 649 for so-called "universal background checks." Our message to politicians in all states was that if they voted for the bill, even the NRA would not be able to protect them in the next election. Our message to the NRA leadership was that we would bleed them of money and members if they supported the so-called "Toomey-Manchin compromise." We motivated the NRA to back off the "compromise" and the bill died shortly thereafter.

Other advantages to forging coalitions include access to mailing lists, email lists, newsletter space, or politicians with whom the coalition partner is close. It gives you access to people who might not otherwise know your organization. Moreover, forging the coalition might be newsworthy and tends to scare the hell out of politicians.

Disadvantages to forging coalitions include inheriting problems of the coalition partner (e.g. enemies, scandals, or credibility issues), that they are likely no better funded than you are, and that you will be at least somewhat beholden to their agenda, which may be significantly different from yours. If they use an access-based lobbying model instead of grassroots mobilization, problems multiply.

Coalitions with left-wing organizations present a host of additional complications. On one hand, when both ends of the political spectrum unite on an issue, it leaves politicians trapped in the middle with no place to hide. On the other hand, you might be giving them (or any leftist organization *they* partner with) valuable information to defeat you on other issues. You might also draw fire from your own supporters.

Suffice to say you should examine carefully any partner with whom you are thinking of getting into bed. If they have meetings, attend some. Approach them quietly, one-on-one, find out who they are beholden to (e.g. donors, other groups, and politicians), and carefully monitor their policy positions, their leadership, and other potentially subtle hazards. You can share voter lists with them, but do not share your membership or contributor lists.

Cautionary tale on coalitions with the left

Back in the 1990s, a national organization fostered coalitions between state-level groups and leftist organizations to kill the "Exclusionary Rule Reform Act of 1995" (which drew the bill number H.R. 666, if you can believe that), that would have allowed use of illegally gathered evidence in criminal cases. My organization forged a coalition with the state American Civil Liberties Union (ACLU), writing a joint position against the bill.

(continued on next page)

241

(continued from previous page)

The good news is that we killed H.R. 666. The bad news is that my coalition "partner" Deborah Ross, who headed the state ACLU, used the power she gained to run for state house where she promptly became a serious thorn in our side. Happily, we used her obstructionism as Judiciary Committee Chair to take out the Democrat House Majority Leader. When she later ran for the U.S. Senate, we defeated her. But then she ran for and was elected to the U.S. House in a district drawn for leftists, making her undefeatable. Was it worth it? In retrospect, perhaps not.

References:

1. Richardson, H.L., *Confrontational Politics*, Gun Owners Foundation, 1998, p.33
2. Foundation for Applied Conservative Leadership, https://facl-training.org/

Chapter 15
Creating & Maintaining Grassroots Organizations

Joe Politician says, "I'd rather receive one well-written letter than a thousand emails" not because he believes in the virtue of writing letters, but because he fears the organization implied by receiving a thousand emails.

People are power. As a lone activist, your leverage is negligible. With a few thousands of what Pat Buchanan called "peasants with pitchforks" at your back, however, you can change the world. The question becomes how to organize those peasants and keep them at your back – something you can do only with an enduring organization.

As always, understand that I am neither a lawyer nor a CPA. Nothing which follows constitutes legal advice. You will need to research Internal Revenue Service (IRS), Federal Election Commission (FEC), and state requirements to ensure you are complying with the law. For example, the FEC publishes a campaign guide for nonconnected committees[1] and your state board of elections (SBE) will publish a similar guide. Get them and scrupulously adhere to them.

Consider too that IRS, FEC, and SBE regulations change with each election cycle, meaning: (1) What you read here could change; and (2) What you know to be true in one election cycle could get you a violation in the next.

Types of political organizations

Different types of organizations can legally do different things, meaning the type of organization you create is determined by your objective. I won't lie: creating tax-sheltered non-profit or not-for profit organizations isn't easy. As demonstrated during the Obama administration, the IRS has been known to discriminate against conservative organizations by denying IRS letters of exemption (although in fairness, I haven't heard of any recent cases).

Simplifying matters slightly, we will discuss three types of political organizations commonly used to influence public policy: political action committees, 501(c)(3) non-profit organizations, and 501(c)(4) not-for-profit organizations. There are others, but these are the ones most relevant to you. As mentioned in Chapter 11, most serious political players operate all three.

What all political organizations must to do survive

Regardless of the type of political organization you choose to create, all political organizations must to the following to survive and thrive:

- ❏ Attract new members or supporters
- ❏ Be perceived as powerful
- ❏ Get media coverage
- ❏ Inspire supporters
- ❏ Build internal morale
- ❏ Provide a public role of dominance for their leadership
- ❏ Deliver value to contributors

Political action committee (PAC)

Typically used to advocate or oppose political candidates, PACs are the simplest and cheapest type of political organization to create. Regulated by the IRS under Internal Revenue Code (IRC) 527, their primary purpose, according to the IRS, is to engage in "exempt functions" such as "…influencing or attempting to influence the selection, nomination, election, or appointment of any individual to any Federal, State, or local public office or office in a political organization…"[2]

Why PACs are poor choices for legislative operations

As noted in Chapter 11, PACs are often the first refuge of scoundrels, who use them to raise untaxable money on the appearance of being active in a cause while actually siphoning off money to contractors (e.g. consultants or mailing houses) they operate themselves, very much on a for-profit basis.

That is not to say legitimate groups don't operate PACs. Every political organization should have a PAC to put "teeth" into its legislative agenda via election operations. Additionally, creating a PAC allows a vehicle for fledgling activists to get started. In the category of political action, however, it should not be a long-term vehicle for legislative (as opposed to election) operations; although the PAC may engage in functions which are not "exempt functions" (i.e. advocating election or defeat of candidates), non-exempt functions such as advocating legislation may not be its "primary activity."

Basic PAC concepts and requirements

Federal elections are controlled by the Federal Election Commission (FEC), while state elections are controlled by individual state boards of election (SBEs). Each will have unique donation limits, reporting schedules and disclosure requirements, with the ostensible goal of transparent reporting of donors and beneficiaries.

No application for tax exemption from the IRS is required to form a PAC, nor is a PAC required to incorporate. Although PAC income for exempt functions (i.e. expenses directly related to influencing elections) is not taxable, the PAC may owe taxes for *non*-exempt functions. The two fundamental ways PACs influence elections are via either independent expenditures or campaign donations. You will see several commonly used terms for PACs, including:

❏ **Campaign contribution:** Anything of value made to (or in coordination with) a candidate to support or oppose the nomination or election of one or more clearly identified candidates; or to a political committee, political party, affiliated party committee, or a referendum committee, whether or not made in an election year. Included are "in-kind" contributions, which are non-monetary contributions such as goods or services. (A common example is sharing mailing lists.) Both the FEC and SBEs specify maximum campaign contribution limits, either by election cycle (e.g. primary, general, special, runoff) or by calendar year.

❏ **Disclosure legends:** Print media, television and radio advertisements purchased by a political committee must have a statement stipulating who paid for the ad, the candidate benefiting, and whether or not it was authorized by the candidate. Because the

FEC and SBEs have unique requirements for verbiage and (if print media) font size, you must check specifics for the race in which you are advertising.

❏ **Expenditure:** Any purchase, transfer of funds, payment, gift, or anything of value whatsoever, whether or not made in an election year, to support or oppose the nomination, election, or passage of one or more clearly identified candidates or ballot measures.

❏ **Independent expenditure:** An expenditure for a communication that expressly advocates the election or defeat of a clearly identified candidate and which is not made in coordination with any candidate. Provided they are not coordinated with candidates, independent expenditures are not considered campaign contributions.

❏ **Report:** PACs are required to report contributions and expenditures on a set schedule. Information reported on contributors typically includes name, mailing address, occupation, contribution amount, and date of contribution. For expenditures, the treasurer must typically report the name and address of payees, amounts paid, purpose, and date. Be aware that the left increasingly uses these disclosures to "doxx" donors. Methods for minimizing that risk include manipulating the timing of PAC reports, or using 501(c)(4) "dark money" for election operations within the IRS limits described below.

❏ **Treasurer:** Each PAC requires a treasurer who is responsible for adherence to applicable regulations as well as reporting contributions and expenditures.

Connected vs. nonconnected PACs

Political Action Committees can either be "connected committees" or "nonconnected committees." Connected PACs are established by businesses, non-profits, labor unions, trade groups, or health organizations and raise money from a "restricted class," which in the case of non-profits generally comprises organization members.

What you want instead is a "nonconnected PAC," which is a political committee that is *not* a party committee, an authorized committee of a candidate, or a separate segregated fund established by a corporation or labor organization.

❑ **Advantage of nonconnected PAC:** The very large upside is that you may take donations from people other than the limited universe of your members. This is vital to raise enough money to impact big races.

❑ **Disadvantage of nonconnected PAC:** The downside is that if your PAC uses services from your main political organization (e.g. supplies, rent, telephone, or printing), if you have one, the FEC treats it as an "in-kind contribution." And if your main organization is incorporated as a non-profit organization (which it should be), contributions from corporations to PACs are generally prohibited. (Some legal or administrative expenses may be exempt from the restriction.) The best way to address this is to have your PAC scrupulously document reimbursement of all expenditures made on its behalf. A sponsoring organization may also loan money to a nonconnected PAC, but loans are subject to calendar year contribution limits.[3]

The two relevant types of PACs

Although the FEC classifies several subcategories of political action committees, the two that matter most to you as an activist (not a candidate) are:

❑ **Traditional PACs:** A "traditional" nonconnected PAC may make contributions (either monetary or "in-kind") to candidates subject, of course, to state and federal contribution limits. However, I consider candidate donations to be an inefficient vehicle for election operations which may actually come back to bite you if the candidate "re-gifts" your money to another, potentially hostile candidate. Far better than candidate donations, traditional PACs can also make *unlimited* "independent expenditures" – mailings, Robocalls, email, etc. – for or against candidates provided the expenditures are not "coordinated" with the candidate who benefits. By using independent expenditures, PACs can funnel more money into a given race than donation limits would otherwise allow.

Traditional PAC characteristics:

- Donation limits per SBE or FEC requirements (currently $5,000/ year for FEC, SBE limits vary)
- No corporate, federal contractor, or foreign national contributions
- Must disclose donors over $200 (FEC) or per state limits
- May conduct unlimited independent expenditures for or against candidates
- May not coordinate Independent expenditures with candidates who benefit
- May contribute to candidates and other PACs within FEC or state limits
- May coordinate with candidates provided services reported as monetary or in-kind donations
- Must file reports of donations and expenditures per state or FEC requirements

❏ **Independent expenditure-only PACs:** Also called "Super PACs," this type can accept unlimited donations and may accept corporate donations, but may not donate to candidates. Super PACs are limited to conducting only independent expenditures for or against candidates.

Super PAC characteristics:

- May conduct unlimited independent expenditures for or against candidates
- May not donate to candidates
- May not coordinate with candidates
- May accept unlimited donations from individuals, corporations, or unions
- Must disclose donors over $200
- Must report donations and expenditures to FEC

Forming a PAC

Having a legislative organization without a PAC is like having laws without jails. Absent a mechanism for enforcing good behavior, the inevitable result is bad behavior. Whether you create a state PAC or a federal PAC depends on the causes and offices for which you plan to be active, but my general rule of thumb is that when in doubt, go federal.

Forming a PAC is relatively simple. The more difficult task is keeping up with reporting and regulatory requirements. Below are steps to form a federal PAC. State PACs will have similar requirements. For detailed federal PAC requirements, see the FEC document "Nonconnected Committees."[4] Basic steps to form a federal PAC include:

1. **File Statement of Organization with the FEC or state board of elections**[5]: The FEC currently requires you to register within ten days of contributions or expenditures exceeding $1,000 per calendar year.

2. **Appoint a treasurer:** The treasurer is responsible for:

    - Filing complete and accurate reports and statements on time
    - Signing all reports and statements
    - Depositing receipts in the committee's designated bank *within 10 days of receipt*
    - Authorizing expenditures or appointing an agent to authorize expenditures
    - Monitoring contributions to ensure compliance with applicable limits
    - Keeping the required records of receipts and disbursements

3. **Get an Employer Identification Number:** You may obtain an Employer Identification Number online or by completing IRS Form SS-4. For questions about obtaining a taxpayer identification number, call the Internal Revenue Service, 1-800-829-3676.

4. **Set up a bank account:** The FEC requires an official depository. If covering both state and federal elections, you have the option of setting up a single account and using federal limits, or setting up two accounts: one for state and one for federal races. The latter option, however, presents the complication of allocating costs between the two accounts.

Dirty PAC tricks

Like everything else in politics, all is not necessarily what it seems. Political operatives sometimes form what I call "dirty tricks PACs," typically super PACs, which attack candidates over issues which may have little or nothing to do with their true motives. (Remember "problem" versus "issue" in Chapter 10?)

One of the more egregious examples happened in the 2020 primary and runoff elections for North Carolina's 11th Congressional District, where a super PAC calling itself "Fix Congress Now!" attacked Lynda Bennett, the candidate endorsed by outgoing conservative incumbent Mark Meadows as his successor when he left to become Donald Trump's chief of staff. In the heavily Republican district, the primary would likely determine who went to Washington.

Taking secretly recorded comments utterly out of context, however, "Fix Congress Now!" spent big bucks viciously attacking Bennett for being a "never Trumper" in mailings and TV commercials. So "Fix Congress Now!" was run by Trump advocates, right?

Wrong. In what is best described as a "false flag" operation,[6] the shadowy Colorado-based super PAC was actually run by centrist R.I.N.O.s ("Republicans in Name Only") who in multiple races opposed true conservatives backed by the U.S. House Freedom Caucus,[7] a conservative element of the House which actually helped unseat R.I.N.O Speaker John Boehner. Ultimately, Bennett lost in the runoffs, albeit to conservative Madison Cawthorn.

Part of the game for dirty tricks PACs lies in hiding who is funding it by manipulating the timing of donations or transfers from other PACs until after disclosure deadlines. To avoid such manipulation, my state instituted a 48-hour reporting requirement for PAC donations over $1,000, but ways can still be found to delay disclosure.[8]

Non-profit organizations

The IRS recognizes a variety of tax exempt organizations, but the two most relevant to you as a conservative activist are those chartered under sections 501(c)(3) and 501(c)(4) of the Internal Revenue Code. Each has advantages and disadvantages. Hereafter, we will refer to them as c3s and c4s.

What they share in common is that no earnings may pass to shareholders or individuals, instead staying with the organization to fund its exempt purpose. That does not, however, mean they can't pay officers, some of whom certain dubious non-profits pay handsomely (such as United Way's Brian Gallagher at $1,578,515 or the $5,110,985 paid by the NRA to Wayne LaPierre in 2014).

501(c)(3) non-profits[9]

Typically called "non-profit" or "charitable" organizations, c3 organizations have the advantage of not only being exempt from state and federal income tax, but donations are also tax deductible, making it easier to raise money from donors who itemize taxes and deductions. In theory, c3s are limited to approved "exempt purposes" which limit their use as political organizations. As you will see below, however, leftist organizations are fond of stretching that tenet – something you, too, can do if you have the chutzpah.

Because we are dealing with impacting public policy, what follows are only the relevant items for your purposes. If some of the IRS criteria are, at best, muddy, I can only say, "Welcome to the wonderful world of political non-profits."

What c3s <u>may</u> do:

❏ **Education:** Because the IRS lists as education functions "lessening the burdens of government" and "defending human and civil rights secured by law", you may "educate" others – including lawmakers – on those issues. So what qualifies as "education"? As usual, the IRS is silent on the issue. Happily, the Congressional Research Service[10] delved into the issue, detailing the IRS "methodology test" and saying the IRS may determine something *not* to be educational if:

- The material distributed are unsupported by facts

- Facts purporting to document the group's position are distorted
- Substantial use of inflammatory or disparaging terms which are emotionally based
- The approach is "not aimed at developing the audience's understanding of the subject matter"

❏ **Legal action:** Presuming you are not running a legal aid organization, the question becomes what type of legal action is acceptable to the IRS? The answer is "a charitable purpose to promote social welfare by defending 'human and civil rights secured by law.' Therefore, organizations, whose purpose is to provide representation to others (or to institute litigation as a party plaintiff) in cases involving the defense of human and civil rights, may be considered charitable organizations for purposes of IRC 501(c)(3)."[11] In practice, this tends to be broadly construed, but the litigation must serve a public rather than a private interest. For example, I have used litigation on Second Amendment issues any number of times against cities, sheriffs, an agriculture commissioner, and a sitting governor. Using a c3 to sue over a property dispute, however, might be construed as not for a "charitable purpose."

What c3s may not do:

❏ **C3s cannot be "action" organizations:** Influencing passage or defeat of legislation may not be "a substantial part of its activities," but you can use a c3 for at least some measure of legislative advocacy. Says the IRS, "A 501(c)(3) organization may engage in some lobbying, but too much lobbying activity risks loss of tax-exempt status."[12] How much is "too much"? Good question. The IRS does not clearly define that phrase, instead relying on "facts and circumstances" determination. That said, the IRS also says: "Organizations may, however, involve themselves in issues of public policy without the activity being considered as lobbying. For example, organizations may conduct educational meetings, prepare and distribute educational materials, or otherwise consider public policy issues in an educational manner without jeopardizing their tax-exempt status."[13]

❏ **C3s cannot do electioneering:** You may not use the c3 for advocating the election or defeat of candidates in any way. There is no muddiness here: It is a hard-and-fast rule. Says the IRS, "501(c)(3) organizations are absolutely prohibited from directly or indirectly participating in, or intervening in, any political campaign on behalf of (or in opposition to) any candidate for elective public office."[14]

A downside to c3s?

Until 2018, *all* nonprofit organizations were required to file a Form 990 Schedule B and disclose identifying information for donors of $5,000 or more to the IRS, which considered donor lists for c3 organizations to be public record, meaning names of members or supporters could be subject to public disclosure.

On the other hand, the IRS was *prohibited* from disclosing donors to *c4* organizations (as well as 501(c)(5) and (c)(6) organizations not relevant to this discussion). Although c4s had to report donors on Schedule B of their Form 990s, donor lists were not considered public record.

Given that many conservatives value privacy (and given that leftists are fond of doxxing conservatives), using a c3 as a primary organization stood to severely depress donations as well as limiting the ability to conduct legislative advocacy as described above. Consequently (and for additional reasons below), it was common to use a c4 as a main legislative organization, reserving c3s for the exempt activities listed above.

However, this drawback of c3s was mitigated by a May 28, 2020 change in regulations which no longer require c4s to report donors, and shield disclosure of c3 donors until they have contributed at least $5,000. In fact, even the $5,000 reporting requirement will probably not apply to you, since you are likely running a "public charity" rather than a "foundation" which relies on a single-source endowment. [15]

501(c)(4) not-for-profits

There are a variety of not-for-profit organizations recognized by the IRS, but the type most useful to political activists is the 501(c)(4), considered by the IRS to be a "social welfare" organization. Most major legislative organizations are chartered as c4s.

To be tax-exempt as a social welfare organization described in Internal Revenue Code (IRC) section 501(c)(4), an organization must not be organized for profit and must be operated exclusively to promote social welfare. The earnings of a c4 organization may not pass to any private shareholder or individual.

The primary advantage of a c4 is that lobbying (what I prefer to call "legislative advocacy") may be the primary activity of the organization. The bad news is that although the organization itself is tax exempt, donations are not tax deductible.

Another big advantage is that unlike the c3, a c4 does not have to publicly disclose donors or members. You still have to file a Form 990 for general financial disclosure, but the privacy of members is kept from the prying eyes of leftists.

What c4s <u>may</u> do:

❏ **Advocate passage or defeat of legislation:** The IRS recognizes "action" organizations dedicated to advocacy as a legitimate goal of c4s[16]. This is the most common activity for c4s, and is the reason it should be your main organization.

❏ **Advocate election or defeat of candidates:** A c4 may also endorse or work to elect or defeat political candidates, provided it is not the organization's "primary" activity. However, this must be done via independent expenditures, not coordination with or donation to candidates, which is prohibited by both the FEC and IRS. Nor may what you do be an "in-kind" donation (e.g. giving use of mailing lists) to candidates. The problem is that the IRS refuses to clearly define what constitutes a "primary" activity. Some have construed it to be more than half of gross expenditures, but that is by no means a concrete definition. Nor does the IRS define exactly what constitute campaign activities, instead claiming to rely on the same sort of vague "facts and circumstances" determination as it does for "primary activity." That said, actions commonly construed as campaign activities include[17]:

- Supporting or opposing ballot measures;
- Endorsing federal and state candidates;

- Distributing communications to the general public – including through get out the vote (GOTV) activities, voter registration drives, billboards, broadcast ads – or to the organization's membership in support or opposition to federal or state candidates. The organization can even encourage voters to vote for or against a specific federal or state candidate;
- Asking federal and state candidates to pledge to support the organization's issues if elected; and
- Producing candidate voter guides or comparisons of where state and federal candidates stand on issues.

What c4s may not do:

❏ **Make a profit for individuals:** In theory, proceeds may not pass to individuals. However, nothing precludes the organization from paying its executives handsomely. Ask the NRA's Wayne LaPierre.

❏ **Advocate candidates as "primary" activity:** See above. Incidentally, "non-scientific" polling designed to influence elections (often called "push polls") are construed by the IRS as campaign activity for the purposes of determining whether it comprises the organization's "primary" activity.

❏ **Be aligned with a political party:** Your c4 must be non-partisan. If the c4's activities are construed as intended to benefit a particular political party, it may be denied tax exemption.

Should you use a c3 or a c4?

So given limited resources, which type of organization should you create first? IRC 501(c)(3) and (c)(4) organizations differ primarily by the following: In exchange for allowing donors to write off donations on their federal income tax, c3 organizations are more limited in what they may do. As "charitable" organizations, they are limited in how much legislative advocacy they may do, and they are absolutely prohibited from engaging in express advocacy for or against candidates.

Because c4 organizations can do legislative advocacy and at least limited express advocacy – and especially in an era when deductibility of donations means less because fewer people itemize taxes – you will generally be better off starting with a c4 "social welfare" organization, then creating a political action committee, and finally adding a c3 as the need arises.

Starting a political non-profit

Although I know people who have done the application process for non-profit status themselves, my general recommendation is to bite the bullet and hire a lawyer specializing in non-profits. It will save you time and headaches, and is less likely to result in the IRS rejecting your application.

Harbor Compliance puts out a state-by-state list of requirements and costs.[18] If you decide to do it yourself, the site also provides guidance and templates for things like articles of incorporation. You can also find information from the National Council of Non-Profits, which can be found at www.councilofnonprofits.org.

IRS Letter of Determination

Once you've jumped through all the hoops to create your political non-profit/not-for-profit organization, your prize is an IRS "Letter of Determination," which is the official, written documentation of IRS approval of a nonprofit's request for 501(c), tax-exempt status. Issued on IRS letterhead, the Letter of Determination includes the organization's legal name and trade name (if applicable), EIN number, and effective date of 501(c) status. In addition, it stipulates exactly which subsection of Internal Revenue Code 501(c) that the approval is granted under.

Using disclosure requirements to damage enemies

In the early 2000s, the usual lobbyists for our state gun control organization suddenly showed up purporting to represent "Americans for Gun Safety."

Research by one of my volunteers, however, found they actually registered for "The Tsunami Fund" which was itself part of the Tides Center, a byzantine labyrinth of radical organizations operating from the Presidio in San Francisco run by a leftist agitator named Drummond Pike. In truth, "Americans for Gun Safety" didn't exist at all, but was instead a non-profit money laundering vehicle (see below) for billionaire Andrew McKelvey of monster.com.

(continued on next page)

(continued from previous page)

We used the information to run a scorched earth campaign against both the gun control group and its bureaucrat supporters, neatly suppressing them for nearly a decade.

Non-profit financial disclosure requirements

The price for either c3 or c4 status is that you might have to disclose your finances to the public. If a c3, names of individual donors may be subject to release. If a c4, only general finances are subject to release. The mechanism for doing so is an IRS Form 990, "Return of Organization Exempt From Income Tax," and the threshold above which filing a Form 990 is required is currently $50,000.

Below the $50,000 threshold, you can file a Form 990-N electronic notice or "e-postcard." If your gross receipts are below $200,000 and your total assets are below $500,000, you can file a Form 990-EZ. Above those thresholds you must file a standard Form 990. A nonprofit's Form 990 must be filed with the IRS on the 15th day of the 5th month after the close of the nonprofit's fiscal year.

Incidentally, the corollary here is that you should research your political opponents, finding out who the officers are, who contributes (if available), how much, and what they spend money on. The best means of doing so is GuideStar, which allows you a free membership and maintains a list of non-profits, mission statements, and Form 990s at https://www.guidestar.org/NonprofitDirectory.aspx

You would be amazed at what you can find in terms of dirt on your opponents. In fact, you might find enough information to damage or destroy them. (See sidebar "Using disclosure requirements to damage enemies.")

But this, too, has a corollary: tax-exempt nonprofits are required to provide copies, upon request, of their three most recently filed annual Form 990s and their application for tax-exemption. That means your opponents can use your Form 990 to dig for dirt or evidence of non-compliance *on you*. Again, comply carefully with all IRS requirements, and think carefully before taking actions that could become public knowledge.

Other requirements

To avoid giving your opponents a weapon to use against you, your organization must rigorously comply with all state and federal requirements. If you plan to operate beyond state borders, you will have to comply with the requirements of each state within which you operate (e.g. charitable solicitation licenses for fundraising).

In the same vein, if you suspect your opposition isn't complying, immediately file a complaint with the appropriate regulatory agency. It might or might not amount to much, but, as I always say, any day you can piss off a leftist can't be all bad.

Depending on your state, the following may be required:

❏ File articles of incorporation with your secretary of state
❏ Apply for a charitable solicitation license
❏ Apply for state tax exemption
❏ Apply for sales tax exemption (if you plan to raise money by selling merchandise)
❏ Register as lobbyist

Non-profit "money laundering"

For reasons for deductibility, some high-dollar donors will only contribute to c3s, which has created a burgeoning industry in what I call "non-profit money laundering" wherein deductible donations go into the c3 arm of the organization and somehow come out of the c4 arm to be used for legislative advocacy. This "dark money" advocacy is a highly popular tactic of the left, for whom leftist billionaires are common contributors.

References:

1. "Nonconnected Committees," Federal Election Commission, May, 2008, https://www.fec.gov/resources/cms-content/documents/nongui.pdf
2. "IRC 527 – Political Organizations," Internal Revenue Service, https://www.irs.gov/pub/irs-tege/eotopici89.pdf

3. "Support From Sponsoring Organizations," Federal Election Commission," https://www.fec.gov/help-candidates-and-committees/making-disbursements-pac/support-sponsoring-organization-nonconnected-pac/

4. Op. cit., note 1.

5. "Registration and Reporting Forms, Political Parties and Political Action Committees (PACs)," Internal Revenue Service, https://www.fec.gov/help-candidates-and-committees/forms/

6. "Fake News in NC-11: 'Never-Trumper' Videos and WNC Congressional Republican Primary Drama," *First in Freedom Daily*, February 27, 2020, https://firstinfreedomdaily.com/fake-news-in-nc-11-never-trumper-videos-and-wnc-congressional-republican-primary-drama/

7. Fix Congress Now! PAC Profile, OpenSecrets.org, https://www.opensecrets.org/outsidespending/detail.php?cmte=C00735670&cycle=2020

8. Maggie Severns, "'Oh that's cool — do that!': Super PACs use new trick to hide donors," *Politico*, August 17, 2018, https://www.politico.com/story/2018/08/17/super-pacs-hidden-donors-disclosures-741795

9. "Exemption Requirements - 501(c)(3) Organizations," Internal Revenue Service, https://www.irs.gov/charities-non-profits/charitable-organizations/exemption-requirements-501c3-organizations

10. Erika K. Lunder, "501(c)(3) Organizations: What Qualifies as 'Educational'?", Congressional Research Service, August 21, 2012, https://fas.org/sgp/crs/misc/R42673.pdf

11. "Litigation By IRC 501(C)(3) Organizations," https://www.irs.gov/pub/irs-tege/eotopicd84.pdf

12. "Lobbying: Charities and Non-Profits," https://www.irs.gov/charities-non-profits/lobbying

13. Ibid.

14. "The Restriction of Political Campaign Intervention by Section 501(c)(3) Tax-Exempt Organizations," Internal Revenue Service, https://www.irs.gov/charities-non-profits/charitable-organizations/the-restriction-of-political-campaign-intervention-by-section-501c3-tax-exempt-organizations

15. "New IRS Rule Allows Many Nonprofits to Withhold Donor Information From the IRS," *Insights*, Nosman LLP, May 28, 2020, https://www.nossaman.com/newsroom-insights-new-irs-rule-allows-many-nonprofits-to-withhold-donor-iInformation-from-the-IRS

16. Raymond Chick, and Amy Henchey, "M. Political Organizations and IRC 501(c)(4)," Internal Revenue Service, https://www.irs.gov/pub/irs-tege/eotopicm95.pdf

17. "Election Year Activities for 501(c)(4) Social Welfare Organizations," Bolder Advocacy, https://bolderadvocacy.org/wp-content/uploads/2012/05/Election_Year_Activities_for_501c4_Social_Welfare_Organizations.pdf

18. "How to Start a Nonprofit Organization," Harbor Compliance, https://www.harborcompliance.com/information/how-to-start-a-non-profit-organization

Chapter 16
Conducting Effective Grassroots Mobilization

"The power of the people is much stronger than the people in power." — Wael Ghonim, Internet activist and founder of Parlio

Having discussed how to make levers for moving public policy and what pressure needs to be applied to move those levers, let's now discuss how to apply maximum possible pressure. Pardon the mixed metaphors, but your job is to act as a lightning rod, drawing energy from the electorate and conducting it to politicians who need to feel the shock.

People are power. The more people you can get to respond to your call, the stronger you will be. But who are the "people" you need to mobilize? Like the 50% + 1 myth of election operations (see Chapter 11), the notion that you need to mobilize a majority of the population is both impossible and wrong. In truth, having one hundred dedicated followers trumps ten thousand lukewarm sympathizers every time. The left learned that a couple of generations ago and have been using it to their advantage ever since. (Which is precisely why your child is receiving "LGBTQIA+" literature in elementary school.) That said, however, the more truly dedicated supporters you can mobilize, the more effective you will be.

Three essentials of grassroots mobilization:

❏ **Capable organizing:** Beyond the obvious need for good leadership, grassroots organizations need dedicated volunteers who work well together. And as much as I have denounced predatory fundraising, legitimate fundraising is vital to success.

❏ **Effective messaging:** To mobilize the "peasants with pitchforks," you need to both reach and inspire them. When communicating with politicians, you must be taken seriously, which requires conveying the persona of a serious person on serious business. When communicating with the media, your message must be one they cannot ignore. All three require clear and convincing communications.

❏ **Accurate targeting:** To effect change, you have to target the people making decisions in ways that will change their behavior. If, despite reading earlier chapters, you think this involves "educating" the politician to persuade him of the strength of your argument, I fear there may be nothing I can do for you. Remember rats in a Skinner Box? (Chapter 7.) Changing a target's behavior involves appropriately applying positive reinforcement and punishment. Period. If it isn't working, it means only that you aren't using the right motivators.

Grassroots organizing

Leadership, baby. It's all about leadership. (See Chapter 14.) But it's important to remember that those qualities should apply not just to you, but also to others you pick to lead your organization. (Exception: I will take a marginally competent volunteer who shows up over a talented no-show any day.)

Recruiting and managing people

As someone who has alternately been called "type A plus" and "a pain in the ass," managing volunteers isn't something at which I am intuitively good. That said, I've made a study of it sufficiently that most of my core volunteers have stayed with me for a decade or more, and a few since the inception of the organization nearly thirty years ago.

Top ten tips for managing volunteers:

❏ **Search for talent:** Treat grassroots leadership as a constant talent search. Regard every meeting with a simpatico individual as a potential recruitment. I once got a call from two people who wanted advice on how to start their own activist project. I said, "Let's have lunch." By the end of lunch, they were working for me (and ended up being two of the best volunteers I have recruited in decades). When I encounter someone at a seminar with potential, I chat them up. If they look good, I pitch them.

- **Pick cohesive leadership:** As a (God help me) union member, I often said that if the egoists of union leadership spent half as much energy fighting management as they did each other, we would own the world. Avoiding infighting doesn't mean recruiting only "yes men," but it does mean that if you have someone in your leadership network in whose Kindergarten file are written the words "Does not play well with other children," get rid of him. Immediately.

- **Delegate:** Perhaps you think you are the only person who can do things to your satisfaction, but you are going to have to delegate anyway. Trying to do everything yourself will burn you out in fairly short order. Also, volunteers are like muscles. The more frequently they are exercised, the stronger they become. Conversely, the less frequently they are used, the more they atrophy. Frankly, I sometimes delegate to certain volunteers just to keep them active.

- **Give people tasks they like:** Early on, I needed a volunteer to manage our membership database and also had a woman who wanted to help, but wasn't especially well versed in database management. I let my needs trump hers and talked her into doing it. After a few months of mediocre performance, she disappeared, nearly crippling my organization. Lesson? If volunteers don't like something, they won't do it, so don't ask.

- **Lead your troops into battle:** Like cavalry commanders who led horseback charges, your volunteers need to see you on the front lines. (Ordinarily, I'd say the good news is that you're less likely to get shot in the process, but given today's leftists, you never know.) I work gun shows, work with the legislative team at the General Assembly, and try to be a presence at rallies and demonstrations even though I live several hours away. Yes, I have capable volunteers who can handle all of those things; but for inspiration, they need to see me doing the things I ask of them.

- **Recognize volunteer contributions:** Frankly, I'm not good enough at this, and I have lost good people because of it. If you aren't paying people, you had better acknowledge their contributions. It's easy to take your volunteers for granted. Don't. We started a "volunteer of the month" program, recognizing the contributions of one person each month and rewarding them, however humbly, with a challenge coin unique to our organization.

❏ **Acknowledge that people have lives:** I tell people who volunteer that I understand they have families, jobs, and other commitments. If something prevents them from doing a task, I ask only that they notify us immediately in order to find someone else to fill the role.

❏ **Keep ego out of it:** If you are contemplating running a grassroots organization, even money says you are not the humblest person in the room. You might find it hard not to make press recognition and political victories all about you. Do so anyway, at least if you want a team to help you. The reality is that volunteers abandon glory-grabbers. In fact, whenever a volunteer or supporter says what a great job I did, I make it a point to say, "We couldn't possibly have accomplished it without the dedicated support of people like you."

❏ **Take input:** Yes, people will give you lots of stupid ideas. After a few years of running political organizations, you will start thinking that your instincts are better than most – and you might be right. But to keep your people involved – and to get ideas you might not have had – listen thoughtfully and carefully to suggestions offered, no matter how dumb they might at first appear.

❏ **Nurture talent:** As a grassroots leader, your job is to attract and train as many talented people as possible. Reward them with more work and responsibility. The tricky part comes when you've trained some "young stud" who now thinks he knows more than you do and challenges your authority. I can't give you hard-and-fast rules for such challenges, except that you should avoid firing aggressive-but-talented volunteers whenever possible.

Creating grassroots organizations

As outlined in Chapter 15, your primary legislative vehicle should be chartered under IRC 501(c)(4) as a not-for-profit organization, allowing you unlimited legislative advocacy and limited express advocacy. You should simultaneously create either a state-level or federal political action committee (PAC), depending on the scope of your activism. (When in doubt, create a federal PAC.) Once you have those two in place, you may or may not wish to create a 501(c)(3) non-profit educational and legal arm, giving you a means for raising tax-deductible donations.

Naming organizations

In Chapter 10, I admonished, "The 'problem' is what you want to solve; the 'issue' is how you frame the debate to solve the problem. Frame the issue to maximize your core constituency of support."

The same holds true for naming your organization. When the lakefront residents of Sherrills Ford, NC needed to kill a sewage treatment plant slated for the community, we didn't call it "Sherrills Ford Residents Against the Plant," we called it "Concerned Citizens of Lake Norman" and did fundraising along all 520 miles of lake shoreline. Because the issue was sewage discharge into the lake rather than a single plant, we raised money for litigation from a far broader constituency.

In naming political organizations, keep the name broad enough to encompass future projects, clever enough to be remembered, and evocative enough to make people care. If you can make it a clever, memorable acronym, so much the better.

Developing a mission statement

Think long and hard about this one, since it will form the basis of your application for non-profit status, including what the IRS considers to be your permissible exempt activities. It will also be considered by the United States Postal Service (USPS) in deciding whether to approve the non-profit bulk mail permit you will need in order to mail at reduced rates. (See Chapter 17.) A concise mission statement clearly defines the specific goals of your organization and tells potential supporters what you stand for. It will also help you stay focused on your objectives and serve as a metric for success.

Together with the mission statement, write a detailed business plan for your political non-profit, just as you would with a for-profit entity. Similarly, every project should start with a project plan stipulating objectives, methods, and required resources.

Marketing your organization

Consider who you are appealing to. Develop a credo or mission statement which both expresses your cause and speaks to likely supporters. For example, I chose "Armatissimi e liberissimi" for my organization, which was first spoken by Niccolo Machiavelli with reference to the universally armed and, therefore, unconquerable Swiss. It means "most armed, most free," which precisely expresses our organizational philosophy. Some have complained that Machiavelli said it not in Latin, but rather Italian, but that is part of our message: Machiavelli was the father of modern power politics – politics we continue to use to defend our rights to this day. (And yes, the fact that I am of Italian heritage didn't hurt either.)

Design or have designed a distinctive logo, with either its name in stylized font or a symbol representing your goals, which is visually appealing and conveys your mission. Avoid clichés. When I see a gun rights organization with a Minute Man in the logo, what I see is lack of imagination.

In designing a logo, consider that a black and white (or grayscale) logo can be more easily reproduced. Incorporating a symbol of importance to your issue might galvanize support. Ours is a snarling Pit Bull with the Constitution clenched between his teeth, daring anyone to try and take it. It gets the message across. Incidentally, avoid mimicking corporate logos that are registered trademarks, and consider trademarking yours.

Messaging for mobilization

Cogent communications are essential for effective grassroots mobilization. Beyond clear, evocative writing, however, copywriting for fundraising, action alerts, talking points, position papers and communications to elected officials (which other activists call "demand letters," but which I prefer to call "Fear of God" or "FOG" letters) each require specific skills.

Commonalities for political copywriting

"Copywriting" means writing text for the purpose of advertising or other forms of marketing. In short, selling. Whether you are raising money, motivating supporters to act, or striking fear into the hearts of targets, you are very much trying to "sell" your perspective. Hence, I use the phrase "non-profit copywriting."

Below you will find particulars for different types of non-profit copywriting. (For fundraiser writing, see Chapter 17.) First, however, let's discuss requirements common to all non-profit copywriting.

Five general rules for effective political copywriting:

❏ **Be honest and be right:** Credibility is your stock in trade. Laziness and dishonesty are punished by obscurity. In Chapter 11, I describe political organizations which engage in what I call "predatory fundraising." One in particular has seen its Form 990 earnings drop to about a quarter of those at its peak. Why? Because people got wise to them and stopped donating. Even beyond fundraising, making false claims about legislation you oppose will permanently damage your credibility. Yes, I often use dramatic examples to take debating points to their logical extreme. But the reason I have so many long-time donors and so many politicians use my talking points for legislative debates is that I do my research and I don't bullsh-t.

❏ **Be concise:** You are not Leo Tolstoy and you are not writing *War and Peace*. In non-profit copywriting, your literary acumen is irrelevant. In training new writers, I routinely slash out half of what they write. Adjectives like "very" and "much" are the enemy. Cut out every non-essential "that," "I believe" and "for example" and restrict topics to those necessary. When you write 200 words, slash them to 100.

❏ **Ask what appeals to your reader:** Too often, people write about what *they*, rather than their audience, find appealing. Think long and hard about who your target audience is and what they want to hear. That doesn't mean pandering, just that the issues you raise and how you frame them should motivate your audience.

❏ **Be clever, not dogmatic:** Satire and ridicule are your friends. Regurgitating dogma makes you sound like a dolt. When the mayor of Durham announced he planned to join other cities in trying to sue gun makers out of business, we gave him the "Fireplug Award"

– a framed caricature of our mascot Max (a pit bull) lifting his leg on a fire hydrant. It made all the local TV stations, serving notice that we would oppose him by all available means.

❏ **Use "inverted pyramid":** People have short attention spans, making it likely they won't read all of what you write. Consequently, journalists present facts in descending order of importance using a short "lead" (also spelled "lede") with essential information first, followed by the "body" with important information, and a "tail" with extra material. (See Fig. 16A.)

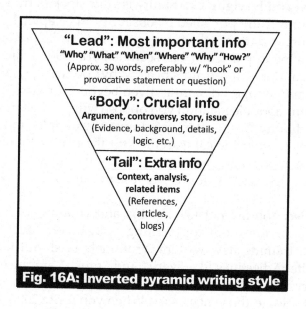

"Lead": Most important info
"Who" "What" "When" "Where" "Why" "How?"
(Approx. 30 words, preferably w/ "hook" or provocative statement or question)

"Body": Crucial info
Argument, controversy, story, issue
(Evidence, background, details, logic. etc.)

"Tail": Extra info
Context, analysis, related items
(References, articles, blogs)

Fig. 16A: Inverted pyramid writing style

Action alerts (aka "calls to action")

"Action alerts" spur supporters to make demands on targets you designate. To write them, start by including everything listed in "effective copywriting" in the section above. In particular, emphasize inverted pyramid style, brevity, scannability, and the use of an alluring "hook." But good action alerts – those that motivate people to demand action from elected officials, corporations and others – have additional requirements. For an example of an action alert, see Appendix VI.

Three requirements for action alerts:

❏ **Piss them off:** Motivating people to act requires emotion, be it fear or anger. (Alas, inspiring love does not work.) Although manipulating emotions *dishonestly* is the hallmark of predatory fundraisers, evoking fear and anger over things that *should* make people fearful or angry – thereby provoking them to act – is not only fair, it is a service to them. To that end, in writing legislative alerts, always assume the worst motivations of opponents, and the worst plausible impact of opposing legislation. Be honest, but take examples to their logical extremes, since those extremes are possible.

❏ **Be imperative:** You aren't making suggestions; you are *telling* your supporters what they need to do. Your calls to action should be clear, simple and direct. Keep sentences short and address the reader directly, as in "*You* must immediately contact Governor Engels..." Tell them to do it *now*, since they will forget about it by tomorrow.

❏ **Make needed actions simple and quick:** Never forget short attention spans and the competing demands of families, jobs, and other interests. The harder it is and the longer it takes to act, the more actors you will lose. In order to channel overwhelming input to a target, you must lose as few of your supporters as possible. If it takes longer than about five minutes to act, you will depress your response to combat-ineffective levels. Practically speaking, that means:

- Focus on as few targets as possible (unless giving supporters a copy-and-paste list of email addresses);
- Condense required actions into preferably no more than three bullet points;
- Give supporters all phone numbers, email addresses, web contact forms, or other contact info;
- Give supporters a copy-and-paste message they can either send verbatim or modify as they see fit; and
- Anticipate lies, misinformation, and spin from targets (particularly for phone campaigns when supporters speak with staffers), and incorporate counter-arguments.

Legislative talking points

To make your bill sponsor feel "loved," you will supply him with talking points at appropriate points, such as caucus meetings, committee meetings, or floor debates. Prior to votes, you should also distribute talking points to all sympatico legislators for use in debating the bill.

Let's be clear: Although your talking points should be well-documented and thorough, you aren't trying to change any minds. In a perfect world, your argument would win the intellectual debate and therefore become law. (Yay!)

But this not a perfect world. And as we discussed in Chapter 7, the merits of the argument rarely influence politicians' behavior. What he responds best to is the application or withholding of votes, money, power, and public accolades. Therefore, talking points are intended to serve as fig leaves for simpatico politicians to cover themselves with the media and the opposition as they argue for positions they would have taken anyway. Does that sound cynical? Welcome to politics.

The week before writing this, my talking points on repealing North Carolina's Jim Crow-era pistol purchase permit law were central to Senate floor debate on the bill, telling me I had done my job perfectly. For an example, see Appendix VII.

Four tips for legislative talking points:

❏ **Use bullet points:** As with other political copy-writing, talking points should be readily scannable. Bullet points make it so.

❏ **Summarize in strong topic sentences:** Each bullet point should start with a bold sentence that encapsulates the point made in the bullet. Again, the politician will likely scan it rather than reading it. If he doesn't see anything that holds his attention, he will move on.

❏ **Include references:** At the bottom of the page in smaller font, include detailed references for the source of your information, including any applicable links.

❏ **Be brief:** Talking points should occupy no more than one page. You can minimize margins or otherwise manipulate formatting to keep it to a single page provided it doesn't make the page too dense to be scanned.

Position papers

Like talking points, position papers on relevant topics aren't intended to win converts. You issue them primarily so ostensibly "friendly" politicians can't screw you and then say, "Oh, *that* bill? I didn't know you had a problem with it." Position papers put friends and enemies alike on notice about what you support and what you oppose. The secondary purpose of position papers is to create additional gravitas that depicts you as serious people on serious business. Draft them like talking points, except their quasi-academic format means they probably won't be bullet-pointed.

F.O.G. ("Fear of God") letters

Also called "demand letters," these are far and away my favorite political writing projects. (I guess I just like messing with a$$holes.) Judging by suggestions from members of my own leadership, however, it appears that people have entirely the wrong idea how they should be written. For a correct example, see Appendix VIII.

The rationale for F.O.G. letters is to convince the target that you are a serious person on serious business, and that you have both the will and the means to inflict significant legal, political, or economic damage if he fails to comply. The objective, by so doing, is to *avoid* having to expend precious time, manpower, and money to actually inflict that damage. Incidentally, letters from lawyers and/or delivered by certified mail tend to be taken more seriously.

Top five tips for writing a F.O.G. letter:

❏ **Write a perfect letter:** Make sure there are no typos or errors of any kind, since errors undermine the aura of infallibility you seek to project. To that end, proofread it (or have others proofread it) as many times as necessary. In a similar vein, put the letter on your non-profit letterhead, use a traditional font (e.g. Times New Roman), and use a business letter template which you can easily find via Google.

- **Don't be nasty:** Tempting though it may be, resist the urge to sling names or otherwise verbally eviscerate the target. Do so not for the sake of the target, but because other people will read it, particularly if the target thinks he can use it to win people to his side. Instead, be saccharine sweet and excruciatingly polite to the point of sarcasm. Except for the demand and required response, imply things rather than stating them. For example, when I expect a politician to stonewall, I say, "Since I'm sure you support transparency in government, I have every confidence that you will supply the information no later than…" (Translation: "I expect you to stonewall, and I will use it against you.")

- **Include all pertinent details:** If a local government is violating state law, list the statute being violated and the consequences for violating it. If you have photographic evidence of non-compliance (e.g. photos of illegal signage), include it.

- **Make specific demands:** Include the action you are demanding the target take, and a reasonable deadline for compliance. For example, here is part of what I sent the City of Raleigh when they whined they didn't have money to replace signs in parks which illegally prohibited firearms:

"The imposition of a local gun law or regulation more stringent that state law is a violation of § 14-409.40 ('Statewide uniformity of local regulation'). Whether or not Raleigh wants to spend the money necessary to remove or replace signs prohibiting lawful concealed carry in parks is irrelevant. If you do not remove the signs, legal action will follow. Please note that under § 6-21.7 ('Attorneys' fees; cities or counties acting outside the scope of their authority'), we will also seek to recover associated legal fees. I can be reached directly at (123) 456-7890. To prevent further action, I look forward to your prompt reply within five (5) business days."

- **Don't bluff:** If the target fails to comply, you should be ready to ratchet up pressure to the next level, carrying out anything you threatened to do up to and including filing litigation. Failure to do so will make it harder to extract compliance in future battles.

Targeting for political mobilization

All the political weapons and ammunition you've built up are for naught if they aren't targeted at the right people. Remember: identify the problem, determine who can solve it, and determine how to motivate them to do so.

Target assessment

I routinely field suggestions from activists to go after Democrats in rock-solid "blue" districts when doing so, while satisfying, would be a waste of time, money, and effort. Similarly, activists often attack un-elected bureaucrats who ignore them with impunity because they don't answer to voters. Each of these represents a failure of target assessment.

"R.V.M.T."

As an acronym for the four essentials of target assessment, remember "R.V.M.T." – responsibility, vulnerability, malleability, and timing. They are explained in detail below.

Four essentials for target assessment:

❏ **Responsibility:** With occasional exceptions, your target should either be responsible for the problem you want solved, or responsible for the person who is. I say "with occasional exceptions" because occasionally you may pick a target solely to serve as an example to others. (Yup. That's unfair, mean, and nasty. Welcome to politics.)

❏ **Vulnerability:** This depends on a variety of factors, including (but not necessarily limited to):

  • **Elected or appointed?** Un-elected bureaucrats don't answer to you; they answer to the politician who appointed them. Consequently, if you have a problem with bureaucrats, don't target them, target the politician(s) who appoint them.
  • **District partisanship:** Does the target represent a heavily "blue" district? If so, he likely won't give a damn what you do. When legislatures draw districts, the party in power draws them to

273

stay in power (surprise, surprise). That might mean drawing districts to concentrate all Democrats (or Republicans) into a small number of districts, in order to give the majority party better control of the chamber. Unfortunately, the resulting district partisanship means politicians in those few districts can't be dislodged with dynamite.

o   If a political organization in your state publishes a reliable measure of district partisanship (e.g. a "partisan index"), use it. If not, rely on state board of election statistics on percentage of Democrats, Republicans, Unaffiliated, or "other."

o   The stronger the partisan bias of a district, the more secure is the politician in his seat. In elections for highly partisan districts, swaying that "3% + 1" we discussed in Chapter 11 likely won't work. Moreover, the more secure a politician is in his district, the more resistant he will be to your demands. The best work-around for heavily partisan districts is to use primary elections to unseat the target or, if not to unseat him, to at least make him feel vulnerable.

- **Seniority:** Sadly, the longer a politician has been in office, the more secure he will be in his seat, making him both difficult to remove and resistant to your demands. By contrast, a junior legislator who has been in office for only a term or so (or better yet, was appointed mid-term) will be more vulnerable and compliant.

- **Other problems:** A target in the midst of scandal is a wonderful thing. One of our most effective operations was against a governor in the middle of a corruption scandal. Such politicians don't need the aggravation you stand to deliver, and will do whatever it takes to make you go away. Scandals can be legal (e.g. corruption), personal (e.g. messy divorce) or political (e.g. attacks by other groups over other issues). Regardless, pile on with everything you have and when the target goes down, stand on his political corpse with his scalp in hand and declare, "We did this!"

❑ **Malleability:** This refers to a politician's inherent personal susceptibility to pressure and depends on two things: personality and ideology.

- **Personality:** In Chapter 7, we discussed how politicians react to pressure, usually by trying to make you go away. One of their tactics is, "If you continue pressuring me, I'll vote against you." Usually, it is a lie … but not always. There is a certain personality type (mine, for example) which, when pressured, responds with "F@ck you." That does not, however, mean you can't target such people. It just means the target might require either a lot more pressure (e.g. a fairly major election effort), or giving the target a face-saving way out of the trap you set (e.g. somebody to play "good cop").
- **Ideology:** If a politician is deeply and ideologically opposed to your issue, applying pressure is generally a waste of time, money, and effort. In every election, one candidate or another approaches me to say they plan to run against Democrat Congressman David Price (North Carolina 4th District). I invariably disappoint them by refusing to invest in the race because he can be neither converted nor defeated. Not only has he never met a gun he wouldn't ban (his wife started the state gun control group), but the district was also drawn for him (and, of course, to ensure a Republican majority in the North Carolina congressional delegation).

❏ **Timing:** An additional variable applicable to both vulnerability and malleability is timing. Close to elections, politicians may either be more or less susceptible to pressure depending on the issue, voters, and the politician's stance. If analysts predict a "red wave" or "blue wave," the effect will be amplified. After elections, politicians feel less vulnerable because they have two or more years for voters to forget what the politician did to them. Other timing issues include recent passage of related legislation, holidays, legislative calendars, national events, natural disasters, etc.

Execution (metaphorically speaking)

I urge you to remember Alinsky's Rule 13: "Pick the target, freeze it, personalize it, and polarize it." We've already discussed picking targets. My version of execution of targeting is: "P.I.P.P." or "prioritize, isolate, polarize, and personalize," in that order.

❏ **Prioritize:** Use Red Fox Four analysis (see Chapter 14 and Appendix IV) to determine priority order of targets. Because victory begets victory, take the low-hanging fruit first: merchants whose customer base overlaps your supporters, corporations losing money, politicians behind in the polls or with the vulnerabilities listed above, etc.

❏ **Isolate:** You have limited resources. Rather than spreading them out over multiple targets, thereby weakening your impact, focus energy on a single target, rotating to the next after the first one falls. The first target's failure sets an example for the next (and make sure to publicly tout your victory).

❏ **Polarize:** In defeating a bill, emphasize the most extreme impact of the proposed law that could be reasonably extrapolated. To beat a hostile politician in an election, take his most extreme past transgressions and make them his defining trait. As detailed in Chapter 10, use "bill branding" to give opposing legislation your own (derogatory) name rather than using the opposition's bill title. Action alerts should be designed to piss off supporters. As I said previously, whatever you say has to be at least arguably true, lest you damage your own credibility.

❏ **Personalize:** Politicians and corporations feel free to screw you because they don't personally have skin in the game. Your goal is to make sure they do. When Catawba County decided to put a sewage treatment plant on Lake Norman, I put a demonstration at a hotel owned by one of the county commissioners. When the commissioner complained, "What are you going after my hotel for? This is a political issue." I responded: "What you call 'politics' is destroying these people's home values. It's personal for them, and it's gonna get personal for you, too."

• **Impugn the target's motives:** Apply the inverse of "Hanlon's Razor" by never ascribing to stupidity that which is adequately explained by malice. When somebody crosses you, damage their reputation. Personally, I try to channel my inner Sean Connery from "The Untouchables": "You wanna know how to get Capone? They pull a knife, you pull a gun. He sends one of yours to the hospital, you send one of his to the morgue." (Met-aphorically speaking, of course.)

- **Go after things that matter to him:** When I encounter a recalci-trant politician whose vote I need, I run Robocalls to voters in his district. If I really want to hurt him, I pull down the list of his campaign contributors from the state board of elections website and give them details of how he crossed them. I have not only put demonstrations in front of a politician's hotel, I have also threatened to do so at another's auto dealership, and even the Speaker's posh neighborhood. Another activist once told me, "You play full body contact politics, don't you?" My response? "Damn right I do."

Delivering 'love' to politicians

In Chapter 10, we discussed different methods of delivering channeled input to politicians. Now let's look at some common scenarios and the specifics of how to address each. Although the section below stipulates tactics for hostile legislation, the tactics for passing friendly legislation are essentially the same, differing largely in sharpness of tone.

Hostile legislation

When your opposition introduces a bill you oppose, use the principles above as well as Red Fox 4 to assess how many resources to apply in killing the bill (if, for example, it has little chance of getting a hearing, my efforts are more modest than for significant threats). Equally, con-sider timing. Do you want to suppress a committee hearing because it is likely to pass, or do you have the luxury of killing it in a recorded floor vote, giving you ammunition to go after legislators who vote for it?

Incidentally, because hostile chamber leadership will give you as little notice as possible when moving bills, make sure to subscribe to legisla-tive and committee calendars and check them each night.

Basic steps in killing hostile bills:

1. **When referred to a committee:** Once the bill is read on the cham-ber floor (First Reading), it will be referred to a committee which

will generally be your first attack point. Send action alerts to your supporters through whatever means you possess (typically email, website, social media, and gatherings of sympatico people), giving them a copy-and-paste list of legislators to contact and the message to send them. In this scenario, snail mail is typically too slow and expensive, but might be used for all-out efforts. It is probably too early to use Robocall and Robotext, instead saving them for later stages.

Do a committee analysis to determine how many committee mem bers will vote your way. You should primarily target "swing voters" on the committee in priority order: namely, 3-star (or "+"), 2-star (or "0"), and 1-star (or "–") committee members rather than stalwart supporters (4-star or "++") and opponents (0-star or "--"). That said, it isn't a bad idea to include your stalwart supporters in the target list for the first alert in order to put them on notice. You will demand that the committee chair(s) deny the undeserving bill a hearing and that committee members vote against it if it gets a hearing. In terms of what to attack, don't immediately use all arguments against the bill, instead saving your more potent attacks for later stages (I call this "layered defense").

2. **Pending committee hearing:** If you have been unable to suppress the hearing, turn up the heat. Have supporters call *and* email the targets with the intent of shutting down office business. To that end, consider concentrating the input into a single morning (e.g. having everyone call between 9 AM and 11 AM on Monday), preferably after a weekend over which you were able to distribute large numbers of action alerts to simpatico groups. Focus entirely on swing voters to deny your opposition enough votes to pass it out of committee. Make sure you have a "committee advocate" – a friendly legislator on the committee who will argue against the bill (give him talking points), make calls for division, run the clock, and try to move the bill to a subcommittee if you face impending loss.

3. **Day of hearing:** If you can't suppress the hearing on a hostile bill (or if you don't want to), your goal becomes dominating the hearing.

- **Distribute talking points:** Make sure simpatico legislators on the committee have talking points using the format in Appendix VII to give them ammunition to debate the bill.
- **Round up votes:** Legislators often have conflicting committee meetings, requiring them to choose between meetings. Make sure all of your votes show up by stopping at offices beforehand to emphasize the importance of attending the hearing.
- **Pack the committee room:** Make sure lots of (politely) angry supporters show up for the meeting. Signs are nice, but likely prohibited by chamber rules. Matching T-shirts of a single color with a coordinated message are a good substitute for supporters, but I still have my legislative action team dress in business attire. (Note: In hostile chambers where leadership gives minimum notice for committee hearings, packing the committee room might not be possible.)
- **Sit up front:** I make a point of positioning my legislative team front and center in the committee room, with me at the center as close as possible to legislators. I do so to deliver the message that I am watching everything they do, even sending volunteers to the committee room early to reserve seats. To ensure legislators get the message, we are not beyond having someone overtly video the meeting.
- **Address the committee … or not:** Addressing the committee will not change the minds of legislators. It accomplishes three things: First, it shows your supporters you are on top of the issue. Second, it demonstrates to legislators how important you consider the issue. Third, it allows you to run the clock in the slim hope that you can get the chair to decide the bill is taking too much time and displace it to another date or, if at the end of the session, table it altogether. Your remarks will likely be limited to less than five minutes, so have a clear idea what you plan to say. Incidentally, if you have the votes to kill the bill, you might not want to address the committee. The hearing at which nobody speaks is the hearing at which "the fix is in" and everybody knows it.

4. **Floor vote:** Even in friendly chambers, you might not get much notice when the bill is calendared for a floor vote, so start prepping as soon as (or even before) the bill clears committee.

- **Hit swing voters:** Start softening up your swing voters with emails and calls as described in Step 2 above. If you have the resources, consider Robocalls and texts to their constituents, social media advertising to zip codes in their districts, and radio spots on stations with appropriate listener demographics.
- **Line up debaters:** Provide friendly legislators with talking points to debate the bill. Depending on the legislative calendar (e.g. if you are running up on crossover deadline), you might be able to use debate to run the clock.
- **Notify legislators:** You can't afford to lose votes from ostensibly "friendly" legislators claiming they "didn't know" your position. Issue position papers to the full chamber, letting them know your stance and reminding them you will track votes for candidate evaluation purposes. (Again, I usually prefer to use votes on Second Reading rather than Third reading because the rats, having seen the results of the first vote, tend to scuttle to the side of the ship still afloat.)
- **Offer poison pill amendments:** Recruit friendly legislators to offer hostile amendments, preferably drafted by you. As mentioned in Chapter 10, watering down bad bills is generally a bad idea because it weakens your core constituency of support and makes hostile legislation easier to pass. Instead, run "poison pill" amendments. We once killed a bill designed to increase posting of businesses against concealed carry by presenting an amendment which addressed the *claimed* intent of the sponsor but was, in fact, wholly unacceptable. Our advocate introduced the amendment saying, "This makes a good bill better." When the amendment passed, the sponsor had it re-referred to committee (the kiss of death) rather than passing it with our language.
- **Hold "fire" until you see the whites of their eyes:** For ambush tactics (e.g. bill branding as in Chapter 10), look for maximum shock value by waiting until no more than a couple of days prior to the floor vote. When we used this tactic for the "Rapist Protection Act" described in the sidebar in Chapter 10, it so unnerved the Feminazi sponsor that she stood before the chamber to defend her bill by saying, "I would *never* introduce a 'Rapist Protection Act.'" Gotcha.

Miscellaneous skills

Running grassroots organizations requires you to be a "Renaissance man," acquiring skills in a wide variety of areas. Below are a few not covered elsewhere.

FOIA requests

Enacted in 1966, the federal Freedom of Information Act (FOIA)[1] is your friend when looking for "the goods" on bureaucrats and politicians. FOIA law gives any person or organization the right to access records of federal executive branch agencies upon request, unless they fall within outlined exemptions and satisfy the "Foreseeable Harm Standard."

In the strictest sense, FOIA applies to agencies within the executive branch of the federal government. According to "FOIA Wiki":

> "Agencies must generally make a determination with respect to an ordinary FOIA request within 20 working days. As a practical matter, agencies generally take much longer than 20 business days to respond to a request. Large requests frequently take months or years to process ... Agencies may extend the normal 20-working day deadline if 'unusual circumstances' apply, such as the need to collect a 'voluminous' amount of records or the need to consult with another agency ... A requester can ask for Expedited Processing of their request if certain conditions are met. An agency must make a determination as to whether to grant expedited processing within 10 calendar days."[2]

State and local records requests

Your state has an open records law, modeled on FOIA, affirming your right to see government documents. Find it and use it. Federal FOIA law permits "any person" to request access to agency records, including citizens, non-citizens, corporations, universities, and state and local governments. Most states mirror those definitions.

The law will have exceptions, such as personal income tax records, adoption records closed, and business information, including trade secrets and privileged or confidential information.

Typically, you should address your request in writing to either the head of the applicable agency or the department responsible for handling requests. Be specific in your information request, making it narrow enough to readily determine which documents you want, but broad enough to avoid omitting relevant information.

Requests granted may include appropriate charges for copying. Requests denied must include reasons for denial including: (1) The requested material does not exist; or (2) Some or all of the materials are exempt from disclosure. If refused, bear in mind that the agency is not the final arbiter of what is or is not public information. Your state will have an appeals process which is probably available from the state attorney general.

Non-disclosure agreements

Once upon a time, I didn't require non-disclosure agreements from my volunteers. But then, without authorization, one of them used our alert list for his state senate campaign, causing a number of (justified) member complaints.

Consequently, I had a lawyer draft a short non-disclosure agreement (NDA) prohibiting the release of any of my organization's proprietary information and stipulating that anyone who releases it will be responsible for resulting financial damages. Any volunteer who advances to leadership level (i.e. beyond basic gun shows or other position that does not involve proprietary information) is required to sign an NDA. I've had no problems with unauthorized release of information since. (Additionally, it discourages spies from opposing organizations, who know they are on the hook for any damages they cause.)

Intra-organizational power struggles

It pains me to have to include this section, but believe me when I say that if you are successful, it will be necessary. For example, Larry Klayman founded Judicial Watch in 1994, using the organization to successfully dog the Clinton administration with litigation. But by 2006, Klayman, Judicial Watch, and the president Klayman hired, Tom Fitton, ended up entangled in litigation.

Cults of personality

For better or worse, political non-profits tend to be cults of personality, often boldly envisioned and created by strong personalities … with attendant egos. The upside is that during the reign of the founder, such organizations can be profoundly successful. The downside is that they often wither and sometimes die with either corruption of the founder or his age- or burnout-related decline.

Politics (particularly conservative politics) attracts people with egos – people who accomplish much but don't necessarily play well with others. The balancing act you will have to learn is to foster leadership, but to keep leaders within the fold.

Vetting volunteers

Free labor is good. Be as inclusive as possible for basic volunteers, who should be screened only for how they might potentially damage the organization. (I once had a volunteer working a gun show table accost a congressman to tell him in no uncertain terms what he ought to be doing about prison rape.)

For positions of greater responsibility (e.g. communications, website design and maintenance, etc.), you need to ensure volunteers are not only personally suitable, but also that they are not working for your opposition. Conduct in-depth interviews encompassing not only their personalities and skills, but also a demonstrated history of commitment to your cause.

Intra-organizational politics

Machiavellian power politics apply not only to legislative bodies, but also to the organizations that attempt to influence those bodies. Consequently, you should apply everything you learn in this book to run your group.

Rules for Anti-RADICALS

Top five rules to keep control:

❑ **Fire malcontents:** Good leaders raise legitimate concerns. Bad leaders whine perpetually, particularly if their ideas are not instituted. If those people remain in your organization, they become a cancer that metastasizes to others of weak mind, will, or character. I make it clear I won't tolerate that type of behavior in my organizations, typically giving wayward volunteers one chance to get their act together before removing them from my leadership network.

❑ **Recruit like-minded people:** This does not mean using toadies and "yes men"; it does, however, mean recruiting people who share your vision. The necessary precursor, of course, is that you must have clear understanding of what your vision is.

❑ **Delegate but monitor:** A corollary of Ronald Reagan's "trust but verify." Keep a close eye on leadership functions delegated to others. Avoid micromanaging because it overtasks you and discourages talented volunteers, but don't be shy about injecting yourself in projects that stray from intended parameters.

❑ **Don't tolerate insubordination:** There is a tendency in volunteer organizations to overlook defiant or noncompliant behavior from volunteers who, after all, don't really need you or your organization. If allowed to continue, however, your instructions will devolve into frequently ignored suggestions, degrading your effectiveness. My leaders are welcome to *respectfully* disagree, with the emphasis on respect, but my word is final. An airline I flew for taught leadership by showing a *Star Trek* episode titled "The Corbomite Maneuver" in which the impetuous Lt. Dave Bailey, on the bridge of the Enterprise, reacts to a potentially hostile object by saying, "We've got phaser weapons; I vote we blast it." Captain James T. Kirk retorts dryly, "I'll keep that in mind, Mr. Bailey ... when this becomes a democracy." One of my board members described my organization by saying, "We are defending a republic, but we are doing it with a benign dictatorship."

❑ **Design bylaws to restrict voting members:** I'm not suggesting you should circle the wagons around corruption the way Wayne LaPierre and his cronies have done at the NRA, but to avoid the nightmare of a hostile takeover of your organization, ensure that only people who are true supporters of your cause, with a vested interest in your organization, get to vote on board members, bylaw changes, etc.

❏ **Know and use parliamentary procedure:** During conflicts at board meetings, annual meetings, or special meetings of the organization, he who best knows and uses Robert's Rules of Order has the best chance of prevailing. When two errant board members tried to take over my organization by calling a special meeting that my schedule precluded me from attending, for example, I simply called other board members and asked them not to attend the special meeting, denying the mutineers a quorum until a date when I could attend. By the time I was done, both resigned.

References:

1. Freedom of Information Act, United States government, https://www.foia.gov/

2. FOIA Wiki, Oct. 27, 2020, https://foia.wiki/wiki/FOIA_Basics

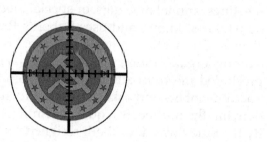

Chapter 17
Fundraising for Political Organizations

Contrary to popular opinion, fundraising is not a dirty word. It is, in fact, vital to activism. Without money, you cannot reach people; if you cannot reach people, you cannot change public policy. The key to both effectiveness and keeping your soul is to be honest in your fundraising rather than, as is popular with certain organizations, inciting fear and anger over things you either cannot or will not do anything about.

Types of political fundraising:

❏ **Direct mail/email solicitation:** By far the most popular form of non-profit fundraising. You undoubtedly receive dozens of these by email and more than a few by snail mail. Although you might not think so, writing direct solicitation is an art form generating debate by professionals over fine points. We will discuss it at length below.

❏ **Fundraising events:** Holding events to raise money is hit-and-miss, with results depending on how expensive the event is to hold and whether you can draw enough donors. For the money raised, fundraising events require more time and effort than other fundraising methods. That said, you should hold them occasionally to give your supporters a feeling of connection. The more outlandish or amusing your event, the better attended it will be. We once had a very popular machine gun shoot.

❏ **Raffles and drawings:** Raffles can be effective providing they stand out from the herd. Although raffling off an AR-15 was once considered edgy, now everybody does it. To raise money for our PAC in the 2016 elections, we held "The Hillary Clinton Special," in which we raffled off an AR-15, a thousand rounds of ammunition, and a framed portrait of Hillary. The byline was, "We're not telling you what to do with the portrait, but we understand that the last time we put Hillary on the front of our newsletter, she was very popular at the range." Happily, a leftist group claimed we were "threatening" Hillary, which caused the raffle to go viral. We were selling tickets for an AR-15 to people in countries where you can't *own* an AR-15; it got me onto Alan Combes' radio show; and it even got us a half-hearted visit from the Secret Service. (Before leaving, the agent asked how to join our organization.) Check state requirements for holding raffles by non-profits and political organizations, which may limit things like the number of raffles you can hold per year.

❑ **Corporate sponsorships:** Presuming you use a 501(c)(4) for which donations are not deductible, structure your program as a marketing and advertising program, giving sponsors an advertising deduction. We use a three-tier program with increasing perks depending on level of sponsorship. Perks include newsletter ads, website links, and mention at the end of email alerts.

❑ **Personal appeals to big donors:** This is the one most people hate, but is crucial to growing your organization, so pick up the phone. Personally, I avoid being pushy and emphasize that we provide a service for their money, the service being defense of their rights.

❑ **Merchandising:** If you do it yourself, it is a time-consuming pain in the ass. If you outsource it, the contractor soaks up most of the profits. At this point, we do it more for comradery and brand recognition than to make money.

Mailing for political non-profits

Good old-fashioned snail mail is not yet dead, and won't be anytime soon. That's why your mailbox fills up as elections loom. As much as "millennial" and later generations believe that all communication can be done by email and social media, the truth is that some people still don't use computers, much less social media.

A 2021 Pew Research Center survey found that fully 25% of people age 65 and older (who are usually your largest donors) don't use the Internet.[1] Meanwhile, Ability PR Solutions reports that due to "email overload," fully 55% of *all* consumers (including younger people) ignore marketing emails.[2]

Types of snail mail

For United States Postal Service (USPS) "snail mail," you have three alternatives. In descending order of cost (and increasing order of complexity), they are First Class, Standard Mail, and Nonprofit Mail. Basically, the more work you do yourself, the cheaper will be your mailing rates, with all bulk mailing done on a "presort" basis in which you are responsible for sorting by zip code.

To make a presorted mailing, addresses in your database will be run through the "National Change of Address" (NCOA) database, comprising approximately 160 million permanent change-of-address records.

Also essential to presorted mailing is "CASS" (Coding Accuracy Support System) certification, which corrects and standardizes addresses and adds missing address information, such as ZIP codes, cities, and states to ensure the address is complete. When choosing a vendor to process your mail, ensure they are CASS certified.

Options for large mailings:

❏ **First Class Mail:** If you try this for more than a few supporters, you will quickly go broke. The rate for a simple letter is currently $.58 and rising rapidly, making a 1,000 piece mailing a $580.00 proposition in postage alone. Rates for large envelopes ("flats") are considerably higher.

❏ **Commercial bulk permit:** You get discounts on bulk mailing because you are required to "pre-sort" the mail before dropping it off to the post office. In theory, you could get a bulk permit ($245/year) and do it yourself. In the ancient past when we did it manually – even before USPS dramatically increased its bulk mailing automation requirements – the workload was daunting even for mailings of 1,000 pieces. At this point, given CASS and NCOA requirements, I doubt it would be practical. The more viable solution is to use a bulk mailing house, with options including online services such as Printing for Less, Amazingmail, Click2Mail, Taradel, Growmail, or AMPlified Mail, as well as countless local mailing houses. We use Click2Mail for smaller postcard mailings that cannot be mailed at non-profit rates (e.g. PAC mailings). There are two options for pre-sorted mail on a commercial bulk permit:

- **USPS Presort First Class Mail:** Depending on counts and zip codes, costs range from $.306 to $.326 for "small" pieces (3½" x 5" to 4¼" x 6") and $.426 to $.485 for "jumbo" pieces (size: 4¼" x 6" to 6⅛" x 11½"). Regardless of size, maximum weight is 1 oz. and the minimum number of mail pieces is 500.
- **USPS Presort Standard Mail:** Cheaper than Presort First Class, rates for Presort Standard Mail range from $.277 to $.33 (minimum size: 3½" x 5", maximum size: 6⅛" x 11½") The maximum weight is 3.3 oz. and the minimum number of mail pieces is 200. The drawback is that Standard Mail is processed by USPS on a "time available" basis with no guaranteed delivery time.

❏ **USPS Nonprofit Mail:** This is the political non-profit's best friend. It is a reduced postage rate within Standard Mail and should be your primary means of mailing. It's processed exactly the same, but gets discounts that can be 70% less than the cost of First Class. As such, rates run $.146 to $.199 with size and weight restrictions the same as Standard Mail above. In theory, use First Class if you have a crucial upcoming event, expiration date, or other time-critical promotion. In practice, I have found that about 80% of mail pieces mailed Standard Mail arrive within a week, and most of the rest within two weeks. A few outliers might take longer. One downside is that you must get USPS approval to mail at non-profit rates via the USPS Form 3624, which we will discuss below; the other is that you cannot use it for political action committee (PAC) mailings.

Getting and using a non-profit bulk permit

Step one to apply for a USPS non-profit bulk mail permit is to complete PS Form 3624, "Application to Mail at Nonprofit USPS Marketing Mail Prices."[3] As you might imagine from a governmental entity, this is not quite as easy as it sounds.

Submitting required paperwork

Along with your PS Form 3624, USPS lists the following documents which must be submitted:

"Required documentation. You must submit some documentation with your application to support your claim for nonprofit prices:

- o *Formative papers—e.g., articles of incorporation, constitution, or charter.*
- o *IRS letter of exemption from payment of federal income tax.*
- o *Other evidence of nonprofit status—e.g., a financial statement prepared by a responsible party such as a certified public accountant substantiating organization's nonprofit status (statement must include balance sheets, income statement, notes, etc.).*

Some mailers provide additional supporting documentation:

- o *List of the organization's activities during the past 12 months.*
- o *Financial statement showing receipts and expenditures for the past fiscal year, plus the budget for the current year.*
- o *Other documents of operation—e.g., the organization's bulletins, minutes of meetings, brochures."*

Are you eligible for a non-profit bulk permit?

The USPS puts out a lovely 62-page tome entitled, "Nonprofit USPS Marketing Mail Eligibility: Nonprofit and Other Qualified Organizations."[4] Here is where it pays to have put forethought into developing your mission statement for your IRS "Letter of Determination," because *"political organizations"* are not eligible for non-profit bulk mail permits, but *educational* organizations are.

Although USPS does not differentiate between 501(c)(3) and 501(c)(4) organizations, it says that the only non-profits eligible for bulk permits are religious, educational, scientific, philanthropic (charitable), agricultural, labor, veterans, and fraternal.

Notice that nowhere does it mention the "social welfare" organizations under which most 501(c)(4) organizations qualify for not-for-profit status. Therefore, I strongly suggest that your IRS application for your Letter of Determination include, in its mission statement, a goal of educating the public on trends which abridge individual liberties (or a similar equivalent). Frankly, our application was first rejected even *with* that statement until I got the office of a U.S. Senator involved.

Once you get approved

You must first pay a $265 "Permit Imprint Authorization fee," which lets you print a "postage paid" box (called a "permit imprint" or an "indicia") on your mail instead of putting a stamp or meter imprint on each piece. There is also a $265 "annual mailing fee." According to USPS: "The organization must make at least one mailing at the Non-profit USPS Marketing Mail prices during a 2-year period or the authorization to mail at the nonprofit prices will be automatically revoked for nonuse."

As you might expect, the USPS manual above contains voluminous regulations on identifying the organization or organizations doing a given mailing, which types of mailings are eligible and much more, which is why it is in your best interest to use an experienced, reputable mailing house.

Mailing with a non-profit bulk permit

Practically speaking, you will probably use a commercial mailing house which will:

❏ Process your mailing list through the NCOA database
❏ De-duplicate addresses
❏ Complete CASS certification
❏ Pre-sort mail by zip code, completing all USPS documentation
❏ Do ink-jet setup, address, and barcode mail pieces
❏ Deliver to post office (although in the past I have picked up shipments and paperwork and delivered them myself, I later found it easier to get approval to mail from the mailing house's post office using our non-profit bulk permit)

List building for political non-profits

Your lists are the life blood of your organization. The more people you can reach, the stronger you will be. Gather names, addresses, and especially email addresses at every opportunity. If you need to kick-start your list building, there are several options.

Fundraising for Political Organizations

Top four ways to build non-profit fundraising lists:

❏ **Petition campaigns:** These are popular among certain political organizations not because they are a particularly good way to impact the legislative process (they aren't), but instead because they are excellent tools for organization building. The caveat is this: *never* use petitions for list building without actually turning in the petition to the target. Incidentally, the best way to create petitions is to use one page for each signatory, then wheel in a hand truck with boxes of petitions to deliver them to the target … taking photos of the event for your supporters, of course. Options for petition campaigns include:

- **Email solicitation with links:** The problem with this one is that you are sending email to people you already have on your list. Encourage them to have friends and family sign the petition to get new people.
- **Website petitions:** Here you can gather people who surf through your website, but,
- once again, your exposure to new people is relatively limited.
- **Social media:** Advertise the petition on Facebook, MeWe, etc. and give links to the petition on your website.
- **Working events:** Using either electronic or good, old-fashioned paper petitions (some data entry required), have volunteers work simpatico gatherings. At gun shows, I have two people forward of our table with clipboards in hand, collaring people as they walk by with something like, "Sir, will you help stop the Biden gun ban?"

❏ **Giveaways:** These can be used in conjunction with petitions; ask people to sign up for a free drawing for something attractive (e.g. an AR-15). No, you will not immediately recoup what you spend on the prize, but if you do solid fundraising solicitation, you will eventually make money. Check state regulations, but giveaways are likely exempt from raffle regulations. To ensure you get valid email addresses, make it clear that winners will be notified only by email.

❏ **List purchases:** These are expensive ($100.00/1,000 names up to $600.00/1,000), but are an excellent way to get started. Make absolutely sure that: (1) The list includes emails, is high quality, and is recently updated; and (2) The people on the list are truly sympathetic to your cause. (I once bought a list of supporters of libertarian-leaning Ron Paul assuming that because Paul opposed gun control, they would be simpatico. I stopped using the list after a significant portion actually took the time and trouble to go to our website to call me a Nazi.)

❑ **Commercial email appends:** This is a slick way to get email addresses for lists which have only physical addresses. It involves having a commercial service with access to millions of records match email to your list. A quality service might be able to match 25% of your list or more. Once again the service is pricey, with rates running around $70.00/1,000 emails obtained, often with a minimum cost of $2,000 or more. Quality services will send an "opt-out" email to addresses matched.

The advantage to commercial email appends is that you can match against publicly-sourced data such as voter databases which are generally too large and non-specific to be valuable by themselves. Other possibilities include handgun permit lists, hunting and fishing licenses, commercial license databases, etc., all of which can be data mined against voter databases to produce supporters who favor your cause.

Potential problems are incorrect matches (the rate for which increases with lower quality services), and the fact that many email providers (e.g. Constant Contact and Mailchimp) will not accept lists compiled in this fashion, instead requiring lists to be "double opt-in" wherein an email is sent to the user which includes a link to click and confirm the subscription. Obviously, anything that requires the recipient to take action will lower subscription rates.

Do anti-spam laws apply to political non-profits?

The "Controlling the Assault of Non-Solicited Pornography and Marketing" ("CAN-SPAM") Act became law in 2003 and applies only to commercial bulk email. Political messages are protected under the First Amendment. However, nothing in CAN-SPAM specifically exempts non-profit organizations, which could fall under its umbrella if sending email to market products (e.g. T-shirts, seminars, etc).

Best practices in sending bulk email:

❏ Provide a clear and conspicuous notice that the recipient may opt out
❏ Provide a functioning opt-out link in all emails
❏ Provide a valid postal address for your organization
❏ Provide a "from" line that clearly identifies the sender
❏ Do not use misleading subject lines

Being in compliance with CAN-SPAM does not mean emails you send won't end up trapped by spam filters. To avoid getting nailed as spam:

❏ Comply with the "best practices" above
❏ Make sure your IP address has not been associated with spam
❏ Avoid "spam trigger words" in subject lines
❏ Ask supporters to "white list" your organizational email address
❏ Check your copy with a spam-checking tool (e.g. Emailable)

Fundraising copy for political organizations

Volumes have been written on the topic, and the professionals (such as they are) will tell you to test each and every approach you make. For better or worse, however, I don't have time for extensive testing, and I'm not willing to let consultants bleed me for results that will likely be no better (and possibly worse) than my own. My personal style is to tell supporters I am asking for money reluctantly, and to do it in self-deprecating fashion. For general rules in copywriting for political non-profits, see "Messaging for mobilization" in Chapter 16. For an example of fundraising copy, see Appendix IX.

Three top tenets for fundraising letters:

❏ **Use good lists:** Develop high quality lists using the methods described above.

❏ **Write good copy:** Beyond being clear, concise, honest, and grammatically correct, here are some of my "rules" of fundraising copywriting. Yes, I often ignore them, but I only do so advisedly and for good reason.

- **Use readable fonts:** The classic fundraising technique is to use `Courier New` as your body font in order to give your appeal that "folksy, personally typed" appearance. While that might not matter in the age of computers, I strongly suggest using a "serif" font (i.e. one with "feet") because the "feet" make it easier for readers' eyes to follow. That said, plenty of professional fundraisers now ignore this in the interest of looking "modern." Your body text should be black and 12-point or larger. Cutesy "personally" addressed envelopes aside, avoid cursive fonts like the plague.
- **Keep it readable and simple:** Your writing style should be conversational rather than formal. Paragraphs should be short. Despite what your English teacher said, feel free to use one-sentence paragraphs.
- **Make it scannable:** In a Twitter world, few people have the time, interest, or attention span to read your entire fundraising appeal. Beyond the inverted pyramid described above, highlight salient points (I use bold underline) to allow readers to get your point by scanning the letter. You get bonus points if the highlight sentences cohere to form a short "letter within a letter."
- **Use a "hook":** The first sentence should command attention and perhaps (within reason) shock the reader.
- **Use strong topic sentences:** The first sentence of every paragraph should clearly describe the content of the paragraph.
- **Make it reader-centric:** The reader should consider how the story you tell applies to *him* and what *he* needs to do.
- **Ask for the sale:** Professional fundraisers divide this into "hard ask" (direct appeals for money) versus "soft ask" (newsletters, alerts, or other publications which develop leads), but regardless, you don't get results if you don't ask. Fundraising is not the time to be shy.
- **Use bullet points:** In the interest of easy readability, summarize your points with bullets.
- **Make it easy to donate:** Anything that requires multiple steps or web pages, more time, or a delay in donating (e.g. taking a donation form home) will suppress response. Similarly, dis-

courage them from waiting to donate by offering a discount or other item of value if they respond immediately.

- **Promise value:** Activists routinely fail to understand they are providing customer service in a competitive world. You should acknowledge that and offer more "bang for the buck" than your competition.
- **Repeat and reinforce:** Unfortunately, making your point once is not as effective as making it repeatedly. In particular, I include several donation links.

❏ **Ask often but not <u>too</u> often:** Many organizations take fundraising too far, and the result is "list fatigue" or "donor fatigue," wherein you ask so often that nobody responds, forcing you to ask still more often in a vicious downward spiral. Even worse than loss of revenue, your supporters will regard you as interested in nothing but money and will also begin to ignore your calls to action, significantly degrading your effectiveness. Professional fundraisers claim donor lists are like muscles, and need to be exercised to avoid atrophy. That said, I err toward the side of too little rather than too much and get good results.

References:

1. Andrew Perrin and Sara Atske, "7% of Americans don't use the internet. Who are they?" Pew Research Center, April 2, 2021, https://www.pewresearch.org/fact-tank/2021/04/02/7-of-americans-dont-use-the-internet-who-are-they/

2. Richard Carufel, "'Inbox overload' is causing over half of consumers to ignore retailer emails," Ability PR Solutions, October 5, 2018, https://www.agilitypr.com/pr-news/public-relations/inbox-overload-is-causing-over-half-of-consumers-to-ignore-retailer-emails/

3. "Special Prices for How to Apply for Authorization to Mail at Nonprofit Prices," United States Postal Service, https://pe.usps.com/businessmail101?ViewName=NonprofitApplication

4. "Nonprofit USPS Marketing Mail Eligibility: Nonprofit and Other Qualified Organizations," United States Postal Service, January, 2017, https://pe.usps.com/cpim/ftp/pubs/pub417/pub417.pdf

Chapter 18
Media Management

"Advocacy journalism is a genre of journalism that adopts a non-objective viewpoint, usually for some social or political purpose. Some advocacy journalists reject that the traditional ideal of objectivity is possible in practice, either generally, or due to the presence of corporate sponsors in advertising."
– Wikipedia

"Never answer the question you are asked. Answer the question you want to answer." – FPV

With a different book in mind, I wrote an early version of this chapter back in 2002. Only when I set about re-writing it for *Rules for ANTI-Radicals* did I fully realize how much American media have changed. Some of what I once did no longer works, not because the tactics themselves are ineffective, but because the leftist media now refuse to even consider alternative viewpoints.

From the mid-1990s until just a few years ago, I was a regularly featured columnist and op-ed writer in many of my state's largest newspapers. By contrast, to get published in the same newspapers today, I have to threaten to boycott their advertisers. Editors no longer bother with the pretense of "fairness," blatantly applying more stringent standards to conservatives than to leftists. Formats, publication timing, and editing all favor leftists. In online newspaper articles, conservative comments, if accepted at all, quickly disappear, leaving only fawning leftism.

"Newspapers?" you say. "What are those?" Yes, newspaper editors are fast destroying their own industry. Unfortunately, however, the online "news" sources replacing them are even more partisan, forcing readers to use news sources which align with their politics and eliminating venues for reaching centrists.

Effective public speaking

Before tackling the big, bad, biased media, you must first be an effective speaker. Because there are scores of books on public speaking, this will be only a brief outline. Speaking techniques specific to interviewing are described below.

Top 5 rules of effective public speaking:

1. **Don't wing it:** Did you ever notice that Donald Trump's worst public comments were the ones he did off-the-cuff? Prepare remarks as bullet points beforehand; practice them, and *glance* at them, don't read them.

2. **Call your followers to action:** Rather than having the audience passively absorb your comments, make them participate. Your speech should rouse them to take specific actions both during and after the speech.

3. **Stir emotions:** Because the goals of public speaking are more about motivating people than educating them, use evocative themes that create emotions in the audience. The most effective emotion in stirring them to action is anger.

4. **Know your audience:** When preparing remarks (especially humor), consider the audience demographic, including age, education, life experience, and geographic area. When in doubt, keep words short, simple and clear. You aren't there to prove you are smarter than they are.

5. **Build to a crescendo:** Your speech should have a beginning, a middle, and an ending, with the pace and volume of the speech increasing to a crescendo. In speaking to a crowd in 2013, I finished my speech against "universal background checks" (aka universal gun registration) by leading the crowd in three successive chants of "We. Will. Not. Compromise!" with the last one literally vibrating windows of the legislative offices above. Incidentally, this also demonstrates what I call "the cadence of threes." To stir an audience, rise to a crescendo three times, with three different lead-ins to

the same dramatic conclusion, preferably with pauses between the words of the conclusion. In the 2013 speech, it was:

"When it comes to our families: "We. Will. Not. Compromise!
"When it comes to the Second Amendment: We. Will. Not. Compromise!
"And when it comes to our freedom: We. Will. Not Compromise!"

The 'advocacy journalism' takeover

I suppose I was like the frog in a pot of tepid water gradually heated to a boil. As an activist, I knew media had become increasingly biased. Still, I didn't fully comprehend the extent of it until I realized that "mainstream media" has given up any pretense of not being advocacy journalism and has become openly hostile to opposing views.

It started nearly thirty years ago, when reporters started expounding that it wasn't possible to be truly objective, that the best they could manage was to be "fair." Destroying the bright line between news and opinion, *USA TODAY* popularized the practice of running editorial on the front page and calling it "news."

But that was child's play compared to current practice, which by philosophy eschews objectivity and neutrality as "antiquated." Journalists for major news organizations no longer consider themselves bound by such curiosities. Instead they, the enlightened, so much smarter than we peasants, have declared themselves free to not only slant news but to lie and even destroy lives in serving their agenda.

The media are channeling Alinsky, who posited that the question of whether ends justify means is "meaningless" with the only relevant question being, "do these particular ends justify these particular means?

How to thrive in hostile media

None of that, however, serves as an excuse for incomplete, half-assed media management. And even against a stacked deck, you can prevail. I know because I do.

Thriving in hostile media requires treating them as quarry to be baited into your carefully set trap. It means getting them to help you by making them think they are hurting you. It means, unfortunately, adopting the leftist tactic of deception; and it means that once you lure game to your trap, you must be prepared to spring it.

Objectives in "doing" media

"Why bother?" you ask. "Who cares what the media thinks?" After all, the Foundation for Applied Conservative Leadership philosophy of political action teaches there is little or no benefit to "educating" the public; that swinging the 3% + 1 to win elections is all that really matters.

I would argue, however, that although the might be true in the short-term, failure to win converts over the longer term will ultimately render you unable to swing 3% + 1. As inefficient as education may be for political action, it is necessary to create an environment in which political action can succeed.

Top three reasons to get your organization into the media limelight:

❏ **To show your supporters you are active:** Being able to point to articles featuring your organization (even if they are unflattering articles) shows your people that you are out there swinging. That translates to increased loyalty by your followers and in donations crucial to political action. I make a point of putting every article mentioning my organizations onto our Facebook and MeWe pages.

❏ **To recruit simpatico supporters:** Unless you have a multi-million-dollar advertising budget (in which case, please give me a call), there will be plenty of potential supporters who have never heard of you. Getting your organization out front in newspapers and local TV stations will help them find you. When local news carried our lawsuits against the sheriffs of two urban counties for failure to issue pistol purchase permits, dozens of people experiencing the same problem called us. Many joined.

❏ **To win new converts:** This is the long-term "educational" part of the effort. While arguably offering a lower immediate return than the other objectives, if we cede the intellectual battlefield to the left, we will ultimately lose.

Ways of getting media

There are essentially seven ways to get media coverage:

❏ Hold an event (demonstration, dinner, forum, etc.)
❏ Hold a press conference (best suited for leftist organizations, but occasionally useful for conservatives)
❏ Issue a press release
❏ Do interviews on talk shows (TV or radio) and social media
❏ Write letters to the editor or comments to online articles
❏ Write op-eds (either in print or online)
❏ Do podcasts, videos, or prepackaged radio shows (either via the airwaves or social media such as YouTube)

Baiting traps for hostile media

Because the increasingly leftist media hates you, your goal is often to convince them they are not doing you any favors by running the piece you want. Inherent in this are two principles. First, any media is better than no media, since it gets your organization's name out into the public arena. Second, bad media is good media. Whenever the media say something unflattering about your organization, use it to incite your people, and to raise money on hostile coverage.

❏ **Shock them:** "If it bleeds, it leads," or so goes the cliché. Use conflict to grab attention. Within the limits of decency, the more outrageous the headline, the better. Examples I have used include "Legislator Defends 'Rapist Protection Act,'" "Court Strikes Down NC Gun Ban," "Gun Group 'Targets' UNC President," and "Latest Salvo in Gunfight Over Raleigh Parks." When gun control advocates Gabby Giffords and Mark Kelly came to North Carolina for what they claimed was a "discussion with gun owners" (which they carefully hid from the gun owners they claimed to want a discussion with), we put out a "Where's Gabby?" press release, using a "Where's Waldo?" theme and offering 1,000 rounds of ammunition to anyone who could locate the event. It was featured in the political "Under the Dome" column read by most of North Carolina's state and federal legislators.

❏ **Fool them:** False flag operations can be loads of fun. When Handgun Control, Inc. director Sarah Brady was scheduled to headline a gun control fundraiser, we put out a "Truth Vigil for Sarah Brady" press release. When throngs of television crews arrived, however, they found a vigil not *for* Brady, but directed *at* her many fabrications.

❏ **Put blood in the water:** Nothing whets a leftist appetite like a whiff of conservative scandal. When pushing restaurant carry legislation through a recalcitrant Republican-controlled Senate, our press release read, "Restaurant Carry Ad Campaign Targets [Republican] Sen. Phil Berger". By the time the dust settled, the Senate President Pro Tempore, arguably the second most powerful politician in the state, was forced to do a rug dance on a conservative radio program, promising that restaurant carry would pass, with the only issue being "not if, but when." (To his credit, the legislature passed it in the next session.)

Advance preparation for media

When you snare a news outlet, things happen fast, meaning you had better be prepared. Failure to take the following steps beforehand will likely result in missed opportunities.

Top three steps for advance media prep:

❏ **Create a press release spreadsheet:** Your press list should include name, phone number, email address, media outlet, and notes on how friendly or hostile the reporter is. This will require research, including reviews of media websites and phone calls to news rooms and editors. Whenever possible, I prefer to email press releases directly to reporters (particularly sympathetic reporters) rather than the general inbox for the news desk. You might be able to find one particular reporter tasked with your issue, and you should work toward being a regular "source" for the reporter. The downside is that reporters change jobs with surprising frequency, making it hard to keep your press list updated. Always work to update press contacts, including getting business cards from any media member you interview with (and yes, that includes hostile media).

❑ **Design an attractive, easy-to-read press release:** Bearing in mind that time is critical when releases must be issued—particularly if you are responding to outside events—have a format ready to go. When the time comes, fill in the details and cut it loose. Using the copy-writing guidelines in Chapter 16, make it easy to scan, with pertinent details (who, what, when, where, why) at the top. Use clean, relatively large fonts (preferably 12 point), bullet point outlines, and bold print highlights. Make sure to use a "hook" in the lead paragraph. Beforehand, delegate an individual or team to send press releases. For an example, see Appendix X. The release should include:

- Company logo;
- Bold headline;
- Subtitle;
- Release date and contact information;
- "Dateline" (date, city, and state, although date is often omitted);
- Intro paragraph (with "hook");
- Body text;
- Relevant quotes (feel free to quote yourself as leader of your organization, but do it in third person); and
- Boilerplate (a short description of your organization).

❑ **Designate spokesmen:** Better yet, designate spokes*women*. Whoever speaks for your organization should be reasonably attractive, well-dressed, articulate, and rehearsed. Give them talking points to work from. The more hard-edged your cause, the more soft-edged should be your spokesperson, and (within limits) vice versa. Make sure she is available for a callback as soon as your releases are issued; reporters quickly lose interest if they don't have a ready contact to meet their deadlines (for local television news, usually around 5:00 PM).

Once you've lured them in...

So the pressure is on. Reporters have responded and now you must give interviews. First, we'll look at general guidelines pertinent to all interviews. Then we will examine specifics for print, radio, and television.

The fine art of being interviewed

If you remember one thing from this section, make it this:

> *Never answer the question you are asked.*
> *Answer the question you* want *to answer.*

Hostile media will do their best to depict you as extremist by asking you loaded questions of the "How often do you beat your wife?" variety. Do not bite. If you say, "I don't beat my wife," you have already lost. The headline will read, "Extremist denies beating wife."

The core strategy of interviewing is to deliver a relatively simple message in a variety of ways and in a format attractive to the interviewer. By looking at the news outlet and any recent news on your issue, assess whether the interview will be friendly or hostile. (Be prepared for surprises: hostility can come from unexpected quarters).

The three primary goals of doing media:

❏ **Be heard:** Giving your interviewer a "hot" topic with a human interest angle or a fundamental conflict will help him, making him more likely to help you (whether or not he intends to).

❏ **Be credible:** Anything that makes you appear fearful or extremist detracts from that credibility. *You* are the voice of reason; *your opposition* is the bunch of whackos (which you imply, but never say).

❏ **"Sell" your perspective to viewers:** In examples below, you will see activists who answered questions within the framework of what matters to *them*, leaving other potential supporters out in the cold.

Before proceeding to specifics, remember that even bad media coverage is better than no media coverage. Indeed, depending on your issue, bad media might be *better* than good. Witness the National Rifle Association, which has raised millions of dollars by demonstrating to members that they are targets of The Evil Media.

Media Management

Keys to effective interviews:

Understand the interview and what motivates it: Although you might accept a hostile interview, you should go into it knowingly and with appropriate caution. Ask the reporter who else he is interviewing and what motivated him to do the piece. Make sure to see it when it airs to ensure you are accurately portrayed.

❏ **Use talking points:** When media representatives call back, do not ramble, equivocate, or hesitate. Your points should be delivered succinctly and clearly. Develop a main theme and no more than two to three sub-themes. Each phrase should be rehearsed for both content and phonetic impact. During print or radio interviews, refer to them often. For TV interviews, don't read from them, but arrange them as large print bullet points you can place in your lap and glance at as the need arises.

❏ **Answer with sound bites:** The more cleverness and punch you can use to deliver your message, the more likely the interviewer will use it. Although particularly true in ultra-short interviews (e.g. local T.V. news), clean sound bites will get better coverage even in longer formats. I just listened to an interview on immigration reform. Although the activist was well versed and made good points, I don't remember most of them. Why? Because rather than delivering short, clean points, he droned on forever. People will remember what you said first and last, but what comes in between may be forgotten. Personally, I like to finish my answer crisply, sometimes with a rhetorical question that provokes thought.

❏ **Back your position with facts:** Too often, people respond to interview questions with opinions or assumptions. If you want to be seen as the master of your issue, do advance research. Be ready to answer with facts, stats, and examples. Whenever possible, cite data from objective sources rather than advocacy groups. Cite the name of the organization: "Well, Bob, according to the National Centers for Injury Prevention and Control, last year only 47 people fell into toilets and drowned."

Rules for Anti-RADICALS

❏ **Exude confidence:** However confident you may or may not feel, the reporter is depending on you to be an expert on your topic. Don't disappoint him. (This is not, however, a license for pomposity.)

❏ **Be the picture of reason and moderation:** No matter how inflammatory the question, never fall back on rhetoric. When faced with provocation, a rational response makes the reporter look stupid rather than you. For example, an activist who opposed county plans to move a cemetery for a light rail line answered a question with: "Why, that is just the most rude, crass, classless and tasteless thing..." Does that inspire you to take action against the county? I didn't think so. Not only did she resort to name-calling, she failed to give good reasons for opposing the plan. Instead, she defined the problem in terms of her own perception of taste which, to you and me, is irrelevant.

❏ **Parse your answers:** If a complete answer to the question paints your issue in an unflattering light, answer the question based on a *subset* of the entire answer.

   Example

   Reporter: "If you succeed in building the border wall, won't thousands of potential immigrants die from disease and malnutrition because they will be denied a better life in America?"

   Activist: "Not at all. Encouraging lawful immigration will allow us to maintain our high standard of health care, not only for citizens but for legal immigrants as well."

❏ **Don't answer the question you are asked, answer the question you *want* to answer:** Yes, I have said it before, but if you get one bit of knowledge from this section, make it this one. Allowing the reporter to frame the question is the most common failing of interviewees. With controversial topics, hostile reporters will attempt to depict you unflatteringly. Don't let them. I've done interviews in which I denied the reporter a sound bite which would have undermined my position, only to have him repeat the question in different ways. Each time, I gave him the same answer, also rephrased. Even in friendly interviews, questioning may diverge from the message you intend to deliver, leaving it to you to steer it back.

Example (done correctly)

Reporter: "Why do you oppose legislation to require mental health checks for all gun buyers, particularly given the lives it will save?"

Activist: "Placing your civil rights in the hands of bureaucrats applying subjective mental health standards that even psychologists acknowledge can't reliably predict violent behavior is a recipe for disaster."

Example (done incorrectly)

Reporter: "Why do you oppose legislation to require mental health checks for all gun buyers, particularly given the lives it will save?"

Activist: "I don't think mental health checks for gun purchases will save lives."

Reporter: "But what about the thousands of suicides committed each year using guns?"

Activist: "Uh..."

❏ **Beware of open-ended questions.** Often the reporter will finish with, "Is there anything else you would care to add?" Check your notes, if possible; deliver any unmade points; but do *not* treat it as an invitation to improvise. Rest assured that if you step on your tongue with a stupid or offensive pontification, it will become the centerpiece of the interview.

Deflecting a NY Times hit piece

When I got a phone call from *New York Times* reporter Michael Luo claiming to center on North Carolina's concealed handgun permit system, I probed until I discovered he planned to make a fallacious claim that thousands of concealed handgun permit-holders are convicted criminals, despite having under-gone FBI background checks.

Forewarned is forearmed: When Luo published the piece, we already had his history of doing anti-gun hit pieces, were ready to debunk his methodology (which used only simple data matching), and demanded to see his raw data. He refused to provide the data, claiming he would only give it to a legislator. So we had a legislator request it, only to have Luo refuse him, too.

We also produced a high quality video debunking his claims which to this day continues to come up when you Google Luo's name,[1] including ridiculing the trivial – and not disqualifying – legal infractions which could have been included in his list of "criminals." (My personal favorite misdemeanor still on the books was "Taking Sea Oats From the Land of Another.") As a result, Luo's hit piece, intended to damage concealed handgun permit laws, got no traction.

Types of interviews

Different types of media interviews require different skill sets. Personally, I sound better than I look (a girlfriend once told me that cameras hate me). So, given a choice, I will take radio or print interviews any day. (Which is why I do a radio show rather than a YouTube video channel.) Unfortunately, however, you generally don't get to pick what type of interview you get, so I have worked hard to improve my visual presentation.

Press conferences

Top five requirements for effective press conferences:

❏ **Press release:** Issue a press release before the press conference giving the "Five Ws" (who, what, when, where, and why) and featuring the names of speakers at the conference, listing the biggest "names" most prominently.

❏ **Press kits:** The handouts should feature your speaker comments, talking points and Q&A for the event, as well as organizational information, including a description of your group.

❏ **Podium or lectern:** Although this can be dispensed with depending on the location (e.g. in outdoor locations such as the steps of the courthouse in which you are about to file a lawsuit), if possible have an attractive, professionally made sign featuring your organization name and website, plus a simple message to visually depict the issue (see Fig. 17A.) Additionally, a professionally made banner behind the podium and/or floor standups or retractable banners used for trade shows can be added. Alternatively, you can position the U.S. flag and your state flag on either side of the podium. (The U.S. flag goes on the left when facing the stage.)

Grass Roots North Carolina
Sues Sheriff
Over Gun Permits
GRNC.org

Fig. 17A: Press conference podium sign

❏ **Sound system with press feeds:** For better sound quality in both audio and video formats, the sound system should allow media outlets to tap directly into the system.

❏ **Visuals, charts, or photos:** If the presentation can be enhanced with visual aids, either have them handy or, better still, have a PowerPoint presentation with appropriate projector and screen. During a Spectrum News town hall, I gave the studio my PowerPoint slides which they flashed to illustrate my points as I made them.

Print interviews

Interviews for newspapers and magazines are generally less hazardous than for other formats. You have plenty of time to check notes and carefully phrase your responses. Odd facial tics will never occupy a camera and detract from your message. If you don't get an answer right the first time, you have an opportunity to change it.

At the same time, however, you have less control over the "spin" the reporter chooses to give your issue. Other sources may be interviewed later. Placement of your key phrases at the beginning or end of the article, where they are most effective, is not up to you. The article may be paired with others designed to undermine or upstage you. Finally, because the reporter is likely to rely on hand-written notes, he may paraphrase your responses rather than giving them verbatim, potentially muddling or misstating your message.

Keys to effective print interviews:

❏ **Ask the reporter who else they will interview:** If you are responding to a topic rather than initiating it, ask what motivated the reporter to cover the topic and what they already know about it. Ask them as many questions as necessary to get a feel for their viewpoint on the topic. (Note: You can also glean information from the reporter, particularly about your opposition's next move. I have actually gotten early warnings from reporters about opposing legislation not yet introduced.)

❏ **Take your time:** Since you aren't subject to time constraints, think carefully about what you say before saying it. If you lose your way, pause and start over.

❏ **Use notes:** I like to put together sample questions and phrase my answers beforehand. The fewer surprises you get, the better the interview.

❏ **Underscore and repeat key information:** If there is a particular phrase I want included in the article, I tell the reporter, "Please emphasize that. Let me say it again so you can write it down verbatim…"

Radio interviews

Radio is my personal favorite. The rise of talk radio has made radio interviews, for some issues, a fantastic source of free advertising. Moreover, it doesn't matter how photogenic you are, or whether you have questionable taste in clothing.

Except for a limited number of national media outlets (e.g. National Public Radio), you will generally get more time to hype your issue than in other formats (particularly TV). Depending on the show format, perhaps as long as an hour. Although I prefer not to (due to inability to get a feel for the host and potentially inferior audio quality), radio interviews are increasingly done by phone or Skype.

Best of all, you may get the chance to debate your opposition ... and decimate them with your superior preparation.

Keys to effective radio interviews:

❏ **Work on your "radio voice":** Yes, babbling into a voice recorder while learning to modulate your voice feels stupid, but sounding like Pee Wee Herman is worse. Other notes: if in the studio, keep the radio microphone about two to four inches from your mouth, speak in a relatively soft voice (don't shout), and learn to listen to both your voice and outside inputs by putting one side of the headphones over your ear and the other behind the ear.

❏ **Avoid silence (or *use* silence):** Radio and television hosts hate "dead air." Therefore, responding to a question with silence or a prolonged, "Duh..." will get cut off before you finish. As in other formats, anticipate the question and have a ready answer. But if you want to make a hostile interviewer look stupid, nail them with a counter-question for which *they* don't have an answer. Early on, I did that with a left-leaning host, resulting in an intentionally awkward silence as he foundered. He actually kept me on the show for an extra segment not because he wanted to hear what I had to say, but so he could make himself look slightly less stupid. I did it again to Alan Colmes on his national radio show, as recounted in the sidebar at the end of this chapter.

❏ **Take calls from listeners:** In a call-in format, you will know you are doing well when the call board lights up (that is, if anybody listens to the show). Presuming you are more prepared on your topic than the callers (and you should be), call-in formats give you control. If callers are supportive, help them out by interjecting examples. If hostile, treat them like the idiots they are.

TV interviews

Television interviews essentially break down into long ("talking head") or short ("sound bite") formats. Unless yours has become the cause célèbre for the fashionably caring (which is unlikely for conservatives), long format television coverage on any show people actually watch is hard to get. Most interviews will be either fifteen second soundbites on the evening news or longer interviews in markets with fewer viewers. Television interviews are also subject to brutal editing, often intended to denigrate or obscure your message.

Short and long interviews require different techniques. Accordingly, we will first look at generalities, and then branch into specifics for each. As a rule, I recommend people video themselves while answering simulated questions. You may discover distracting gestures or facial expressions you never knew you had.

Keys to effective TV interviews:

- ❏ **Dress appropriately:** This might or might not mean business attire. Think about who you want to influence. If you are targeting politicians, wear a business suit. To mobilize the working class, dress in chinos and an open-collared shirt. But whatever you do, don't look cheesy. Ill-fitting clothes, oddball ties, and nose rings will undermine your credibility. I avoid bright colors, plaids, and horizontal stripes on shirts. For small media outlets with cheap cameras (e.g. cable TV), white shirts may "bloom" in the image.

- ❏ **Control the setting:** Certain topics get certain standard treatments from the media. Every gun control interview, for example, starts with stock footage of "gun nuts" blasting away at firing ranges. When contacted for an interview, apply as much control as possible over the interview backdrop and how the issue is framed, including the "B-roll" footage used as a cutaway, ostensibly to provide context and visual interest.

- ❏ **Avoid excessive gesturing or facial expressions:** Not only do hand gestures detract from your message, they can also make you look like a fanatic. Your overall goal is to demonstrate to viewers that you are an expert, not a whacko. Consequently, try to keep your hands in your lap or on a tabletop. Equally, avoid facial expressions. As noted above, practice in front of a video camera is highly instructive.

- ❏ **Look at the interviewer, not the camera:** Looking into the camera gives the interview a deer-in-the-headlights quality that distracts from your message and detracts from your credibility.

Sound bite interviews:

These are short interviews most often done by local news outlets in response to significant state or local news events. Even five minutes of interview will likely be edited to one or two five to ten second clips, meaning that you have to express your perspective in pithy "sound bites." Over the years, I've done hundreds of such interviews, typically in response to pending legislation, local angles on national issues, horrific crimes, and important litigation.

❏ **Don't pontificate:** You've heard people whine about how sound bites oversimplify issues. Perhaps, but the sad reality is that you will never go broke betting on the stupidity of the American public. If you expect them to care, much less help, you'd better deliver a short, simple, compelling message.

❏ **Take your time:** Before answering, think carefully about what you will say. Because most of the footage from a soundbite interview ends up on the cutting room floor, how much time you take to phrase your answer is irrelevant.

❏ **Start over:** If you mangle your words, don't worry, just start over. (It happens to everybody, including George Bush and especially Joe Biden.) Because only a small portion of the footage will be make it through editing, your mistake probably won't be used.

❏ **Render bad answers unusable:** If you make a gaffe that is unflattering to your issue, don't pause before correcting it. If you do, they may use it to make you look bad. Instead, immediately use a run-on sentence to deliberately screw it up, thereby making it difficult to edit the clip down to the unflattering section. Example: "Illegal-aliens-shouldn't-get-free-health-care-disregard-that-it's-not-what-I-meant. What I meant to say is, [pause] 'We intend to preserve our high level of health care for citizens and all *lawful* residents.'"

Talk show interviews:

Remember this: You are the voice of reason. As such, you must confidently present yourself as the resident expert on your topic – someone who has carefully considered the facts and made a logical, fact-based decision on your issue. Dress and behave accordingly.

❏ **Determine whether the interviewer is friendly or hostile.** Because television talk shows, like radio shows, tend to be editorial in nature, your host may or may not be on your side. And he has the power to flame you if he isn't. I'm not saying you should avoid hostile interviews, particularly if the interviewer is someone your people love to hate. But anticipate traps and have glib sound bites ready. To see how it should be done, check YouTube for the episode featuring then-Gun Owners of America Executive Director Larry Pratt dismantling host Piers Morgan on CNN.

❏ **Glance at but *don't read* from talking points:** It is perfectly all right—even recommended—to use interview notes. But because you are dealing with a visual medium, don't read from them. Print them neatly, in large type, arranged by highlighted key phrases which will trigger pre-rehearsed responses. That way, you can simply glance at them from time to time. Hold them low, so they aren't obvious to the camera. "Talking head" interviews at a desk or table are best, since you can place your talking points in front of you on the table to glance at as needed.

❏ **Dominate the debate:** Get in the first word and the last word using crisp sound bites. At a Spectrum News town hall debate against state Representative Christy Clark (whom we later unseated) and Sheriff Garry McFadden (whom we later sued), I carefully prepared my spot at the table, arranging my microphone and cord to be invisible and placing large-print talking points on the table. I wore a dark suit and navy blue tie (navy blue ties evoke trust, red projects power), and kept my reading glasses low on my nose to look slightly pedantic. Using pre-prepared facts and sound bites, including PowerPoint slides which the studio broadcast, I got in the first word, the last word, and dominated nearly everything between.

❏ **Know when to shut up:** "Hot mic" moments have destroyed political careers. During the countdown to the beginning of the interview, be quiet, and position yourself comfortably for the cameras. At the end, say nothing, even when the host bids farewell, until he or she says something which obviously indicates that they are no longer recording. Even then, watch your words.

Thin 'Gruelle' for debate

On one of the state's talking head television shows, I once debated gun control with a Feminazi named Kit Gruelle (really) of the NC Coalition Against Domestic Violence.

What made the debate remarkable was that she sat down at the table and spread out reams of notes and photos while I set before me a single typed page of talking points.

I destroyed her. Every time she would search through stacks of papers for information to answer a question, I would glance at my notes and nail her with the sound bite I had already prepared. I got in the first word and the last word. Thanks to my preparation, she never stood a chance.

Social media interviews

In terms of format, social media interviews are similar to radio and TV interviews except they are typically less formal. What differs is that *you* control your surroundings. Accordingly, get a high quality webcam or conferencing camera and/or microphone. Run tests to check its positioning and ensure you are depicted from the most flattering angle. And finally, use an appropriate backdrop, whether real or digitized, and ensure you aren't disrupted by barking dogs, ringing phones, or other extraneous noise. At the beginning of the pandemic, when TV talk shows started doing "virtual" interviews, I was amazed at the disruptions interviewees allowed.

Problem interviews

Opposition or host won't let you talk: Unfortunately, freewheeling debate-style formats, in which the moderator fails to adequately moderate, seem to be in vogue. (See the sidebar for "The Great Gun Debate".) In such formats, your opposition may refuse to yield time, even interrupting you (a favorite of leftists). CNN's "Crossfire" was an early adopter of exactly such a format. In the ensuing noise, few intelligent arguments are made. The best I can tell you is that if you are subjected to this sort of abuse, dominate it. Repeat a single (important) phrase, if necessary, until your opposition shuts up. I've even seen James Carville, lacking anything intelligent to add, resort to making what can only be called animal noises to talk over his opposition.

❑ **Your host, the heckler:** As an example, think of Rosie O'Donnell ambushing Tom Selleck for his support of the NRA. How you respond will depend on your personality and who the host is. Your options are basically to remain a class act and let the host make a fool of herself, fight back, or simply walk off. Personally, I fight back, ceding absolutely no ground to hostile interviewers.

❑ **Ambushes:** Occasionally, a hostile interviewer will try to lead you into verbal traps. Anticipate them and have ready responses. If necessary, ignore the question and answer the question you are prepared for. Sometimes entire forums are set up as an ambush (again, see "The Great Gun Debate" sidebar). I refused to participate in one such forum but now regard that as a mistake since they just went ahead with their dog and pony show anyway. My policy now is to take all comers. There are, however, several things you can do to mitigate the ambush:

- **Control the audience:** Regardless of what the hosts say, bring your own people and seed them into the audience. At "The Great Gun Debate," they told me they already had an audience, but I brought my own cheering section anyway, and, considering the cabal they had assembled, was glad I did.
- **Control what the cameras see:** Although the Spectrum News town hall reserved front-and-center seats for gun control activists, I entered the studio early, removed the "reserved" signs and seated my own people at the front of the audience. The host didn't have the cajones to challenge me.
- **Feel free to reject the assigned seat:** If you feel the seat they assign is designed to depict you unflatteringly, refuse it.
- **Reject anything you don't like:** At "The Great Gun Debate," they seated us on stools without an accompanying table. They tried to tell me not to use my talking points, to which I replied: "Bullsh-t. I won't read from them, but I either keep them or I walk right now." Faced with having to cancel the forum (which was slated to stream live on the station website), they conceded.

The talking points later unnerved one of the leftists so much that he whined, "It's not fair that you have notes and we're just using our feelings." Gotcha.

'The Great Gun Debate'

I was invited by WXII in Winston-Salem to participate in "The Great Gun Debate" at the Southeastern Center for Contemporary Arts. Using a "Crossfire" format, it was ostensibly four conservatives versus four leftists and would be aired live on the station website and in four parts on TV. For reasons that eventually became clear, I was not allowed to pick conservative debaters. I was also told not to bring audience members, since they had already selected the audience. (I was very glad I ignored that demand.)

Upon arrival, we were met by a cabal of limousine leftists and aged, Birkenstock-wearing hippies. "My side" was essentially worthless, making it one against four. Worse, the moderator introduced the topic and then stepped out of the debate, leaving it unmoderated.

The leftists immediately started trying to talk over me, which didn't work out well for them when I came out swinging. Early on, one of the leftists started name-calling (as leftists are wont to do), saying, "You're a hater." Instead of saying, "No, I'm not," I responded, "Isn't that just like a leftist? You don't have a cogent argument, so you start slinging names."

Despite a hostile format, including being outnumbered, by any objective standard I won the debate. In fact, the slugfest caused the leftists to utter precious gems we turned into a video entitled, "Out of the Mouths of Leftists."

Wanting media too much

Activists often enjoy being "big shots." To do that, they are drawn to the media limelight ... and sometimes end up fried like a moth in a bug zapper.

Such was the case of a certain state-level gun rights activist who was routinely featured in national media. One might debate the actual effectiveness of his organization, but its leader was nationally recognized ... until what became known to some activists as "The Puppy Pistol Incident." It seems that satirist Sacha Baron Cohen, according to Wikipedia, "disguised himself as an Israeli ex-Mossad agent and invited [this individual] to Washington, DC to receive a 'Friend of Israel' award in honor of Israel's 70th anniversary by a fictitious pro-Israel group created by Baron Cohen. In the segment [this individual] endorses 'Kinderguardians,' a phony program to teach and arm schoolchildren as young as three to protect themselves in the classroom."[2] Unfortunately, the rather graphic result ended up on Baron Cohen's television show, "Who is America?"

Similar spoofs have been directed to other leading conservatives with varying degrees of success. The lessons are: (1) Don't want media too much; (2) Examine each media offer with a somewhat jaded and cynical eye; and (3) If it doesn't smell right, don't bite.

Other media considerations

When you are lucky enough to find a friendly reporter, treat him like gold. Give him the first "scoop" on any press release you plan to issue, and respond immediately to requests for quotes or information. As another possibility, I used to periodically take a friendly editorial page deputy editor to lunch at a nice restaurant.

As another weapon, wherever possible, use op-eds in newspapers and online publications to supplement paid media and press releases. In the era when Knight-Ridder would publish most of my op-eds, I often used them to supplement our legislative efforts. As the leftist media became increasingly intolerant of opposing views, I later got a Republican Lt. Governor to co-author one of my op-eds to ensure the editorial department couldn't ignore it. (They did, however, print a leftist rebuttal which violated nearly all of their claimed editorial standards.)

Political advertising

Typical venues for political advertising include radio (relatively cheap and effective), TV (expensive), print media such as newspapers (all but dead), direct communications (e.g. snail mail or email), or social media platforms (e.g. Twitter, Facebook, etc.).

Issue or express advocacy?

Political advertising divides into issue-oriented advertising and "express advocacy." Because violating either election laws or IRS regulations for non-profits can have substantial penalties, when conducting election ads make absolutely sure you are in regulatory compliance with your state board of elections, the Federal Elections Commission, and IRS regulations.

Issue advocacy refers to political advertising focused on "broad political issues rather than specific candidates." In theory, it does not advocate particular electoral outcomes, instead seeking to highlight broader political or social issues. Express advocacy, by contrast, directly and clearly supports or opposes a particular electoral outcome, typically recommending election or defeat of a candidate or candidates or the passage or defeat of specific ballot propositions.

Express advocacy may be conducted using political action committee (PAC) money or, occasionally, (501(c)(4) funds. (See Chapter 11 for limits and restrictions.) Issue ads may be done with money from individuals, corporations, not-for-profit 501(c)(4) organizations and, to a limited extent, non-profit 501(c)(3) organizations.

The problem lies in determining which is which, with SCOTUS and lawmaking are all over the map. Although a 1976 Supreme Court decision (Buckley v. Valeo) established a test using "magic words" such as "vote for" or "support," in 2003 SCOTUS declared such magic words to be "functionally meaningless" (McConnell v. Federal Election Commission), instead applying a vague "reasonable person" standard.

Worse still, the 2002 "Bipartisan Campaign Reform Act" (also called the BPCRA or "McCain-Feingold Act") defined broadcast ads naming federal candidates within 30 days of a primary election or 60 days of a general election as "electioneering communications" and prohibited such ads when paid for by corporations (including non-profit issue organizations).

But then in Citizens United v. FEC (2010), SCOTUS held that the BPCRA prohibition on all independent expenditures by corporations and unions violated the First Amendment's protection of free speech. Although much hated by the left (which, of course, hates *any* free speech with which it disagrees), Citizens United represented a turning point on campaign finance, allowing unlimited election spending by corporations and labor unions and fueling the rise of Super PACs.

Are you confused yet? The good news is that you can avoid problems (albeit with a loss of efficiency) by simply funding your advertising through political action committees and treating it as express advocacy. The bad news is that since you are not a candidate, radio stations will charge you exorbitant issue advertising rates regardless.

Issues & education

We've already noted that educating politicians is generally a waste of effort. They respond best to leverage in the form of votes, money, power, and public accolades. Such cannot be said, however, of the public. While you don't need vast numbers of supporters to make an impact, broadening your base of support beyond your core constituency gives you added power. Do not, however, try to win over groups with interests at variance with your own. Doing so not only represents a waste of money and effort, it also telegraphs your tactics to the opposition.

At whom should you direct political ads?

Political ads can serve any of several goals. Your target depends on the intent of the advertising. Equally, your messaging should vary depending on the target audience.

Top four types of advertising targets:

❏ **Your core constituency:** These are people you know will support you. Although they might not be familiar with your organization, they have already demonstrated commitment to the issue. Consequently, the action-based ads which target them won't waste time and money selling them the issue. Rather, you will leverage your strength by alerting them to particular threats and succinctly telling them what to do about it. Conservative talk radio formats are a perfect instrument for these.

❏ **Natural allies:** To broaden your base of support, appeal to natural allies. Marion Barry, the ever-colorful (and occasionally arrested) mayor of Washington, D.C., did this by campaigning at prisons. The felons couldn't vote, of course, but their relatives could. Ask who will be most helped or harmed by your issue. Will it cost them money or freedom? Once you identify potential sympathizers, identify the organizations representing them and the media serving them. To reach people in these markets, run issue-based ads which alert them to their dilemma. Again, conservative talk radio is a good choice, but you might also consider other radio formats if their market demographic includes potentially simpatico listeners.

❑ **The target himself:** While activating your core constituency, ads can also deliver a clear message to the target that you will hold him accountable for his actions. The ad should run in media the target or one of his cronies (or better yet, donors) will see. It should not only depict the issue in the starkest of terms, it should instruct listeners—usually members of your core constituency—to phone the target. For ads directed at the target, use radio, TV, social media, or print media that he or his donors will likely see.

❑ **Centrists and swing voters:** As an "educational" effort, these are the types of communications the Foundation for Applied Conservative Leadership (FACL) discourages as ineffective. Without doubt, targeting centrists gets less "bang for the buck." But I maintain that if you don't do some form of "education," you will eventually be unable to swing the "3% + 1" that FACL describes. (See Chapter 11.) This can be especially useful for "false flag" operations. We once created a dirty tricks PAC named the "North Carolina Medical Privacy Council" to go after a Democrat in a heavily Democrat district, effectively appealing to soccer moms.

"Politics of personal destruction" exemplified

Perhaps the clearest example of destroying a candidate occurred with the 1987 nomination by President Ronald Reagan of Judge Robert Bork to the Supreme Court. As one of the nation's most respected jurists, the American Bar Association judged him "exceptionally well-qualified." Although a professor of law at Yale and Solicitor General, he was a conservative whom leftists vowed to destroy. Democrat Senator Ted Kennedy claimed, "Robert Bork's America is a land in which ... blacks would sit at segregated lunch counters, rogue police could break down citizens' doors in midnight raids, and children could not be taught about evolution."

Confirmation hearings were so vicious that to "bork" became a verb, meaning to render someone politically ineffective by destroying them personally. Using smear tactics that included digging up lists of his past video rentals, Democrats derailed his nomination. They unsuccessfully tried similar tactics in 2018 to kill the confirmation of Brent Kavanaugh.

Top four types of political advertising:

- **Express advocacy:** The most common form of political advertising is intended to elect or defeat candidates, or to support or oppose ballot proposals. In this case, your target audience is, first and foremost, your core constituency of supporters whom you are motivating to get out and vote. That said, some campaigns might also target low information voters, particularly if the "issue" you are using is only tangentially related to the "problem" you are trying to solve. For example, we defeated one of Michael Bloomberg's "Moms Demand Action" gun control organizers, Representative Christie Clark, largely using mailers which denounced her support for defunding police and were directed at marginally attentive voters who voted in presidential elections but not off-year elections.

- **Legislative advocacy:** Here you are motivating voters to contact a legislator to support or oppose specific legislation. Targets include voters in the legislator's district likely to support you on the issue. But the target also includes the legislator himself, whom you hope to scare into voting your way.

- **Destroying politicians:** Despite claims that "attack ads" don't work, in truth they work very well indeed, especially when used to tie a politician's name to one particular derogatory phrase or nickname. In 2020, we ran social media ads against Joe Biden over his refusal to answer questions on packing the Supreme court, dubbing him "Hidin' Joe Biden." (Trump won in my state, incidentally.) But there has probably been no greater use of derogatory nick names than "Tricky Dick" (and you know exactly who I am talking about).

- **Issue advocacy:** These are educational in nature and intended to bring general awareness to a problem. In this category, plan to spend lots of money to change very little. Your target will be centrists and swing voters.

References:

1. "GRNC responds to Michael Luo and the New York Times," December, 2011, https://www.grnc.org/home/grnc-in-the-media/280-paul-counters-michael-luos-nyt-article

Employing (and enjoying) the "Sound of Silence"

Prior to the 2016 presidential election, we held an AR-15 raffle to raise money for our political action committee. To make it stand out, we raffled off the gun, a thousand rounds of ammunition, and a framed portrait of Hillary Clinton, calling it the "Hillary Clinton Special." The byline for the raffle was, "We're not telling you what to do with the picture, but we understand that the last time we featured Hillary on the cover of our newsletter, she was very popular at the range."

Predictably, leftists claimed we were "threatening" Hillary, garnering media coverage and sending it viral. (In thousands of tickets sold, some went to people in countries where they couldn't even *own* AR-15s.) Among other media, it got me onto the Alan Colmes (as in "Hannity and Colmes") national radio show. Knowing Colmes was a particularly nasty example of leftism, I was ready. Below is the exchange which opened the show.

Colmes: *"So you're having a raffle where people can get an AR-15, right?"*

Valone: *"Correct."*

Colmes: *"And along with that, what, ammunition?"*

Valone: *"A thousand rounds. That's correct."*

Colmes: *"And a picture of Hillary Clinton?"*

Valone: *"Yes, indeed."*

Colmes: *"Now let's do the math here..."*

Rather than defensively justifying the raffle, which was what he intended, I let him twist for a very long five seconds (an eternity on radio), before finally burying him with a simple question.

Valone: *"What 'math' is that?"*

More silence.

Colmes (flustered): *"You know what I'm talking about, right?"*

Valone (laughing and changing subject): *"We call this the 'Hillary Clinton Special' because if elected, she will undoubtedly be the gun salesperson of the century."*

If I had taken the bait and answered, "We're not threatening Hillary," he would have destroyed me. Instead, I evaded his trap by using silence and feigned ignorance to destroy *him*. Notice that even in my parsed answer, I did not raise the fallacious claim that we were "threatening" Hillary. Colmes was smart enough not to go there himself, because if he had, I would have responded: "Alan, that you would think such a thing says more about you than about me."

325

 # In Conclusion...

I hope you find utility from this little foray into what Representative Jay Adams, in his foreword, described as "hard core, no holds barred, political reality." He exactly encapsulated the goal of the book when he said I "refined Alinsky's methods and turned them mercilessly against the left." (Thanks, Jay. The many nasty things I've said about politicians do not apply to you.)

My aspiration is for *Rules for ANTI-Radicals* to become the standard textbook for conservative political activists and, as such, apply just a little restraint to western civilization's headlong rush toward the yawning precipice of nihilism.

But I harbor no illusions that *Rules for ANTI-Radicals* will meet with universal acclaim, even among conservatives. To those who will claim I'm giving tactics to the opposition, I would note that the opposition has been using variations of them against us for generations. The Evil Party gets it. Only the Stupid Party seems blithely unaware.

To those who will claim I am wrong about political players and the nature of politics, that educating politicians and appealing to their better natures is the only way to go, please return to golfing and watching football. You are fools.

And to those who will claim I am stooping to Alinsky's level by refining and adapting his subterfuge, please allow me to quote what is said to be the original motto of Israel's ruthlessly effective intelligence service, the Mossad, which has long understood the realities of facing existential threat.

"By way of deception, thou shalt do war."[1]

References:

1. Clair Hoy and Victor Ostrovsky, *By Way of Deception: The Making and Unmaking of a Mossad Officer*, Stoddart Publishing, 1990.

Appendix I
Elections Terminology

What follows is a short glossary of basic elections terminology. Because each state's requirements and definitions are unique, check your state election board for specifics. For a more complete election glossary, check "Glossary of Election Terminology," U.S. Election Assistance Commission, available at: https://www.eac.gov/sites/default/files/glossary_files/Glossary_of_Election_Terms_EAC.pdf

Bundling: Practice in which multiple contributions from a single industry, interest group, company, or group are channeled to candidates. Under federal law, legal bundling can occur in two ways: (1) an individual or group (a "conduit" or "bundler") collects and delivers the contributions in a "bundle" to a candidate; or (2) a coordinated effort by individuals from the same industry, interest group, or company to send separate contributions to candidates. Bundling allows contributions whose total exceeds individual contribution limits. Check state laws for legality.

Campaign Committee: Registered fundraising committee set up by a candidate to finance a campaign for state or federal office. Campaign committees must file regular (at least quarterly) campaign finance reports with the Federal Election Commission or state election board detailing donors and expenditures.

Citizens United v. Federal Election Commission: U.S. Supreme Court ruling in January 2010 which struck down limits of the Bipartisan Campaign Reform Act (BCRA) of 2002 by allowing corporations (including non-profit organizations) and unions to use general treasuries for political advertisements expressly advocating election or defeat of a candidate and allowing nonprofit groups to air electioneering communications within 30 days of a primary election and 60 days of a general election.

Coordination: Campaign activity made in cooperation, consultation, or concert with or at the request or suggestion of, a candidate, a candidate's authorized committee, or their agents, or a political party committee, or its agents. Such activities must be reported to the FEC or state election board as "in-kind" contributions to candidates who benefit. Coordination by independent expenditure ("super") PACs is prohibited. The FEC three-pronged test of coordination (communications must meet all three to be considered coordinated) includes: (1) the source of payment (payment prong); (2) the subject matter of the communication (content prong); and (3) the interaction between the person paying for the communication and the candidate or political party committee (conduct prong).

Electioneering communication: Broadcast advertisements which: (1) air within 30 days of a primary election or 60 days of a general election; (2) mention a federal candidate; and (3) are aimed at 50,000 or more members of the electorate of the office the candidate is seeking. Expenditures must be reported to the FEC. Although the 2002 Bipartisan Campaign Reform Act barred special interest groups from spending unregulated soft money on electioneering communications, the U.S. Supreme Court rejected that prohibition as unconstitutional in Citizens United v. FEC.

Express advocacy: Political advertisements which explicitly advocate the election or defeat of clearly identified candidates.

Federal Election Commission (FEC): The independent regulatory agency responsible for civil enforcement and administration of campaign finance law.

Hard Money: Regulated contributions from individuals or PACs to federal candidates, party committees, or other PACs of money used for federal elections. Hard money is subject to contribution limits and prohibitions and may be used to directly support or oppose candidates.

Independent expenditure: Also known as "express advocacy," independent expenditures are advertisements (e.g. TV, radio, or social media), mailings, or email that expressly advocate election or defeat of clearly identified candidates by using words such as "vote for," "defeat," or "support." Independent expenditures have the advantage of not being subject to campaign contribution limits, but they may not be coordinated with candidates who benefit.

Internal Revenue Code (IRC) 501(c)(3) organization: Non-profit organization for religious, charitable, scientific, legal, or educational purposes. May conduct limited legislative advocacy (lobbying), but it may not be a "substantial" part of its activity. May not conduct express advocacy. These organizations are tax exempt and donations are tax deductible.

IRC 501(c)(4) organization: Commonly called "social welfare" organizations, they may engage in limited express advocacy provided political activities do not become a "substantial" part of its activities. These organizations are tax exempt but donations are not tax deductible.

IRC 527 Committee: Tax-exempt groups organized under section 527 of the Internal Revenue Code to raise money for political activities including voter mobilization efforts, issue advocacy, and, in some cases, express advocacy. The FEC requires 527 groups to file regular disclosure reports only if they engage in either activities expressly advocating the election or defeat of a federal candidate or in electioneering communications. The Citizens United ruling allows 527 committees to raise unlimited funds from individuals, corporations, and unions to expressly advocate for or against federal candidates, causing many 527 groups to register with the FEC as "super PACs."

Issue advertising: Political advertising framed around an issue which does not specifically instruct the audience to vote for or against a candidate. Issue ads that mention a federal candidate and are broadcast within 30 days of a primary election or 60 days of a general election must be reported to the FEC as electioneering communications. Issue ads may address public policy issues and the position of particular public officials on those issues, but due to wording or timing do not qualify as either independent expenditures or electioneering communications.

Lobbyist: Individuals working to influence public policy and how legislators vote. Federally, lobbyists must register with the Senate and House, and must disclose who hired them, how much they are paid, what issues or bills they are lobbying on, and what federal agencies they are contacting. State legislature lobbyist registration requirements vary and are summarized by the National Conference of State Legislatures at: https://www.ncsl.org/research/ethics/50-state-chart-lobbyist-registration-requirements.aspx

Political Action Committee (PAC): A political committee registered with the FEC or SBE which raises and spends money to elect or defeat candidates. PACs may be either "separate segregated funds" or "nonconnected PACs." Separate segregated funds are administered by corporations, labor unions, member organizations, or trade associations and can only raise funds from individuals associated with the connected groups. Nonconnected PACs are not affiliated with those groups and may solicit funds from the public: They are financially independent and pay for themselves via contributions they raise. PACs may either donate to candidates, in which case they are subject to FEC or SBE donation limits, or they may conduct unlimited independent expenditures for or against candidates.

Soft Money: Contributions legally made outside the framework of contribution limits to state or local parties, state or local candidates, or outside interest groups.

State board of elections (SBE): Here we are using "SBE" as shorthand for state elections boards which vary widely between states and must, therefore, be individually researched.

Super PAC: Also known as an independent expenditure-only committee, this type of political action committee came into existence in 2010 following a federal court decision in SpeechNow.org v. Federal Election Commission. Super PACs may raise and spend unlimited sums of money for the sole purpose of making independent expenditures to support or oppose candidates. Unlike traditional political action committees, super PACs may not donate money directly to candidates, nor may they coordinate with candidates. Super PACs are required to disclose donors to the FEC.

Appendix II
Issue Plan Example

Issue Plan:

Judicial Fairness Project "Defund Police" Mailings

Using our super PAC, the Judicial Fairness Project (JFP), "defund police" petition mailers are intended to use the issue of individual and family safety to defeat North Carolina House candidates who also support gun control legislation.

Objectives

Defeat seven leftist Democrat candidates who are gun control supporters and who signed a national "defund police" petition: Brian Farkas (NCH009), Sidney Batch (NCH037), Frances Jackson (NCH045), Nicole Quick (NCH059), Ray Russell (NCH093), Christy Clark (NCH098), and Brandon Lofton (NCH104). The mailings will be timed to arrive just prior to the first weekend of early voting.

Target Demographic

Polls find roughly two-thirds of Americans oppose defunding police, suggesting the issue will resonate with voters. In a highly polarized election year, voters affiliated with Democrat or Republican parties will likely align closely with party affiliation. Therefore, the JFP mailings will target unaffiliated voters, particularly "low information" voters who are not intensely "political," as demonstrated by voting only presidential elections (as opposed to off-year elections). Because security-minded males can be reasonably expected to be more likely than females to oppose defunding police, the target demographic for the mailings will be unaffiliated male voters who vote only presidential elections.

Message

Targeting the second level of Maslow's Hierarchy of Needs, mail pieces will stress that by signing a national petition to defund police, the candidate opposed has prioritized a radical leftist agenda over the safety of the recipient and his family. The front of the postcard will feature buildings aflame. The back will feature statements by well-known people either forced to defend themselves against rioters or who lost loved ones in riots. The people featured will be suburbanites similar to the target demographic.

Delivery Method

Mailers will be half page flats mailed at USPS Presort First Class rates using the mailing house bulk permit (since we can't use our non-profit bulk permit for PAC mailings). Total mail count will be 45,725 pieces with a total cost, including printing, of $22,685.85.

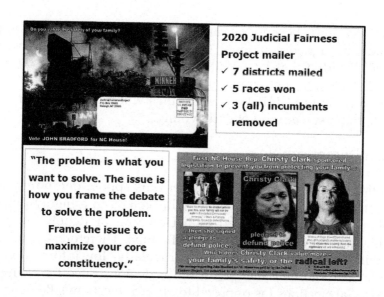

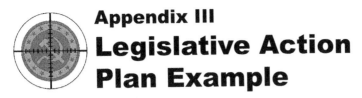

Appendix III
Legislative Action Plan Example

Legislative Action Plan:

Defeat H. 1744, "Gun Trafficking"

Analysis

In June of 2002, Representative Jennifer Weiss introduced House Bill 1744, which would create a "Gun Crime Interdiction Task Force" to harass lawful gun owners and promulgate gun control. It would also create a new Article 53D under North Carolina statutes entitled "Mental Health Records Access" which would give the North Carolina Department of Health and Human Services access to mental health data for the ostensible purpose of determining who is prohibited from owning firearms, but which would actually serve to discourage gun ownership due to deterioration of medical privacy, as well as giving bureaucrats new means for restricting gun ownership.

Objectives

Because Democrats control both chambers of the General Assembly, as well as the governorship, it is highly likely that if the bill gets a hearing, it will pass. Therefore, our objectives will be to:

1. Suppress a hearing for the H. 1744.

2. Make the concept of releasing mental health records politically radioactive to discourage future introduction.

Methods

We received information that the state gun control group, North Carolinians Against Gun Violence (NCAGV), received a grant for $60,000 from the Tsunami Fund, a "pop-up" front group for the left-wing Tides Center, which it used to hire the preeminent North Carolina Democrat lobbying firm, Parker, Poe, Adams and Bernstein. Thanks to Parker/

Rules for Anti-RADICALS

Poe lobbyist Bruce Thompson "sunshining" the bill to the NC Child Fatality Task Force (CFTF) to secure a CFTF endorsement, we procured a copy of the grant proposal to the Tides Center, which had been endorsed by anti-gun Democrat Governor Mike Easley. Fortunately, Easley was embroiled in a legal controversy over misappropriation of state resources, including the gubernatorial helicopter, making him vulnerable. Therefore, we will utilize the following steps:

1. Create a "dirty tricks" PAC called "The North Carolina Medical Privacy Council" to run radio spots, transferring money from the GRNC Political Victory Fund to the new entity.

2. Make the issue medical privacy rather than guns. To do so, we will bill brand H. 1744 to draw opposition not only from gun owners, but also suburban mothers in Rep. Weiss' heavily Democrat district who would logically be fearful of children's medical records for things such as ADHD being disclosed and permanently damaging children's future prospects with such diagnoses. Therefore, we will bill brand H. 1744 as "The Medical Records Disclosure Act."

3. Because Gov. Easley signed the NCAGV grant proposal for the bill, we will brand it "Gov. Easley's Medical Records Disclosure Act" and direct all opposing input directly to the governor's office via both email and telephone calls.

4. We will run radio spots on all prominent radio stations in the state capitol, Raleigh, while the General Assembly is in session, implying that "Gov. Easley's Medical Records Disclosure Act" will permanently stigmatize children with ADHD or other behavioral problems, giving the governor's office phone number, and instructing people to call. The intent is for the Democrat governor to call the Democrat speaker of the house, instructing him not to give the bill a hearing because the governor already had enough problems. Budget for radio spots: $6,250.00, giving us approximately fifty spots concentrated over three days in Raleigh and intended to be heard by the governor and his staff.

5. Burn lobbyists for Parker/Poe with the governor by identifying on our website the fact that it was their lobbyist from whom we got the grant proposal endorsed by Easley.

6. Burn the left-leaning CFTF with the governor by identifying on our website that it was the CFTF which is the source of the governor's pain.

Results

On day two of the radio campaign, I called the governor's office, saying: "I would like to register my opposition to Governor Easley's Medical Records Disclosure Act." The governor's secretary gave me a weary sigh and replied, "Thank you." I said, "Don't you want my name and address?" Sounding utterly fatigued, she replied, "No, at this point we're just keeping a tally." Gotcha.

The following day, Bruce Thompson, the lobbyist for Parker/Poe and NCGV, stopped me in the legislative office building stairwell, saying, "That is the lowest thing you have ever done." I replied, "From you, Bruce, I will take that as a compliment." The exchange suggested that Gov. Easley had indeed been displeased with Parker/Poe.

Meanwhile, the Raleigh *News & Observer* "Under the Dome" political column ran a piece entitled "Gun Group Behind Medical Privacy Ads," quoting Weiss as saying, "There's a real subterfuge going on here." Because legislators routinely read the column, it delivered a message that we would use any method to go after legislators, even in supposedly "safe" districts.

Ultimately, H. 1744 died a quiet death for lack of a hearing, NCGV's grant proposal dried up for lack of results, and the CFTF got its funding dramatically cut. This project rendered NCGV combat-ineffective for nearly ten years. Overall, a highly satisfactory outing.

Appendix IV
Example of
'Red Fox Four' Analysis

Below is an example of Red Fox Four (RF4) analysis of a legislative project, in this case using the bill branding of "Medical Records Disclosure Act" and subsequent advertising campaign to kill H. 1744 ("Gun Trafficking") as described in Appendix III. Depicted are the analyses of three activist leaders, averaged to produce a final score. Note that there is no "good" or "bad" score. RF4 is merely a tool to provoke thought on whether or not a project is worthwhile.

	A	B	C	D	E
A11	ƒₓ 4) The cost to liberty if we lose? (Rate 0 to -10)				
	RED FOX FOUR ANALYSIS	SCORE 1	SCORE 2	SCORE 3	AVERAGE
1	**RED FOX FOUR ANALYSIS**				
2	Win **or** lose:				
3	1. Just by fighting the fight, will it attract more money or people to my cause? (Rate +10 to -10)	3	5	6	
4	2. Will it help friends or allies? (Rate +10 to -10)	2	4	4	
5	3. Will it hurt enemies or their allies? (Rate +10 to -10)	9	10	10	
6	• Will it defund them?	Yes	Yes	Yes	
7	• Will it help beat them in the next election?	No	No	No	
8	Win **and** Lose:				
9	4. What is:				
10	• The value to policy if we win? (Rate 0 to +10)	8	9	9	
11	• The cost to liberty if we lose? (Rate 0 to -10)	0	0	0	
12	**TOTAL:**	22	28	29	26.3

Appendix IV: Red Fox Four analysis, "Medical Records Disclosure Act"

Appendix V
Candidate Evaluation Spreadsheet

Our "Remember in November" project offers objective evaluations of where individual candidates stand on the gun issue. Voting records on relevant legislation, as well as survey scores, bill sponsorship history, and leadership history of either moving or killing gun-related legislation are plugged into an Excel spreadsheet which calculates the percentage of the time a candidate can be expected to concur with a control group of conservative gun owners. Candidates agreeing at least 90% of the time receive four stars (****), those agreeing at least 80% of the time get three stars (***), etc. Objective evaluations, together with district demographic data, are then used by our federally registered PAC to more efficiently prioritize "focus districts" in which the PAC does independent expenditures for or against candidates.

Incumbent	Last Name	Name on ballot	Race	Party	Star	GRNC-Val	Surv Avg	Voting-recent	Voting-All	Bill Sup-Recent	Bill Sup-All	Other	Race type	Elec_Year
Y	GOODWIN	Edward C. Goodwin	NCH001	R	****	99	93	100	100	100	100		NCH	2020g
	NICHOLSON	Emily Bunch Nicholson	NCH001	D	0	0							NCH	2020g
Y	YARBOROUGH	Larry Yarborough	NCH002	R	***	86	87		85				NCH	2020g
	DEPORTER	Cindy Deporter	NCH002	D	0	0							NCH	2020g
	WHITE	Dorothea D. White	NCH003	D	*	67	67						NCH	2020g
	TYSON	Steve Tyson	NCH003	R	***	82	82						NCH	2020g
Y	DIXON	Jimmy Dixon	NCH004	R	****	97	100		96		100		NCH	2020g
	SCHULTE	Christopher Schulte	NCH004	D	0	0							NCH	2020g
	KIRKLAND	Donald Kirkland	NCH005	R	***	88	88						NCH	2020g
Y	HUNTER	Howard J. Hunter III	NCH005	D	0	11		11				NCH	2020g
Y	HANIG	Bobby Hanig	NCH006	R	****	100	98	100	100	100			NCH	2020g
	FULCHER	Tommy Fulcher	NCH006	D	0	0							NCH	2020g
	WINSLOW	Matthew Winslow	NCH007	R	****	95	95						NCH	2020g
	STOVER	Phil Stover	NCH007	D	0	0							NCH	2020g
	MOORE	Tony Moore	NCH008	R	****	90	90						NCH	2020g
Y	SMITH	Kandie D. Smith	NCH008	D	0	0	0	0	0			NCH	2020g
	FARKAS	Brian Farkas	NCH009	D	0	0							NCH	2020g
	JONES	Perrin Jones	NCH009	R	****	100			100				NCH	2020g
Y	BELL	John Bell	NCH010	R	****	100		100	100	100			NCH	2020g
	MARTIN	Carl Martin	NCH010	D	0	0							NCH	2020g
Y	DAHLE	Allison Dahle	NCH011	D	0	0	0	0	0			NCH	2020g
	POPE	Clark Pope	NCH011	R	0	0							NCH	2020g
	TRAVERS	Adrian Lee Travers	NCH011	L	0	0							NCH	2020g
Y	HUMPHREY	Chris Humphrey	NCH012	R	****	97	92		100				NCH	2020g
	COX-DAUGHERTY	Virginia Cox-Daugherty	NCH012	D	0	0							NCH	2020g
Y	MCELRAFT	Patricia (Pat) McElraft	NCH013	R	****	95	98		92	100	100		NCH	2020g
	BAYLIFF	Buck Bayliff	NCH013	D	0	0							NCH	2020g
Y	CLEVELAND	George G. Cleveland	NCH014	R	****	99	100		100	100	100	95	NCH	2020g
	WOFFORD	Marcy Wofford	NCH014	D	0	0							NCH	2020g
Y	SHEPARD	Phillip Shepard	NCH015	R	****	96	96		95		100		NCH	2020g
	GOMAA	Carolyn F. Gomaa	NCH015	D	0	0							NCH	2020g
Y	SMITH	Carson Smith	NCH016	R	****	95	84		100				NCH	2020g
	FINTAK	Debbi Fintak	NCH016	D	0	0							NCH	2020g
Y	ILER	Frank Iler	NCH017	R	***	86	89		85		100		NCH	2020g

STAR_RATING Final Draft Surveys Voting Other Incumbents Elec_Raw LookUp G_Verify Instructions Current_Survey_Score ⊕

Remember in November Candidate Evaluation Criteria

Candidate evaluation formula

$$\text{Evaluation\%} = \frac{(\text{Vote\%}) \times 2 + \text{Survey \%} + \text{Bill Support \%}}{4}$$

Rules for Anti-RADICALS

Methods

1. To determine a baseline, surveys are issued to a control group of "conservative gun voters." Candidate metrics measure correlation between the candidate and control group.

   a. "Survey %" measures how closely the candidate's survey score correlates with the control group

   b. "Vote %" measures how closely candidate's voting record correlate with the control group

   c. "Bill Support %" includes the bills sponsored by the candidate and also the willingness (or lack of willingness) by the speaker or president pro tem, rules chair and committee chair to give or deny hearings to relevant bills.

   d. "Evaluation%" is the mean of the variables above with the exception that voting score, as the most accurate metric of candidate evaluation, is over-weighted by a factor of two.

2. Past year voting and bill sponsorship data compiled back to 1994. Survey scores and chamber leadership bill support metrics included in 1998.

342

Appendix VI
Example of Legislative Action Alert

GRNC Alert:

CCW in Parks & Restaurants Hits Floor Tuesday

Sponsored by Reps. Hilton, Barnhart, Steen and Hastings, HB 111, "Handgun Permit Valid in Parks & Restaurants," would enable concealed handgun permit-holders to protect themselves in restaurants, and in both municipal and state parks.

<u>NC House members need to hear from you ASAP</u>: Even if you have already contacted them, do so again. There are still a few problems getting the Republican caucus to hang together.

Give your rep instructions to do 3 things:

1. Vote for final passage of HB 111;

2. Vote for an amendment to be offered to remove the "Ross Amendment" which would encourage restaurant servers to ask patrons whether they are carrying firearms. In committee, Rep. Deborah Ross used the amendment to get the NC Restaurant & Lodging Association to oppose the bill (she failed); and

3. Oppose any and all weakening amendments made to the bill, including a plan reportedly afoot to carve out a "gun free" zone at any sporting event (e.g. Little League games) held within public parks.

IMMEDIATE ACTION REQUIRED

❑ <u>CALL YOUR OWN NC HOUSE REP</u>: Do so even if you know he or she supports the bill, telling them to support removing the weakening Ross amendment and to oppose any other weakening amendments proposed for the bill. Again, find out who represents you in the NC House by going to: **http://www.grnc.org/contact_reps.htm**

❏ CONTACT REP. DAVID GUICE: (Name pronounced "Gice"). Let him know that no "carve out" for sporting events is needed in parks because concealed handgun permit-holders have proven themselves responsible. In fact, creating another "victim disarmament zone" might well cost lives. Guice represents Henderson, Polk and Transylvania counties. Reach him at: David.Guice@ncleg. net or 919-715-4466.

DELIVER THIS MESSAGE

Rep. Guice:

NC concealed carry has reduced violent crime: Since 1995, when our concealed carry law passed, the rate of overall NC crime has dropped by 27.7%, while the rate of violent crime dropped by a whopping 37.1%. This mirrors the study by John Lott and David Mustard which found that concealed handgun laws deter murder, rape, and aggravated assault.

State parks have not seen the same drop: An extrapolation of partial data for the same years estimates only an 8.9% drop in crime within state parks. Although crime in municipal parks is not tracked, news accounts and the urban location of many suggest that crime is actually increasing in these "victim disarmament zones." HB 111 will not only benefit permit-holders, it will deter violent crime.

NC permit-holders are overwhelmingly responsible: Of 336,743 concealed handgun permits approved since 1995, only 1007 have been revoked for any reason (that's less than a third of one percent, or 0.29%). Although the SBI doesn't keep reasons for revocation, other states' experience suggests that few of those revocations are for misuse of firearms.

Respectfully,

Appendix VII
Example of Legislative Talking Points

Grass Roots North Carolina, PO Box 10665, Raleigh, NC 27605, 877-282-0939, www.GRNC.org

Issue paper:
H. 398: Pistol Purchase Permit Repeal

In North Carolina, legal purchase of a handgun requires either a pistol purchase permit or a concealed handgun permit. The purchase permit is turned in at the time of sale, no record of the sale is kept by the sheriff, and the permit is valid for five years, raising the possibility that an applicant could become disqualified after obtaining the permit but still use it to bypass the FBI's computerized National Instant Background Check System (NICS).

- **Purchase permits are used to deny minorities**: Passed in 1919, North Carolina's archaic pistol purchase permit law is a vestige of the Jim Crow era, when it was used by sheriffs to deny gun purchases to blacks by abusing its subjective "good moral character" requirement.
  - **Racism continues today**: Worse, a recent North Carolina Law Review[1] paper noted that **discrimination in issuing permits continues to this day**. In Wake County, for example, 23.54% of black applicants were denied permits between 2015 and 2020, but only 8.37% of whites – **a rejection rate for blacks which is three times higher than whites**.

- **Purchase permits are used to obstruct gun purchases**: No case is more clear than that of Wake County Sheriff Gerald Baker who, citing COVID-19, **stopped issuing permits altogether,** denying citizens the ability to protect themselves at exactly the moment civil unrest was increasing across the U.S. Sued three times, Baker only recently began complying with NCGS 14-404(f), which requires permits be issued to qualified applicants within 14 days. Meanwhile, **months-long delays continue in Mecklenburg County** and elsewhere.

- **NC Sheriffs' Association supports repeal of purchase permit law:** NCSA president Sheriff David A. Mahoney of Transylvania County has confirmed that the association recently voted in favor of repealing North Carolina's archaic, Jim Crow-era purchase permit system. Lobbyists for the NCSA now call the law "duplicative."

- **NC Law Review excoriates purchase permit law:** A recent UNC School of Law paper entitled "Misfire: How the North Carolina Pistol Purchase Permit System Misses the Mark of Constitutional Muster and Effectiveness,"[2] even beyond noting racism in both the law's origins and current application, notes that it falls short of appropriate levels of judicial scrutiny, making it **unconstitutional** under the Second Amendment and violating the equal protection clause of the Fourteenth Amendment.

- **Only three states have purchase permit laws:** The UNC paper listed above goes on to note that only Maryland, Michigan and Nebraska (and New York City)[3] have purchase permit laws similar to North Carolina's.

- **Purchase permit law is ineffective:** Comparing states which have permit laws with states which do not, the UNC paper finds that **states without permit laws have 7% fewer handgun murders** than states with the laws. While a basic tenet of statistics is that correlation does not imply causation, the data make it difficult to substantiate claims that permit laws increase safety.

- **Point of sale background checks increase safety:** If the purchase permit law is repealed, background checks would be done at the point of sale via NICS. Because purchase permits are valid for 5 years, are untraceable, and allow gun buyers to bypass NICS, *The Charlotte Observer* found 60 felons and 230 substance abusers who could potentially continue to hold permits enabling them to buy firearms.[4]

GRNC strongly urges you to support H. 398
to repeal North Carolina's pistol purchase law!

References:

1. "Misfire: How the North Carolina Pistol Purchase Permit System Misses the Mark of Constitutional Muster and Effectiveness," Nicholas Gallo, *North Carolina Law Review*, UNC School of Law, Volume 99, Number 2, Article 7.
2. Ibid.
3. Ibid. Although the UNC paper lists Iowa, the state has since repealed its permit system:
   https://www.legis.iowa.gov/legislation/BillBook?ga=89&ba=hf756
4. "Dozens of felons hold gun permits in Mecklenburg Country, Gavin Off and Bruce Henderson, *The Charlotte Observer*, May 12, 2013:
   http://www.charlotteobserver.com/2013/05/12/4036604/dozens-of-felons-hold-gun-permits.html

Want more information on activist tactics?
Find online seminars or schedule an in-person
seminar for your organization by going to

www.RulesForANTIRadicals.com

Appendix VIII
Example of
'F.O.G.' Letter

Grass Roots North Carolina
P.O. Box 10665
Raleigh, NC 27605
877.282.0939 www.GRNC.org

October 22, 2013

Charlotte-Mecklenburg Police Department

601 East Trade Street

Charlotte, NC 28202

Attn: Chief Rodney Monroe

Dear Chief Monroe:

Reports from gun dealers at two recent gun shows, as well as internal communications within your department, indicate you are attempting to regulate gun sales from individuals to dealers, and possibly between individuals who are not dealers under N.C.G.S. Article 45, (Part 1, "Pawnbrokers and Cash Converters") by classifying them as "cash converters." Specifically, your officers have been distributing and requiring use of the enclosed "CMPD Gun Show Gun Purchase Form."

Please be advised that: (1) As outlined below, the "cash converter" statute clearly does not apply to gun shops or private transactions; and (2) The imposition of a local gun law or regulation is in violation of § 14-409.40 ("Statewide uniformity of local regulation").

As passed in Session Law 2011-325 and then re-codified in S.L. 2012-46, § 66-387(2) defines "cash converter" as follows:

> *(2)   Cash converter. - A person engaged in the business of purchasing goods from the public for cash at a permanently located retail store who holds himself or herself out to the public by signs, advertising, or other methods as engaging in that business. The term does not include any of the following:*
>
> > *a.   Pawnbrokers.*
> >
> > *b.   Persons whose goods purchases are made directly from manufacturers or wholesalers for their inventories.*
> >
> > *c.   Precious metals dealers, to the extent that their transactions are regulated under Part 2 of this Article.*
> >
> > *d.   Purchases by persons primarily in the business of obtaining from the*

Rules for Anti-RADICALS

public, either by purchase or exchange, used clothing, children's furniture, and children's products, provided the amount paid for the individual item purchased is less than fifty dollars ($50.00).

e. Purchases by persons primarily in the business of obtaining from the public, either by purchase or exchange, sporting goods and sporting equipment, provided the amount paid for the individual item purchased is less than fifty dollars ($50.00).

Please note that neither gun show vendors who purchase firearms from individuals nor private transfers between individuals meet the definition of "cash converter" for the following reasons:

1. Although your form is entitled "CMPD Gun Show Gun Purchase Form," nothing in the statute addresses gun shows any more than it addresses flea markets or other venues, leading any reasonable person to conclude that you are attempting to stigmatize gun shows;

2. A gun show vendor is not "a person engaged in the business of purchasing goods from the public for cash at a permanently located retail store." Not only do gun show purchases **not** take place at a "permanently located retail store," many gun show vendors do not even possess such locations.

3. By any reasonable plain language interpretation of the statute, it even more clearly excludes private transfers between individuals not engaged in a firearms-related business;

4. I am unaware of any gun show dealer who "holds himself or herself out to the public by signs, advertising, or other methods as engaging" in the business of buying firearms particularly at the show itself, with the possible exception of pawnbrokers, who are specifically exempt as described below;

5. The cash converter statute specifically exempts both "Pawnbrokers" and "Persons whose goods purchases are made directly from manufacturers or wholesalers for their inventories," which would, in all likelihood, encompass nearly all gun show dealers.

Accordingly, Grass Roots North Carolina strongly advises you to cease and desist in your apparent attempt to register guns and gun owners in contravention of both Article 45 of the North Carolina General Statutes and § 14-409.40. Failure to do so will result in legal action. Please note that under § 6-21.7 ("Attorneys' fees; cities or counties acting outside the scope of their authority"), we will also seek to recover associated legal expenses.

I can be reached directly at (123) 456-7890. To preclude further action, please reply within five (5) business days.

Respectfully,

F. Paul Valone
President, Grass Roots North Carolina
Executive Director, Rights Watch International

Appendix IX
Example of Fundraising Copy

Grass Roots North Carolina

Armatissimi e liberissimi

877-282-0939
Fax: 919-573-0354
P.O. Box 10665
Raleigh, NC 27605

Gun Rights Supporters:

It's been a busy pandemic for GRNC. Earlier, I promised that Grass Roots North Carolina was devoted to safeguarding gun rights during the coronavirus emergency. **Please allow me to update you on our progress.**

Building on previous success

You may recall that **in 2011, GRNC and the Second Amendment Foundation sued then-Governor Beverly Perdue** over what had previously been a complete ban on carrying firearms outside the home during a declared state of emergency (SOE).

We won in federal court on Second Amendment grounds and, even though we were disappointed that the decision never became precedent-setting law in the Supreme Court (since Perdue chose not to appeal her loss), we did go back to the General Assembly, where **in 2012 GRNC forced repeal of NC's state of emergency gun ban**, making it possible for lawful North Carolinians to protect their families when most needed.

Counties try

take advantage of emergency

to curtail gun rights

But nobody envisioned a multi-week (month?) state of emergency. When most states issued stay-at-home orders, closing "non-essential" businesses, **counties and cities across NC started trying to close gun shops**.

349

Worse, the closures and other restrictions starting taking place exactly during the huge rush to
buy guns for family protection during the emergency, with restrictions in North Carolina taking two
forms:

➤ Sheriffs started restricting issuance of pistol
purchase permits and concealed handgun permits;
and

➤ Counties started closing gun shops as "non-essential."

GRNC is "seven for seven" against
anti-gun local governments

GRNC fought back immediately, as reports came in of
local government malfeasance. The game-changer occurred on March 28 when, thanks to Gun Owners of
America, the **Trump administration added firearm-related businesses** to the non-mandatory "critical infrastructure" guidelines for federal stay-at-home
recommendations.

In little more than a week:

➤ **GRNC sued Wake County Sheriff Gerald Baker**: When
Baker announced he was suspending issuance of
purchase permits and concealed handgun permits,
GRNC, together with the Firearms Policy Coalition and Second Amendment Foundation, filed suit
in federal court on a variety of grounds. Baker
is now under a consent order forcing him to start
issuing permits again in a few days.

➤ **GRNC threatened suit against Wake County**: When
Wake County issued a declaration effectively shutting down gun shops, GRNC and Gun Owners
of America sent a "Fear of God" ("FOG") letter
to county commissioners. Although Chairman Greg
Ford first scoffed at GRNC supporters who called
him out, when he got the letter he immediately
reversed course and followed the federal guidelines, immediately opening gun shops.

➤ **GRNC threatened suit against Greensboro**: Again
joining GOA, GRNC issued a FOG letter to Greens-

boro Mayor Nancy Vaughan, who had publicly announced gun stores would be closed. After getting the letter, Vaughan immediately (and tersely) responded that she had been "incorrect" in her gun-hating interpretation of Guilford County guidelines.

➢ **GRNC threatened suit against Guilford County**: After receiving the "FOG letter" from GRNC and GOA, Guilford County commissioners responded that they were following federal guidelines, and that gun shops would remain open.

➢ **GRNC threatened suit against Orange County**: After receiving the "FOG letter" from GRNC and GOA, Orange County commissioners responded that they were following federal guidelines, and that gun shops would remain open.

➢ **GRNC threatened suit against Durham County**: After receiving the "FOG letter" from GRNC and GOA, Durham County commissioners responded that they were following federal guidelines, and that gun shops would remain open.

➢ **GRNC threatened suit against the City of Durham**: Like Vaughan in Greensboro, City of Durham Mayor Stephen Schewel is a virulently anti-gun leftist. But in response to the GRNC/GOA FOG letter, **even he backed down**. Although he refused to make a public statement, effective April 4 at 5 PM, the city deferred to Durham County guidelines, leaving gun shops open. (I'm sure signing that order stuck in his craw.)

These victories don't even include:

➢ **Mecklenburg County**, whose declaration appeared to keep firearm-related businesses open but where a Charlotte-Mecklenburg Police representative was telling people on Facebook that gun shops had to close. When GRNC contacted the CMPD attorney, he removed the offending post; or

➢ **Anti-gun Gov. Roy Cooper**, who didn't include gun businesses among "essential" businesses, but was smart enough to avoid getting sued by issuing "FAQs" that stipulated gun businesses could

Rules for Anti-RADICALS

stay open provided they follow social distancing guidelines.

Please help make continued victory possible

Even in this time of uncertainty, many of you have contributed generously to GRNC in order to make victories like this possible. If you have not, I very much hope you will go to:

www.grnc.org/join-grnc/contribute

As always, the many volunteers of Grass Roots North Carolina will endeavor to put your money to more efficient, effective use in defending your rights than any other organization.

Armatissimi e liberissimi,

F. Paul Valone

President, Grass Roots North Carolina

Executive Director, Rights Watch International

Radio host, Guns, Politics and Freedom

P.S. *Believe me, I've watched my 401(k) evaporate with everyone else's, and I know lots of people out of work. I know times are hard. But if you can contribute $100, $50 or even $25, we will use those precious funds to continue our string of victories in defending your rights.*

Appendix X
Example of
Press Release

Grass Roots North Carolina
Post Office Box 10665, Raleigh, NC 27605
877.282.0939 (Phone)   919.573.0354 (Fax)   www.GRNC.org

FOR IMMEDIATE RELEASE
Press Contact: 123-456-7890
E-mail: presscontact@YourURL.org
Release date: August 4, 2021
Press release link: XXXXXXXXXXX

Mecklenburg County Sheriff Sued
Over Handgun Permits

Grass Roots North Carolina, Gun Owners of America and Mecklenburg residents sue to ensure permits issued as required by law

[Charlotte] Grass Roots North Carolina (GRNC) and Gun Owners of America (GOA), together with three Mecklenburg County residents, today filed suit and a request for preliminary injunction against Mecklenburg County Sheriff Gary McFadden over McFadden's refusal to issue North Carolina pistol purchase permits and concealed handgun permits as required by law. The suit can be found at: **XXXXXXXXXXXX.**

Press conference: A press conference will be held on the steps of the Mecklenburg County Courthouse to explain the reasons for the suit and possible outcomes.

- **Where:** Mecklenburg County Courthouse, 832 E 4th St, Charlotte, NC 28202
- **When:** 2:30 PM, Thursday, August 5.
- **Who:** Representing the plaintiffs will be GRNC President Paul Valone and attorney XXXXX
- **Why:** The days of sheriffs denying lawful North Carolinians the right to self-defense are **over**.

Background: Either a pistol purchase permit or a concealed handgun permit is required under North Carolina law to purchase any handgun, whether from a dealer or in a private transaction. McFadden's office is taking up to six months to schedule appointments and up to an additional six months to process permit applications, denying lawful citizens the right to firearms for protection of themselves and their families.

McFadden becomes the second sheriff sued by GRNC for malfeasance in refusing to issue permits. The first suit, against Wake County Sheriff Gerald Baker, was recently settled when Baker agreed to issue permits as required by law and to pay court costs, attorney fees and damages totaling nearly $30,000.

Said GRNC president Paul Valone:

> *"The days of sheriffs obstructing North Carolina citizens from exercising their right to keep and bear arms under the United States Constitution and North Carolina Constitution are over. GRNC intends to ensure the rights of lawful citizens to protect themselves are respected. To that end, we will file as many lawsuits as necessary. Other non-compliant sheriffs would do well to heed our warning."*

Background: Founded in 1994, Grass Roots North Carolina is an all-volunteer 501(c)(4) organization dedicated to preserving individual liberties guaranteed by the U.S. Constitution and Bill of Rights with emphasis on the Second Amendment right to keep and bear arms.

##############

Made in the USA
Middletown, DE
29 July 2022

70189285R00215